Pre-Inca Art and Culture

HERMANN LEICHT

———

PRE-INCA ART
AND
CULTURE

Translated from the German by
MERVYN SAVILL

THE ORION PRESS
NEW YORK

MANUFACTURED IN GREAT BRITAIN

FOREWORD

SINCE the days of the discovery of the New World, the imagination of the West has always been fired by the ancient American civilisations.

The first to arouse attention were the Aztec State in Mexico and the Inca Kingdom in Peru which, from the tales of the Spanish conquistadors, immediately appeared miraculous. In both instances it was merely a question of descendants—they survived for a comparatively short time—of races that had taken over a far older civilisation, part of which they no longer even understood.

Within the last thirty years, as the result of well-subsidised research into the New and Old kingdoms of the Maya, an immense quantity of material from 800 excavation sites has come to light. These have been dealt with fully in specialised literature.

On the Peruvian coast, however, long before the Inca, an ancient civilisation flourished for over 1,000 years. Its artistic creations include some of the most beautiful objects ever fashioned by Indian hands. Its moon worship allows us many a glimpse behind the veil of early religious thought. The very few serious revelations in this field are to be found in great works on some other theme or in learned journals which are seldom available to the layman.

It was well worth while, therefore, to treat this kingdom and its inhabitants as a whole, and from the various sources to present its history, art and culture. This could only be done by constantly bearing in mind the general history of the human race and by taking into account the lastest knowledge acquired by modern Americanists.

New theories have been propounded on the connection between moon-worship and the water-worship of the Indians, on the symbolical, mythological significance of the countless finds, and in particular on the position of canines in the religious concepts of the ancient American world.

Nevertheless, while observing all the requirements of scholarship, this book had to be readable. That is why I chose an easy style and did not hesitate to banish all the cumbersome, scientific apparatus to the appendixes. I have dealt in the same way with the relative historical notes and short biographies.

The illustrations, in addition to the better-known treasures and various comparative drawings, represent much that is new and hitherto unreproduced, above all from the very valuable Peruvian treasures in Swiss collections.

The bare necessities of the language to be found on the drawings are explained in note 1, and later in the text on page 42.

TABLE OF CONTENTS

7

logical table—The tree ring calendar—Reliable com-
putation—The problem of the Maya time reckoning—
Moon worship as a time factor—Stylistic comparisons—
Ancient cultural ties—The late races—Overall survey

Tumbes, the invasion gateway of the Spaniards—The
scales of the Indian merchants—In sight of the vol-
canoes—First meeting between Whites and Indians—
Contour map of the frontier region—A cock crows—
The blunderbusses ring out—A forgotten language—
The peoples of the tropics—In the rich Chira valley
—Stepped pyramids—The late style of the Chimu

The treasure sites of Lambayeque, Chiclayo and
Etén—Typical building forms—Calancha's description
of the Pacasmayo valley—The ruined city of Pacatnamu—The relic with two heads—The god with the
carapace—The early style of the Chimu—The Chavín
influence—Burial customs—Coffins and mummy
bundles—Tomb artifacts—The death masks

The Chicama valley—The mature style of the Chimu—
Portrait ceramics—The Trujillo valley—The capital
Chan-Chan—The first palace—The second palace—
The treasure seekers—The temple of Moche—The
treasures of the cult—Water worship—Historical
parallels—Colour symbolism

The upper Santa valley—Tombs and stone circles—
The Chulpas—The art of the Huarás—The Recuay
style—The water cult in the *altiplano*—The shrines of
Chavín—Building plans and stylistic features—The
sacrifice of the heart—The Raimondi monolith—The
Colla Indians—The Sun Gate of Tiahuanaco—The
culture of Lake Titicaca—Contour map of the Chimu
land

A*

INTRODUCTION

WHEN the ship on its way to Peru, after days of sailing, leaves the Equator and the tropical splendour of Panama with its luxuriant vegetation farther and farther behind, and continues down the coast some distance off-shore, the sensitive traveller cannot fail to be impressed by the complete change in the landscape.

Behind the small, interminable strip of sandy desert which, monotonous and deserted, fringes a shore barely ruffled by the even Pacific swell, rises, from a gentle slope to an unending chain, the majestic wall of the Andes, with its monstrous naked peaks. Above the snow-covered summit vaults a pale, leaden sky, and there is no breath of wind to chase away the lazy cloud masses which pile up over the sea, and hardly ever burst in refreshing rain. Bare and frowning, casting spectral shadows, occasional mountain spurs descend towards the coast, rigid and immutable as on the first day of Creation.

But when the ship approaches nearer to the land, at intervals between the dunes can be seen rivers, beggarly watercourses, which often trickle away into the sand without ever reaching the sea. Very seldom, like an oasis, a larger valley breaks the monotony of this desert. Then the picture changes. The slopes of the Sierra with their fissured porphyry and granite walls are covered at the bottom of the valley with green; signs of fertility and the settlements of men appear.

By the rivers and the seashore, and today, too, in barren spots which once, thanks to artificial irrigation works appeared like smiling gardens, slumber in the driven sand the remains of countless temples, palaces and forgotten rows of tombs. These are the sunken cities once inhabited by the ancient races of the Peruvian coast; the northern part formed the great kingdom of the Chimu, the centre the sanctuaries of Pachacamac, while the southernmost end represented the Nazca civilisation in the land of the Chincha.

11

In the Chimu kingdom, where the Spanish conquerors first arrived, the sources of historical tradition flow clearest and the finds are most coherent. From here the entire coastal art and culture can best be explored and understood. That is why it must be our first consideration. An understanding of the inter-related civilisations of the southernmost shores can best be acquired by a regional treatment of the material.

Pre-Inca Art and Culture

CHAPTER ONE

The Kingdom of Chimu

THE name Chimu,[1] like the word Inca, did not originally mean a race but was used by the Indians to denote the most powerful rulers of the coast.

Just as today the Quechua-speaking inhabitants of the *altiplano* and their civilisation are grouped together under the name of their princes as 'Inca', in the following work the ancient inhabitants of the north Peruvian coast, using mainly the Mochica language, and their very homogeneous art and culture, will be described as 'the kingdom of the Chimu'. Thus the reader need not be confused by such terms as Mochica or Chimoid culture and the countless, even stranger designations and qualifications according to language, location of the finds or the techniques employed in individual artifacts, often inaccurately called styles, which archaeologists with varying degrees of justification have introduced into their specialised field.

★ ★ ★

At the time of its greatest expansion during the rule of the later Chimu, approximately between the years 1100 to 1400, this kingdom extended from Lat. 3 to 11° S. for about 600 miles along the coast, while the distance from the sea to the mountains varied between thirty and 100 miles (Map page 182).

The natural northern frontier of this coastal stretch of desert, divided by about twenty streams of varying sizes into flowering valleys, was the region round the valley of Tumbes on the Gulf of Guayaquil (Map page 138).

Beyond this gulf the entire Ecuadorian coast appears as a typical tropical landscape in which man, under the enervating influence of heat and damp, waging a desperate struggle with luxuriant primeval vegetation or living in barren, marshy regions, could not possibly have developed a permanent culture. With

15

Puña Island in the Gulf of Guayaquil there first appears a kind of parkland in which handsome trees raise their heads above the pampas. But even this pearl of the Ecuadorian coast is dotted with large marshes, a breeding ground for yellow fever. To the south and east of Puña and on the mainland opposite the island we come at last to the first forests, which extend as far as the valley of Tumbes.

To the east of this valley stretches a mountain chain, the Cordillera de Chilla, which separates the hot, damp tropics in the north from the equally hot but dry land in the south with its cool nights. This is the natural frontier between the ancient cultural region of the Chimu and the coastal desert of the north.

The western frontier is the Pacific Ocean, while the eastern frontier is no less clearly defined by the mighty Cordillera range, which attains an average height of 12,000 feet, rising at its peaks to 18,000, and farther south to 21,000 feet in the realm of eternal snow, each of the passes lying at the same altitude as Mont Blanc.

To the south, however, the land is open and the strip of desert with its forty-odd oases of life in the valleys and streams extends over 1,000 miles into Chile, slowly altering its character and becoming ever higher and less suitable for agriculture.

If we accept this region round the Pativilca as the southern frontier of the Chimu kingdom, we shall find that this is also the Mochica language frontier where in this valley today stands the mighty fortress of Paramonga on the Rio de la Fortaleza (Map page 182 and Plate 38).

Here in the realm of the Kings Cuismancu and Chuquimancu, the Chimu kingdom ran up against new and powerful intellectual influences, the cult of Pachacamac and the art of Tiahuanaco. This is by far the most interesting frontier of the kingdom, although not the only one, but together with the valley of the Rio Santa, represents its most intensive point of contact with neighbouring civilisations and at the same time the bridge to the closely related world of Nazca.

Into the region we have described, at the dawn of history, in the course of the general population of the two American continents from the Bering Straits to the southernmost tip of

Patagonia, came the first Indians as hunters and fisherfolk with the knowledge of primitives—simple ceramics and weaving. Upon planting the mandioca they soon made their earliest acquaintance with agriculture, although not in a very intensive form, learned how to grow the native maize and potatoes and to domesticate the llama of the highlands.

There is absolutely no archaeological evidence to show that the later Chimu culture gradually grew on the spot from these first inhabitants. On the contrary, the most ancient art of the Chimu is easily distinguishable from the finds which can be attributed to the autochthonous population. In its first stage can already be seen quite clearly its connections with Central American culture, connections which we shall examine in detail in the course of this book. There is no possible doubt that the ancestors of the Chimu, in possession of a culture that had already evolved from the archaic stage, migrated here from the north in the second or third century of our calendar.

Some may have descended overland from the Straits of Panama, despite the obstacle of wild Indians with poisoned arrows, following the course of the river, slowly pressing forward south over the mountains, where the transverse valleys and the water led them once more out of the mountains to their later abode.

It is certain, however, that the greater part of them came by the more simple route along the coast by sea. Today we must set man's knowledge of the ship very much farther back in time than has previously been envisaged. To take a simple example, if a word like sceptre, in Greek *skeptron*, is split into the ancient syllables, *skep* = ship and *tar* = to turn, it signifies no less than the concept of the man at the helm. But the man who worked the tiller was the most important, and this sceptre was adopted by the rulers as the staff of dignity, symbolising his power, an age-old memory of the era when man had easier access to his places of settlement by water than by land.

In order to accept that the bringers of civilisation crossed the sea, one does not have to create fantastic theories of an ancient Phoenician merchant fleet or to turn one's eyes in the direction of the South Seas. The Chimu, even at the time of the conquest, possessed a capable sea-going craft which amazed the

Spaniards. This was certainly no new discovery but an ancient possession of the Indian coastal-dwellers.[2]

Pizarro's bold and experienced pilot, Ruiz, on his first reconnaissance along the north Peruvian coast in 1526, soon caught sight of a strange Indian vessel; from the distance it looked like a large caravel and sported a huge sail which billowed gaily in the wind. The Spanish sailor was very surprised by this phenomenon, for he was convinced that no European ship had been in these latitudes before him.

On drawing closer he realised that it was a huge raft, known to the Indians as a balsa, consisting of a number of planks of exceedingly buoyant wood bound together and a deckhouse of reeds and bamboo. Two tall masts had been erected amidships carrying a large square cotton sail. The steering of the vessel was accomplished by a rudder and perfected by a movable lee-board secured between poles, like the so-called 'blade' in modern sailing boats, to increase the balance. This simple but practical type of construction was more than adequate for coasting, and similar balsas with thatched deck-huts and quarters were used as freighters by the Spaniards after the conquest along the coast and on the larger navigable rivers (Plate 4).

A popular recollection of the migration along these coastal waters had certainly endured for many centuries. Miguel Cabello de Balboa,[3] an intelligent and scholarly Jesuit, during the last quarter of the sixteenth century studied the accounts given to him by the Indians of their ancestors and their origin. He carefully collected as much information as he could and committed it to paper in his *Miscelánea Antarctica*. The original manuscript has unfortunately been lost, the two printed editions of the chronicle are of great rarity and mutilated, but a serviceable translation exists of the third part of the work dealing with Peru.[4] Finally there is a good unpublished holograph copy of the original manuscript dating from the first quarter of the eighteenth century in the New York Public Library.[5]

When we carefully discard, as we shall endeavour to do, everything which appeared vague or dubious to the chronicler in his honest attempt to describe the popular traditions and make allowances that he was a child of his age with his own views and moreover a Spaniard, we are left with the following saga.

THE SAGA OF KING NAYMLAP AND HIS RACE

In times so long ago that no one today can describe them, a large, foreign fleet of Indian balsas with many sails appeared off the coast in the region of Lambayeque. The vessels came from the north and anchored at the mouth of the Faquisllanga river.[6]

A powerful prince came ashore, accompanied by his wife, a host of concubines and children and a number of subjects who were devoted to their ruler. The name of the king was Naymlap and his queen was Ceterni. They were attended by a magnificent retinue, forty of the most trusted men forming their court, among whom were Fonga Sigde, the royal forerunner, Ninacola, the guardian of the throne and protector of the royal litters, Ninagintue, the cup-bearer, Occhocalo, the head cook, Xam Muchec, a valet, particularly skilled in strange dyes and unguents used in the king's adornment, Ollopcopoc, the overseer of the king's baths, Pita Zofi, the herald who blew on a powerful marine conch, and finally Llapchillulli, the artistic designer of the beautiful feathered ornaments which the ruler greatly loved and prized.

With a wealth of possessions and magnificent objects, such as had never been seen before, the newcomers penetrated a short way inland and founded a city with a temple which bore the name of Chot. In this temple they erected a column which they had brought with them. It was deeply revered, was a likeness of the prince and consisted of several pieces of green stone. The column was called Yampallec, a portrait and memorial of Naymlap.

For a long time the settlers lived there contentedly, improving their standards of life and increasing in numbers. When Naymlap died his retinue buried him secretly in the room in which he had lived, telling his subjects, who must never learn that death had power over their deified prince, that he had come on wings out of the sky and had donned his wings once more of his own accord and flown away.[7] Great grief descended upon the land, and many of the most faithful made a vain attempt to find their lost ruler, wandering through the neighbouring valleys never to return.

The crown, however, fell to Naymlap's eldest son and heir, Cium. He was married to a princess named Zolzdoñi, who had presented him with twelve sons, each of whom became the founder of a race that went forth into the land. Nor colonised the Cinto valley, Cala settled in Tucume and a third brother in Collique. Llapchillulli, Naymlap's chief courtier and relative, left with a particularly large following for the valley of Jayanca,[8] where his issue continued to live happily.

In the meantime Cium ruled for many years in the temple city of Chot. When he felt the approach of death he went down into his crypt and retired of his own free will to eternal rest in order to demonstrate to his followers his immortality and divinity. Down the ages followed him as rulers Escuñain, Mascuy, Cuntipallec, Allascunti, Nofan Nech, Mulumuslan, Llamecoll, Lanipatcum, Acunta and Fempellec.

Fempellec was the twelfth, last and most unfortunate ruler of Naymlap's dynasty. He decided to move the Yampallec column from the temple of Chot to another place. He made various unsuccessful attempts to do this, until the Devil suddenly appeared in the guise of a beautiful woman to punish his sacrilege. So great were this woman's arts of seduction and so weak the powers of resistance of the prince that he married her. But hardly had this impious union taken place than the rain began to fall to an extent that had never before been seen in this district. The downpour lasted for thirty days and thirty nights, to be followed by a year of appalling drought and a dreadful famine. Since it now became clear to the priests and worthies of the land that their prince's crimes were to blame, they rose against him, bound him in chains and flung him into the sea. Thus ended the dynasty of the first rulers of Lambayeque, which still bears their name today.[9]

In actual fact the words Lambayeque, Naymlap and Yampallec are closely connected. When one takes the Spanish orthography into consideration and removes the syllable from the last word—lec—there remain lam, naym, and yam, which have an affinity, while pal or in reverse lap recalls the several pal and pol words in the many different languages; in the queen's name Ceterni, too, we must see an age-old star word. The belief that the human race originated from the stars was widespread among the coastal Indians, and the Archbishop of Lima, Don Bartolomé Lobo Guerrero, tried in vain at a later date to eradicate this belief.

The legend of King Naymlap cannot be dismissed as the myth of a primitive race. Apart from the mythical number of twelve rulers and once more of the twelve sons of Cium, the tradition clearly embraces a very large time-span, at the end of which the priesthood seems to have come to power. Obviously the high cultural standard of the nomads and the colonial character of their undertaking comes to light. That ever more groups of newcomers pushed forward into the country is repeatedly and clearly indicated, justifying the theory we shall propound in the following paragraphs.

Of particular interest is the fact that the Yampallec column is accurately described as the portrait of a prince carved from a piece of stone, an additional detail being given that it was green. Now a six-feet-tall column of dark green diorite is one of the most valuable exhibits in the Lima National Museum. This is the famous so-called Raimondi monolith (page 178). It was found at Chavín de Huántar in the valley of the Puccha, a tributary of the Marañon, and we shall discuss it later in detail. In view of the great importance held by the Raimondi monolith in the art history of ancient Peru, the reason that no one has perceived its remarkable connection with the tale of Miguel Cabello de Balboa is due to the fact that his work is so inaccessible.

When one compares the contents of this chronicle with what the Augustinian historian Antonio de la Calancha[10] relates in his *Crónica moralizada* we can say for certain that Fempellec's end also denotes the end of the first dynasty in the Lambayeque valleys. The overthrow of Fempellec succeeded with the help of the first Chimu, the rulers of Chan-Chan, who now usurped the land by electing a prince of their race called Pongmassa to rule as a vassal of the Chimu; he was succeeded on his death by his son Oxa. At the time of this Oxa, news of the rising power of the Inca had already spread through the land. They gradually pushed forward into the valley of Cajamarca and finally wrested the power from the Chimu. Oxa must have lived in the first quarter of the fifteenth century. According

to tradition he was succeeded by his son Llempisan, followed
by a certain Chullumpisan and his brother Cipromarca and
once more by his younger brother, Fallenispan. The last vassal
ruler on the arrival of the Spaniards was Pecfunpisan. Thus far
the history of Lambayeque.

★ ★ ★

The history of the remaining valleys must have followed the
same pattern. They too absorbed caravans of Central American
nomads, who were already possessed of a culture far higher than
the merely primitive. They arrived sometimes over the mountains
and sometimes by sea, making their way up the estuaries and
settling at suitable fertile spots. An eloquent proof that such
migrations took place by sea not only in the north at Lambayeque
is to be found in the Gretzer and Bolivar[11] collections of richly
carved parts of leeboards and handles decorated in the fresh
naturalistic style of the early coastal inhabitants (Plate 4).

These proofs of ancient shipping found in the south at Pisco
and Ica and outside the domains of the later Chimu rulers cast
a significant light in the darkness that veils the origin of the
civilisations on the southern Peruvian coast.[12]

Pattern on a vessel in early Chimu style

Wherever a primitive population was found in the valleys of
the northern coast it was conquered and to a large extent
absorbed, so that only a few traces remained by the time the
Spaniards arrived. These people spoke a raw, guttural dialect

which Calancha refers to as *la Pescadora,* the fisherman's language.[13]

A few families and descendants of the nomads dispersed or, sometimes, in places increased to become rulers over a whole valley. With the expansion of the population, the question of food assumed ever-greater importance. Soon the first artificial irrigation works were built, gradually improving and finally becoming so fantastic that even today they arouse universal admiration and are still largely in use. By the time the first Spaniards arrived the thickly populated valleys were strewn far up to the slopes of the mountain with superimposed, terraced fields.

At the moment the local settlements grew into cities, which, in their natural need to expand, began to conquer the surrounding land and smaller places, developed the battle for land and water rights. This battle naturally produced strong leader personalities and created a new type of ruler (Plate 3). More than an original patriarchal family chief, he was a general who, according to the laws inherent in power, gradually expanded beyond his narrow realm, burst the bonds of a mere valley rulership and sought to conquer the neighbouring valleys, until finally it came once more to battles between the big rulers for the hegemony of a far more extended region—a process which constantly repeats itself in history.

It was logical that the rulership was not determined solely by the rights of the first-born but that the princes should choose from the ranks of their sons, nephews and relations, successors most suited by their natural talents. This heir was already made known to the people during the lifetime of his predecessor so that he might be recognised as the future ruler. The one chosen was then carefully educated to assume the reins of government when his time came. Particularly capable women too (Plate 2) were occasionally chosen as rulers and were known as Tallapona or Capullana.[14]

On his first coastal journey as far as Chimbote, Pizarro was invited near Santa Cruz by one of these Indian princesses, who gave an exceedingly elegant banquet in his honour. Arbours were erected beneath a luxuriant roof of leaves from which hung sweet-smelling flowers, while the tables were laden with a host of magnificent dishes unknown to the Spaniards. When the banquet came to an end, the guests were entertained with music and dancing by young people in simple garb, who displayed great grace and agility. Probably in such dances and mimes by conjuration of the idols the demons were often questioned. They were represented or believed to be present and uttered oracles, as Calancha reports in his chronicle.

But Pizarro showed little understanding for this cordial welcome, and, before he left, revealed to his friendly hostess the reasons which had brought him to the land by unfurling the royal banner of Castile, seeking to make those present recognise it as the symbol of their subjection by the Spanish crown. This they did with the greatest willingness and much laughter, whereby, according to this contemporary writer, they must have had a very vague concept of the gravity of the ceremony.

Calancha, in agreement with other sources,[15] mentions that the first princes to break out from a purely local regency with limited powers and rule over a far larger kingdom were called Chimu. He adds categorically that this word signified something similar to the word Pharaoh in Egypt. The wife of the first Chimu, according to the legend, was called Chacma, a name which still survives in the naming of the valley of Chicama. A powerful leader, the Great Chimu towards the end of the fifth or the beginning of the sixth century founded a consolidated kingdom which may primarily have stretched from the Chicama to the Viru valley but later embraced all the Lambayeque valleys as far south as the lower Santa valley (Map page 182).

The Great Chimu took tribute from all his vassals and is reputed to have had in his service 6,000 Indians whose sole occupation was to bring him gold, silver, copper and valuable minerals from the mountains. The Chimu increased their wealth and power from generation to generation; their fame and power radiated from their capital, which was later called by the Spaniards Gran Chimu, but was known to the Indians as Chan-Chan. Even today, in their ruins, this ancient metropolis together with the pyramids of Moche give an impressive picture of the power and might of the Indian civilisation which first blossomed in these temples and palaces (Plates 32 and 33).

The accounts of Balboa and Calancha, upon which the foregoing history of the Chimu is based, in so far as they corroborate the archaeological finds and the results of scientific spadework in the field, were written completely independently of each other, with a lapse of fifty years beween them. Nevertheless they supplement each other magnificently, because both of them deal with everything that the coastal peoples possessed in the way of a common tradition. For further study two more sixteenth-century accounts are important, that of Jerónimo de Román y Zamora[16] and that of Bishop Bartolomé de Las Casas, the famous, well-meaning apostle of the Indians, who, by a tragi-comic whim of fate, helped to found American traffic in negro slaves.[17]

According to Las Casas, popular tradition on the coast had preserved the memory of a first period of civilisation lasting some 500 to 600 years. According to this, the whole country at that time was split up into a host of small kingdoms with rulers who had their own establishments and their own economical life. Between the neighbouring races a simple type of barter prevailed. On the other hand there was hardly any traffic between the regions which were remote from each other. The coastal inhabitants during these first centuries mainly used the catapulted spear, whereas the inhabitants of the highlands used slings and stones in their attacks. For defence both nations possessed shields. This conforms to countless designs found on pottery from earliest times illustrating the weapons in question, the shield being either round or square in shape. Javelin quivers, battle-axes and clubs completed their armament. This was the age of the early Chimu style.

Román y Zamora gives a further chronological hint when he says that the Golden Age of the Chimu may have lasted many hundred years, coming to an end 600 years before his own century, thus towards the middle or the end of the tenth century. This is the most accurate detail we possess from the old chroniclers.

The separation into an old and a new kingdom, or, as has become more generally accepted by North American anthro-pologists, into an 'early' and 'late' Chimu civilisation, is hardly satisfactory from an art-historical point of view, since between the two periods the foreign influence of the form world of

Tiahuanaco, which never entirely subdued the art of the coast, must be taken into account.

A separation into 'early' and 'late' is too comparable with a beginning and an end without middle and maturity. Many of the most magnificent and most artistic creations of the Chimu are described as early, which could not possibly be correct by reason of their development and their innermost nature. In the description of the magnificent portrait ceramics from the Chicama and Moche valleys and also in the general chapters on the chronology I shall deal with this at greater length. For the moment I shall be content, without taking unduly into consideration the political conditions reigning at that time in the Chimu kingdom, to postulate that from the evidence of countless finds a truly early, stylistically archaic age which may have lasted until the end of the fifth century was followed by a renaissance under the Great Chimu; this reflected the gradually increasing influence of Tiahuanaco in the ninth century, to be reanimated, from the year 1000 onwards until the conquest by the Incas, into a typical late style.

To maintain an 'old' and a 'new' kingdom one must endow the old kingdom with a long lease of life, above all in its early period, and a certain elasticity, for its artistic achievements embrace both the early style of the Chimu and its maturity. The new kingdom, then, between 1100 and 1400 of our calendar was at its peak of brilliance, showing a well-articulated feudal state with the Chimu at its head in Chan-Chan. The art of this kingdom was the easily recognisable and very unique late-Chimu style with which I shall deal in Chapter Six.

A huge, main road which had only to be taken over and used by the Inca rulers, and today still serves in many places as the foundations of a modern autobahn, ran the whole length of the country. In all the desert regions Chimu guides were available to accompany the travellers and lead them safely through the desert.

An interesting account of this last period was rendered between 1541 and 1544 to the contemporary Governor of Peru, Don Cristóbal Vaca de Castro;[18] it contains everything that the surviving readers of the Knot script knew about the last Chimus. A Quipu custodian related that before the Incas arrived an important ruler called Chimo Capac ruled the entire coast from Nazca in the south to Piura in the north. According to him this prince levied enormous tribute in the form of costly jewels, in particular emeralds and turquoise, magnificent apparel embroidered with precious metals and a great variety of textiles.

This account is particularly interesting since it shows the kingdom of the Chimu to have extended far beyond what has already been accepted in this book as the actual frontier, the Rio Pativilca valley, in fact as far as Nazca in the south. This embraces a region which will be dealt with in a later chapter on account of its cultural peculiarities. It is questionable whether the political sphere of Chimu influence, even if only for a brief period, was actually so extensive. The natural southern frontier of their kingdom will have to be considered, as before, as the fortress region of Paramonga, in agreement with Calancha's account.[19]

Chimo Capac, the last great ruler of the Chimu, is also mentioned by other sources. The wealth of his temple was fantastic. Gold and silver looted by the Spaniards in the temple of Moche amounted to 800,000 pesos at the current rate of those days, and from a smaller temple called Tasca, on the road to Huanchaco, Escobar Corchuelo and one of his friends looted treasures to the value of more than 600,000 pesos, 'not counting what they buried'.[20] At the end of his career Chimo Capac raised a huge army against Tupac Yupanqui, the tenth Inca, by whom he was finally defeated at the beginning of the fifteenth century.[21] After this the kingdom of the Chimu ceased to exist as an independent state and the age of Inca rule had arrived for the whole of Peru. The culture and art of the Chimu, however, continued to have an influence for a long time, with a gradual transformation, and only died out during the Spanish age.

★ ★ ★

The material for the above history of the Chimu kingdom is a combination of the results of archaeological and ethnological research and contemporary Spanish accounts which have survived.

Although this is not the place to write a history of American anthropology as a science, we must give some details of the early Spanish chroniclers whom we have to thank for so much information. They were certainly a mixed but very admirable brotherhood. Among them were priests, laymen, jurists, civil servants, knights, adventurers and soldiers; the majority were ambassadors of the Spanish crown, although a few were of mixed blood, having married into the best native families.

All of them were children of their age whose tales were a mixture of fact and fiction, and since they delved in many out-of-the-way and turbid sources they have to be very carefully checked. It was the age which Shakespeare called the 'age of curiosity', its most outstanding feature being a series of the greatest discoveries and inventions mankind has ever made. Nevertheless it had a natural sense for the preservation and unravelling of facts and analogies of life and past history.

Far more than is commonly accepted, many of the chroniclers were innocent of the brutality and impatience which have been attributed to the Spaniards of that age. Most of them, on the contrary, were men of great insight and enormous sympathy, who admired much that they saw among the Indians and found in their institutions. Thus it is still a delight to peruse these old books, if only to see how little human nature has changed down the centuries. The tales of the individual chroniclers naturally differ extensively, according to their temperament, their age and their education. They differ as much in their sources as on the grounds why they wrote their books. Possibly Garcilaso and Sarmiento represent the greatest contrast. The former was inordinately proud of his Inca origin and felt himself in duty bound to write their history. As a result his work is primarily dedicated to them and in content is continually pro-Indian, at times painting them in far too glowing colours.

Sarmiento on the other hand had every cause to please the viceroy Francisco de Toledo, and it is not in the least surprising that he became the official Spanish historian. This viceroy, a man of the world and a fatalist, played in Peru a role not dissimilar to that played in the Netherlands by his namesake Toledo, better known as the Duke of Alba. The history of the Inca kingdom commissioned by the viceroy was to make it clear to everyone that Peru had not been ravished by the

Spaniards but that the latter, by setting aside the rule of the Incas, had restored it to the original condition intended by the Christian God. Despite this bias, Sarmiento's work, if read with understanding, is a very useful historical source. The attitude of the other writers stands somewhere between the two extremes.

Further details of the individual chroniclers will be found in the notes at the end of this book; in the bibliography they are printed systematically in bold type.

CHAPTER TWO

The Indians, their Origin, Race and Language

W HO then were these Chimu? Whence did they come and what place must we accord them in the brightly coloured yet unbroken series of pre-Columbian cultures?

When the Spanish knights in the sixteenth century, driven by greed of gold and religious fanaticism, broke into the ancient American world they often walked about as if in a dream. Although with their superior steel weapons and blunderbusses, mounted on their horses, a beast unknown to the Indians, and armoured cap-à-pie, they easily overthrew armies which could only muster arrows, spears and slings, they felt most deeply that they had come here to a new and different world, in many respects not much inferior to their own, in fact of equal birth and sometimes superior. This strange clash of European and Indian cultures was much the same as if a modern man were suddenly to be set thousands of years back in time among the builders of the pyramids in ancient Egypt and out of the present to wander about in a world which has long since disappeared.

The Europeans found roads far better laid than any that were to be seen in their own land, superior even to those of the time of the Roman Empire. In Mexico they had already met with a completely unknown science, an arithmetic which used a symbol for zero unknown even in antiquity; had given a value to numbers thousands of years before pre-historical Chinese civilisation, and had produced a calendar which, at the time of the discovery, appeared to be the most accurate ever possessed by mankind. The ruined Indian pyramid of Cholula is still today the largest artificial mound among all the antiquities of the world; the largest buildings in the Nile valley approach nowhere near its basic length of 500 yards. The wealth in precious metals which aroused such furious greed in the Spaniards needs no special mention. In Peru they found whole walls and floors laid and inlaid with gold, saw the Inca eating and drinking from vessels of pure gold and, in the land of the Chimu, beautifully dressed people wearing sandals of pure silver.

It was really as though the Europeans had arrived on another planet. They met with completely new types of plants and unknown beasts, while man, the peak of creation, bore no resemblance to them in the colour of his skin, his speech and his social activities. And yet at the same time they discovered in what they called the New World so much which was familiar, although they could not understand how it had reached this land. They constantly encountered the sign of the cross, monasticism and a priesthood, even nunneries, baptism with water and the tradition of a great flood. They heard that two men had survived this flood and saw them depicted in the old pictures with an ark swimming on the waters at the foot of a mountain. A dove too was painted with hieroglyphics in its beak. The people of Mechuacan had a legend of an ark in which Tezpi, their Noah, survived, carrying countless species of birds and an impressive collection of four-footed beasts.

One could elaborate these amazing similarities with the faith of the whites, and it is no wonder that the first Spaniards already connected the New with the Old World, and this doubt as to the origins of Indian civilisation has never been silenced. At the time of the discovery of America, the Europeans were convinced that the residents were survivors of the deluge. Later it was thought that they had migrated there from Atlantis or Lemuria, when those legendary continents sank below the waves.

No less a scholar than Alexander von Humboldt wrote in 1810:[22] 'One is surprised to find towards the end of the fifteenth century, in a world which is called new, these ancient institutions, religious ideas and architectural forms, which seem to lead back to Asia in the first dawn of civilisation. . . . Although the languages show but a faint connection between the two hemispheres, nevertheless this connection can undoubtedly be substantiated in the creation legends, the buildings, the hieroglyphics and the institutions of both the Asiatic and the American races.' While Humboldt had seen only a vague relationship in the languages, in 1871 Vicente Lopez, the Rector of Buenos Aires University, tried to prove no less than that the Inca language was an agglutinating Aryan language and that the population itself was of Aryan[23] descent.

Much ink has been spilt since then to impose European, Polynesian or Phoenician origin upon the Indian cultures, and not all the arguments were as weak as those of the Dutchman Van Zonteven, who maintained quite simply that the Phoenicians invaded Central America 2,000 years ago with elephants.[24] French ethnology has developed a school which has for a long time contended that America was populated from the South Seas, from Oceania and Polynesia, their main argument being philological similarities. Ernst Fuhrmann, following in the path of Lopez, maintained in 1922 that the ancestors of the Inca were white-skinned, 'even though this cannot be proved', and migrated from Western Europe, whereby the 'actual colony which came from Europe to America' settled at first in the Central or Upper Amazon, until 'a damming of the waters in the river basin of central Brazil' drove that race, traces of which can still be found today deep in the heart of the high-up jungle, into the Andes.[25] And finally in 1938 Werner Wolff broke the Maya alphabet and explained its uncontested similarity with the Phoenician script by the theory that the Phoenicians must have reached America by ship.[26]

When one sees in Wolff's[27] book the Maya hieroglyphics compared with the Phoenician script, one is in fact surprised at the many echoes and conformities. It is understandable that the opinion voiced as early as 1685 by Bircherod,[28] that Phoenician and Carthaginian ships reached the American coast and that a Phoenician colony actually existed there, should have continually cropped up again in the most varied forms, not only in popular but in scientific literature. This idea is too good to be true. Either one must accept that unintentionally, in other words by pure accident, a few Phoenician seafarers were driven off their course to America and settled there, or one must reckon on a planned voyage.

In the first case, which is naturally credible, the question arises as to how such a small group of shipwrecked mariners could introduce civilisation to two huge continents and impart

1 Clay head in mature Chimu style

2 Women's heads

it to a population estimated, at the time of the Spanish conquest, at between eighty to a hundred million, split up over great distances into states which knew nothing of each other's existence. Or are those stranded men the forbears of these countless million Indians who had nothing in common with the Phoenicians, not to mention Fuhrmann's Europeans? But even if men from some part of the Old World appeared as the *bringers of civilisation*, at the same time exercising this or that remarkable influence, the question of the *origin* of these many million Indians is still not clarified.

One is left, therefore, with the second premise, i.e. a well-organised Phoenician colonisation. But then let us remember the first journey of Columbus, who was pursuing a very particular goal: he had calculated most accurately the course he must steer and was equipped with nautical aids far superior to those available to the Phoenicians; he had carefully estimated his provisions and water supplies, and rigged his sailing ship for a very long journey—and yet at the end of it, after incredible hardships and in great distress, he reached one of the West Indian islands. If we are clear, then, about the difficulties which did not deter a Columbus and opt for the hypothesis of a true communication with Phoenicia in the most favourable circumstances, namely that the first expedition for some reason succeeded, that it returned in good order to its point of departure, to be repeated on a larger scale, then there would certainly have been some tradition of this. We have not altogether been left in the dark as to some of the voyages of this nation of traders.

And finally it must be recorded that none of these suggested migrations to America left behind a single household plant of recent date.[29] Every great migration undertaken by the civilised peoples of the Old World, even if it had included no domesticated animals, would at least have retained a memory of these, with the natural consequences on the American side. Here it is important to remember that the Indians, on the arrival of the Europeans, with the exception of the dog, the guinea-pig and the llama, indigenous to the Andes as the turkey is to Mexico and a species of duck to Peru, knew neither cattle nor horses nor a single one of the domesticated animals of the Old World.

B

The use of milk, too, was completely alien to them. I mention this for the sake of completion; it means comparatively little, because the llama, as I shall explain later, is impossible to milk, and the North American buffalo cow is hardly a very amenable subject for this operation. More significant is that the Indians knew nothing of the wheel of the Old World and the many uses to which it was put, nor did they even possess a potter's wheel. All these domesticated animals and utensils of civilisation were an age-old possession of the various races presumed to be nomadic. Could they possibly have forgotten all this?

Admittedly within historical times Chinese, Japanese and South Sea Islanders have been driven many hundreds of miles from their home in light craft.[30] There is no doubt that in the seventh and eighth centuries, as their annals maintain, both Chinese and Japanese reached Kamchatka and Alaska. It has also been proved that since the year 1000, when Leif, the son of Erik the Red, discovered the coast of North America, that for three and a half centuries there existed a never completely interrupted although sporadic traffic between Iceland and North America.[31] But what do these communications signify, since they occurred long after a magnificent Indian culture was already in existence and when the first kingdom of the Maya already lay in ruins?

It is high time to be rid of all these idle theories and dreams. Modern science has better methods. As the result of a meticulous and tireless work of excavation in the past few years, material has come to light which can be soberly and chronologically checked to illustrate what was temporally possible and impossible.

As an important clue, since the deciphering of the calendars and various inscriptions, we possess a complete Maya chronology although it is slightly elastic compared with the European calendar. Morley[32] and Spinden[33] set the conjunction of the Maya and European calendars very far back in time. Goodman,[34] Martinez,[35] Teeple[36] and Thompson[37] take a middle course and Vaillant,[38] approaches the later dating of Zeler and Lehmann.[39] All these serious scholars arrive at figures for by no means the oldest but the most impressive known Indian cultures, which definitely rule out any mass migration of non-American peoples in historical times.

It is immaterial that the historian in the field of ancient American civilisation dismisses the knowledge and the latest discovery of modern natural history. At Copilco, near Mexico City, is an extensive field of basalt lava, the so-called *pedregal*, which ranges between three and thirty feet in depth. Beneath this basalt covering in ancient times stood a fertile and well-irrigated, thickly populated plain until a violent eruption of the volcano Ajusco buried everything, creating an Indian Pompeii or Herculaneum. Adits have been driven below the lava top layer, and a host of antiquities of the culture which Gamio[40] has termed subpedregal have been found.

This indubitably archaic culture is very rich in treasure. There is great conformity in the small figures, and the other finds produce a personal effect which remind one vividly of the early naturalistic figures which crop up from time to time in Peru. In these, as in the Mexican finds beneath the basalt covering of pedregal, hieratic stylisation is completely missing.

The date of this volcanic eruption can be assessed by the climatic erosion and by the piling up of earth on the surface of the lava; although geologists differ somewhat in their figures we arrive at a date between 1000 and 3000 B.C., an average, therefore, of 2000 B.C. This race had progressed to an archaic stage with all the attendant features, and in order to date its more primitive condition a large span of time must be taken into account.

When Virchow, as early as 1877, declared[41] that he did not believe America possessed any aborigines he was forced to accept that America was populated from outside; this is the concerted opinion of the leading ethnologists today. To corroborate this, prehistoric human bones are lacking in the New World and nothing has been discovered comparable with the finds in the Old World such as Neanderthal man. Even the oldest skulls differ very little, if at all, from those of modern man.

Nor have any artifacts been discovered dating from the Chelléan, Moustérian, Solutréan or other European palaeolithic age. On the grounds that in the Argentine as well as in Ecuador and Nevada, human remains as well as those of extinct animals such as the giant sloth and perhaps also the mastodon, have been found it can be presumed that man lived in America far earlier than has generally been supposed, even if these beasts survived there long after they had become extinct in the Old World.

But it is certain that the first men who broke into the New World had not evolved culturally from the Stone Age. Not only was everything I have referred to on page 34 unknown to them; they had no agriculture, did not know how to grind with stone tools, and were ignorant of many other inventions which appeared during the Neolithic Age and which they obviously would have brought with them to their new home had they possessed any knowledge of them.

The arrival of these first Americans naturally cannot be dated to within centuries, since it occurred in such a far-distant past. Friends of chronology can accept, however, that the first migrations took place at the earliest before 1500^0–2000^0 B.C., and at the latest towards the end of the Neolithic, *circa* 3000 B.C., for it was obviously a case of several migrations in strength which took place during the course of centuries, possibly aeons.

The question, then, of the origins of Indian culture can only be answered in an undogmatic and objective manner in the light of modern chronology, which differentiates basically between man as a mere creature and man as a bringer of civilisation. All further speculations as to when the first settlement of the American continents took place continue to remain in the air and are at best entertaining topics for drawing-room discussion.

The Indians of both Americas as mere creatures are without doubt and without exception of Mongolian origin.[42] Apart from easily recognisable external features—straight black hair, sparse beard growth, pronounced zygomatic arch, etc.—they bear all the other Mongolian signs and particularly, unless they have intermarried with negroes, the characteristic Mongolian mark.[43] The thoroughbred strains belong without exception to the blood group D. These Mongolian Indians are actually the first discoverers of America. It is one of the great ironies of history that the white man, who has put up so many memorials to a variety of discoverers of America, should never have raised one to these first discoverers, namely the Asiatics, to whom today he almost refuses access to this land.

But if the Indians are to be portrayed merely as one of the great outposts of Asia, the well-defined similarities with other

Asiatic frontier zones such as Phoenicia or Polynesia are not surprising, and it is hardly a matter for astonishment when one finds points of contact with this or that language or when the description of the Indian king Montezuma could have applied equally well to the court of the great Khan and the Mongolian princes as Marco Polo described them.[44]

Furthermore it must not be forgotten that with similar premises man develops in the same way. In the last analysis pots can only have a limited number of shapes, hair styles are not inexhaustible, and doors to be practical can only have a certain shape whether they are in the land of the Chimu or in Europe. As regards the pyramids, which are found both in America and among other races, it must be remarked that in ages lacking great technical aids, sloping ground offered the only possibility of lifting great weights. And finally if further similarities are to be found between Central American and Phoenician letters, the latter developed these not in a day but perhaps inherited them just as the Greeks did.

If one feels inclined to dream, it is more intelligent to accept that, instead of founding a Phoenician colony in America many thousand years ago, all these races of Asia, the cradle of the human race, possessed a common primitive speech, a speech of roots which at the beginning was more stammered than spoken and accompanied by explanatory gestures. Before the first predicative phrases were evolved many hundreds and perhaps thousands of years may have elapsed.

Such words, gestures and the inherent ideas could have been preserved over enormous spans of time and it is at least plausible that from them similar alphabets may have developed. Words could then be occasionally older than the stones themselves and revert to the deepest roots which made man develop from a mere creature into a human being.

As a primitive creature, however, we must repeat that all Indians in prehistoric times were of Mongolian origin. As bringers of civilisation, on the other hand, their own culture was due neither to a large-scale migration of foreigners in historical times nor to some kind of grafted foreign travel. The ancient American civilisation is far more the age-old possession of the Indians; it is autochthonous and has developed on American soil.

When Virchow[41] in 1877 also said that in reply to the question as to how America was populated he could only counter with a number of problems, so today no satisfactory answer has been found. As soon as the Mongoloid characters of the Indian race has been unanimously determined, there are no plausible grounds against, but a great many more in favour of, the natural and most simple solution, that the migration took place from north-east Asia along the nearest route from Siberia across the Bering Straits and the Aleutians, where in those days there was possibly a land bridge.

Presumably for a very considerable period newcomers continued to stream into the land, driven by their quest for food and love of travel. The newcomers forced the already resident races farther down the continent, until, finally, both continents from Alaska to Patagonia were inhabited. A certain counterstream began to travel northwards once more from central South America so that on the promontory of Panama a veritable circular movement ensued, to be clearly reflected in the bright-coloured mosaic of Indian dialects there.[45]

A final reinforcement from the north, a bare 3,000 years before our era, already met with resistance from the earliest nomads who had become resident, and came to a halt in North-West America, from the same climatic and ethnographical causes which in historical times prevented the union between the American and Asiatic fisherfolk of the north from becoming more active. The stream had dried up.

The story of the internal American wanderings, however, will probably never be elucidated. It seems fairly certain that the first northern races arrived some 5,000 years ago in the upper valleys of Central America, where the land must have seemed to them a godsend. These valleys offered them a wealth of game and fruit; to east and west were the warm regions of the coastal area, where, after a few days' journey, the magnificent products of the tropics were to be had in plenty.

Thus in the blessed fields of Mexico and Guatemala as well as in the upper valleys of the South American Andes and in the tiny paradisal spots on the Peruvian coast, so suitable for the development of a higher civilisation, some of the races became agricultural settlers, while others in less propitious conditions travelled on to less suitable regions and never emerged from Stone Age culture.[46]

The picture of alternating civilised and savage nomadic races which America offered when the Europeans arrived is by no means a unique phenomenon. In Europe too, during the time of the migrations, a few hundred miles from the highly developed Roman Empire in the forests and wilderness lived the younger Indo-Germanic peoples who were related by blood, race and language to those Romans.

In the magnificent pageant of fluctuating ancient American civilisations the Peruvian coastal regions now assume an important place. Observation of their thousand-year-old flourishing culture is in many respects far more interesting than that of the later races. That an element of truth resides in the saga of King Naymlap and that the ancestors of the Chimu did in fact come from North and Central America and not from some part of the Old World need not be doubted in view of all that has been propounded in the way of migration hypotheses. The archaeological finds furnish sufficient proof, and if the South Sea Islanders' balsas had approached the Peruvian coast from Polynesia they would have been driven farther northwards by the powerful Humboldt stream which flows up from the south. Seafaring in Peru was and remained a simple coastal traffic,[47] which, like the entire culture of the coastal region, varied little in the course of twelve centuries. Since the days of their migration in the second or third century A.D. these races already worked in metals and had already emerged from the level of Stone Age culture.

What then distinguishes and differentiates the Chimu as a race from their neighbours? Firstly, together with the inhabitants of the coast farther south, from a purely anthropological standpoint they form in their pronounced brachycephalism a particular group, in contrast with the more dolichocephalic inhabitants of the highlands. Too much weight must not, however, be given to this evidence; for the shape of skulls, ruling out frequent artificial deformations, is extraordinarily transient. In one and the same family are often to be found the most deviating types, and in every large necropolis, both in the land of the Chimu and in Europe, one can make a collection of skulls showing almost every form and measurement.

Even less does the lighter or darker pigment of the skin allow us to draw a final conclusion. The term 'redskins' for all the Indians is completely false and is based on a faulty translation of the first Spanish chronicles. When these spoke of *'hombres colorados'* or *'gente colorado'*, the translators found in their dictionaries that red, being the brightest colour, was called in Spanish *rojo* and also *colorado*; they overlooked the fact that this word also meant dyed and coloured, in which latter sense it was used by the old chroniclers, who merely told of coloured people. This error on the part of the translators has crept into many languages, never to be eradicated. The misnomer 'copper red' is far removed from the true colour of the Indian's skin, since in the case of the mummies and also in the present-day Indians and Mongolian peoples it runs the entire gamut of colour from the lightest to the deepest brownish-black. The Indian skin has not the same velvety softness and suppleness as is to be found in the negro. It is rougher and dryer and in the present-day natives gives the appearance of having been tanned.

To mention another very obvious fact, one found and still finds, among the Indians races with definitely long noses and snub noses. Usually, however, when this develops among small family communities, intermarriage begins and it would be ridiculous to try and make distinctions on this point. A careful comparison of the magnificent portrait heads of the Chimu, the pride of many collections, clearly shows that in the shape of the skull and nose there was no characteristic type—one for the rulers and the other for the serfs. It will suffice to look through the many plates in this book and to compare the portraits of the nobility with those of the common people.

Language is of far greater service than physical features for a closer distinction of a race. We know comparatively little of Mochica or Muchic, as the Chimu called their language, since later it was very much submerged by Quechua, the tongue of the victorious Inca. The preponderance of undeveloped words in the coastal idiom as compared with the highland dialect would make it appear to be a far older language.

Fernando Carrera, a grandson of the Spanish conquistador Pedro Gonzalez, was of Indian blood on his mother's side. He spoke Mochica from his babyhood, and after studying theology

in his homeland and taking Holy Orders he compiled a grammar
of his mother tongue in the year 1644.[48] Conforming to the
custom of the Inca, who dubbed all the coastal inhabitants as
Yunga, he called it 'Lengua Yunga'. According to him it was
spoken at that time by more than 40,000 people from the Viru
to the Motupe valley, corresponding precisely to the area of the
original Chimu kingdom (Map page 182).

With the help of his grammar and the individual accounts of
the chroniclers one can obtain an overall view of the nature of
this language, which later naturally fell more and more under
the influence of Spanish, so that researches today carried out on
the spot are of little value. Like all Indian tongues, Mochica was
capable of agglutination, or, to be more precise, of running
together entire word-sequences and trains of thought which can
be considered, as one wishes, to have arisen either as the expression of a philosophical spirit or of primitive clumsiness. Much
was made of this peculiarity of the Indian language by the first
Spaniards and in later times. In reality the practice is neither rare
nor peculiar. The French liaison goes in a similar direction, and
in German it is possible to build word-monsters such as *Auto-
mobilmotorenbetriebsstoffüberwachungsaktiengesellschaft* (motor-
car fuel supervision limited company) and similar oddities which
need not necessarily be a straightforward stringing together of
nouns. All adverbial parts of speech can be used, and ugly but
comprehensible coinage such as *Nichtnachhausegehenkönnen*
(the inability to go home) are more strongly agglutinative than
many Indian constructions. These combinations can all be dis-
solved just as the Indian word-sequences for the initiated can be
split up into their individual parts.

It may be of interest to introduce here a few words from the
Chimu language: a neighbour—*anmann*; idle—*taeraeg*; a
young animal—*jungeis*; the breast—*tsitsu*, which has a similarity
with teat; the mouth—*sapp*, which recalls words like *saufen* in
German or *soup* in English, to make a few comparisons with the
Anglo-Saxon languages. To lie or to be hypocritical—*fein,*
is reminiscent of the French *feindre*, whilst the comparative *pire*
in the same language corresponds in Mochica to the simple form
pis—bad. Here once more there is comparison, because the
French final letter is silent and the 'r' and the 's' in language

B*

are usually interchangeable. Since in Mochica mother is either *eng* or *inga*, according to its position in the sentence, one needs only to change it slightly to get the Greek word for a woman, *gyne*. In the word *ssoy* for blind one can perhaps read 'ex-oy', whereby an otherwise ancient word for eye not to be found in Mochica comes to light.

I—*moin*, resembles the German *mein*, the French reflexive *moi* and the Slav languages; the word *joig* for south is found in the Jugoslavian *jug*, and finally the Mochica word *per* for feather is similar to the Russian *pero*, thus one finds a direct Mongolian bridge. The differently derived word 'seven' in all European languages in Mochica is *nite*; this is nearer to the *nadan* of the Tungus and Manchurians, while the Quechua word *llama* for the indigenous mountain animal brings to mind that the Dalai Lama in Tibet means 'the one who lives up aloft'.

These examples should suffice for the reader to form his own judgment on this question, particularly when he reflects that many other words bear not the slightest resemblance to each other, or that sounds, as for example a bird not unlike the long-eared owl called *pucu*, can simply be explained as onomatopoeic. These similarities can be considered as pure coincidence, or in the light of the theories discussed on page 37. One thing is certain: words are often older than the myths and other racial tradition. They are born inversely but also anew and arise like the phoenix from its ashes. They derive from the speech-creating foundations of the psyche. Words change and are frequently transformed, and it always possible that what today seems alike may in an earlier age have been completely different.

In the foregoing examples of Chimu words, they have been spelt as far as possible phonetically to conform to the English sound values, just as in the old days the Spaniards wrote down Mochica as they heard it so that it could best be translated into their mother language. As a result of this necessity a great many confusions arose; the Indians, to quote from many examples, possessed a sound, unknown to the Spanish, comparable with the English 'w' in 'what'. They helped themselves, therefore, as best they could, and for this sound wrote the Spanish 'hu' and then 'gu' and 'vu' and also 'b' and 'u'. An example was the Quechua word *huaca*, which actually means 'I from here', a revelation of their ancestor worship, the general Indian term for the large and small shrines to be found all over the country. It is not surprising, then, that this word constantly rang in the ears of the Spaniards. They wrote it alternately as *huaca, uaco, vuacum* and frequently as *guaco*.

Apart from the above-mentioned word-comparisons, in writing Indian names we have generally conformed to the current Spanish orthography and pronunciation as being the best known internationally, and have refrained from all attempts at a more precise description of the sounds, since they can never be completely recaptured as they were pronounced and since they differed considerably in the old days, even at the time of the conquest, between north and south. A language by fixation in a script is less subject to change and can usually better preserve its unity. So far nothing has been discovered which would allow us to presume that the Chimu possessed a script.

Fernando Montesinos,[49] however, related that the ancient Peruvians possessed a script reputed to have been written on banana leaves and parchment, but that, as a result of invasions from enemy races at the time of 'Titu Yupanqui', the alphabet was lost and their king 'Topa Cauri Pachacuti VII', strictly forbade the continued use of it. A priest who invented a new alphabet was hanged. Montesinos further reports that the same Topa Cauri invented the quipu knots in order to record for his successors the great deeds of their ancestors.

Unfortunately this tale stems from a chronicler who often indulged in pure fiction.[50] As long as no evidence appears to disprove it, we must accept that the Chimu had no alphabet, although the possibility can by no means be ruled out. In olden days the script was often a secret and the exclusive property of the priesthood or the ruler and could for a great variety of reasons have disappeared with them. They may have been purposely destroyed, just as the Spanish invaders of Mexico in their blind fanaticism carried away countless beautiful and valuable illuminated manuscripts before the eyes of the terrified 'savages', and burned them as the works of the Devil.[51] Very few of these books with their doubly folded leaves of stag leather or agave fibre coated with fine chalk have survived.

Moreover, Sahagun relates that not only the Spaniards but the

Mexican princes themselves once burned the scripts under their king Itzcoatl so that they should not be profaned or their subjects corrupted.[52] There is nothing to disprove that something similar may have occurred among the South American civilisations. Bingham alone of modern American ethnologists is of the opinion that the ancient Peruvians possessed a script.[53]

The quipus (Plate 20) or knotted cords, also reported by Montesinos, who on this occasion corroborates various other chroniclers and recent finds, were by no means the exclusive property of the Incas or the Chimu. They existed in other regions both in South and North America. In China, Tartary and a great part of east Asia, a form of knot script was also used before the invention of ideographs. The quipus were naturally closely bound up with the textiles. Apart from the use of the cords, anyone who wished to tax his memory had to count. It is certainly no coincidence that this latter word in German is *Erzählen* and in the French *raconter*. The ancient Spaniards in their account often attribute a strong telling significance to the quipus.

No word-sequence has yet come to light in the different excavations. Recent researches, however,[54] have shown convincingly that with most of the quipus the decimal system, unknown to the Romans, was used extensively in the knot groups for 1s, 10s and 100s and probably for 1,000s and 10,000s. Apart from statistical purposes these cords were certainly of great importance in completing the calendar.[55]

But all this together with the language is comparatively insignificant. The most powerful language in which the coastal peoples still speak to the modern world resides in the sum total of their well-preserved art treasures, which not only boldly portray with a wealth of naturalistic detail their daily physical life but also their entire spiritual stature. Where the examination of skulls, skin pigmentation, speech and much else fails, art as one of the most primal utterances of the human race comes to our aid. The excavations of the last few decades have provided material which gives a clear picture of the lives of the coast inhabitants, of their whole existence and, last but not least, of their religious ideas. But in order to understand on what foundations this entire culture developed it will be necessary in the following chapter to describe their ordinary daily lives.

CHAPTER THREE

The Material Foundations of the Civilisation

T H E external conditions of life in the coastal area were far more favourable to the development of an indigenous civilisation than might appear at first sight.

The warm, in fact rather hot climate in those regions is by no means enervating, thanks to the dryness of the air and to the fact that a cold sea-current, the Humboldt stream, runs the whole length of the seaboard, only veering west when it reaches the Gulf of Guayaquil in the north. Thanks to this cooling stream the land cools off comfortably at night and a light dew occasionally descends upon the valley vegetation, upon those small isolated oases among the deserts and shifting sands.

Many of the rivers only bring down their waters between October and May, during the rainy season in the highlands; those, however, with sources deeper in the mountains flow throughout the whole year, although in the dry season the waters shrink to a tenth of their normal volume. Many of the watercourses which today fertilise the valleys only at certain seasons were formerly perpetual, because in those days the western slopes of the mountains were covered with trees, which the Spanish colonials proceeded to cut down.[56]

The forests alone, however, were in a position to collect the necessary water from the regular downpours in the highlands, because in the lower parts of the valleys rain only falls in very exceptional years. In this event the water is not considered at all fortunate, but as an appalling, destructive power which is to be feared like some natural cataclysm.

Normally in the winter, from June to November, the coast affords rather a gloomy picture; a thick mantle of metallic grey cloud hangs about 15,000 feet above the turbulent sea, producing an unpleasant grey light beneath which the whole land appears hostile and abandoned. During these months the only relieving note is the carpet of short-stemmed flowers, nourished by the night dew, which grow in huge patches on the otherwise bare slopes.

The bottom of the valleys, as a result of the mud brought down from the mountains by the rivers in the rainy season together with washed-out minerals and other rich and fertile deposits, makes agriculture easy and rewarding. To till the soil in the loose floodland requires very little effort.

It was not difficult by the use of the so-called 'cultivation at depth' to lift the layer of sand until a fruitful and rich soil was reached at a low level in the damp earth, in which the crops could be planted. The water, trickling down from the slopes, led very early to the terraced cultivations and encouraged artificial irrigation.

To facilitate matters, on the nearby islands manure was available in the form of enormous quantities of bird droppings, in Indian *huanu*, a word which has entered our vocabulary as guano. Soon the droppings of countless small fish were also used as manure; mixed with fresh earth and a little lime it was placed round the plants.

For tilling this fertile soil very simple implements, similar to those used by the North American Indians, sufficed. To plough the soil they used long, pointed spades and small hoes either of hardwood, or wooden hafts with solid stone and copper blades attached. These have been found in great numbers. In addition, to loosen the soil, spades of algaroba wood with the digging surfaces of metal and in the northern region a simple plough were used. The latter consisted of a six-feet-long pointed stake below, attached about twenty inches above the soil to a cross-bar on which the peasant could set his foot and bring his added weight to the plough. Normally this implement was drawn across the field on a rope by three or four men, two of whom took the stake and pressed it by the cross-bar as deeply as possible into the soil.

Other finds have come to light which point to the use of leverage, the cross-bar being filled on both sides with stout stakes which with the aid of both arms gave a substantial pressure on the plough itself. Harrowing and raking, on the other hand, were unknown both among the Chimu and the Incas. To split up the sods and to level the furrows a number of women followed the plough with pointed stakes and hoes. Most of the additional work in the fields, including sowing, planting and harvesting, was left to the women.

Many wild plants capable of cultivation were available; the luxuriant reeds by the coast furnished material for plaiting and mats; there was plenty of clay for their pottery and plenty of mineral and vegetable dyes for the decoration of bowls, pots, pitchers and other utensils, which soon inspired the artistic genius of this race. Finally the material for tiles was easily obtainable, and the loam did not even have to be fired to acquire rigidity but merely to be laid out to dry in the hot sun. Thus all the requisites for the development of a higher civilisation were to hand and life was by no means arduous.

The best possible conditions for growing mandioca were to be found in the coastal valleys. Like many tropical, cultivated plants, this shrub afforded a great yield for very little work. A few stalks had to be planted in the soil, and the bulbous roots needed no attention but remained the entire year in the earth and could be dug up at any time for food. This tuber did not call for a settled population. After several months' wandering the hunters could return to a field and leave it again if he felt so inclined. The Chimu, however, cultivated a number of nourishing plants such as maize, sweet potatoes, melons, beans and gourds, the latter providing them with practical bowls and pitchers. Countless fruits, nuts and spices such as pepper must be added to the rich diet enjoyed by this fortunate race.

In addition they cultivated a host of useful shrubs, above all cotton and toquilla, a reed from which the so-called panama hats are made and since time immemorial has served for all manner of woven straw and matting. The American agave, the fibre of which was much used, grew wild in vast quantities and was only seldom an object of planned cultivation.

They bestowed their greatest attention on the maize and the sweet potato; maize was their staple diet and a bad harvest meant disaster on a national scale. As a result of the importance it held for the agriculture of the country, it naturally played a very significant role in the people's worship, and for this reason we must say a few words on this subject.

The maize, or Indian corn, is a child of the American soil. Legend maintains that it stems from a kind of grass that once grew in the Mexico valley which the Aztecs called Teocintli, the sacred maize. It was many a long year from the day some Indian hunter carelessly let fall a few straws outside his tent to discover how easy it was to raise this cereal to the time when the maize was cultivated throughout the two Americas. For it has been found in this guise since prehistoric times everywhere the climate allows it to grow. The knowledge of a common origin is not to be found and the different Indian races have the most varied names for the plant,[57] which would hardly be the case had its distribution started from one particular spot. The maize adapts itself to a whole range of climates and changing soil conditions. Grains of this Indian corn found in tombs show that at a very early date several varieties were produced. They are often found with huge, long cobs, while other types exist with yellow, red, grey and even with spotted grains.

Among the serviceable woods we must mention in particular the algaroba and the balsa tree. The former has an extremely gnarled and writhing trunk of more than thirty feet, spreading out into countless branches. Its roots do not descend deep into the ground, so that in a gale it is often blown on to its side, whereby it continues to grow in the strangest possible forms. Such a trunk naturally produces very little serviceable wood, and what is to be had is very uneven. Nevertheless, in default of anything better the algaroba wood was the one most used for building, all along the coast.

The balsa tree, on the contrary, is erect, slim and tall and above all extraordinarily porous; on this account it was used for the building of balsas or rafts. Since this soft, light wood was susceptible to strong pressure, it could very seldom be used for building purposes.

In strange contrast to this otherwise so barren coast, a bright-coloured and variegated life rules above the waves. Countless birds, above all gulls, geese, pelicans, cormorants and many other species fill the air in their hosts, as they have done since time immemorial. Less easy to see but no less plentiful is the marine fauna. The bays and shores of the coastal islands teem with schools of seals, sharks and dolphins sporting in these waters.

3 Heads of
rulers

4 *Above:* A Peruvian Balsa from a later age. *Below:* Carvings on ancient Indian leeboa

5 *Above:* Tethered llama kid *Below:* North-west Argentine clay vessels with crucifix symbols

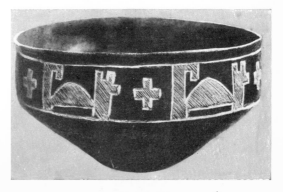

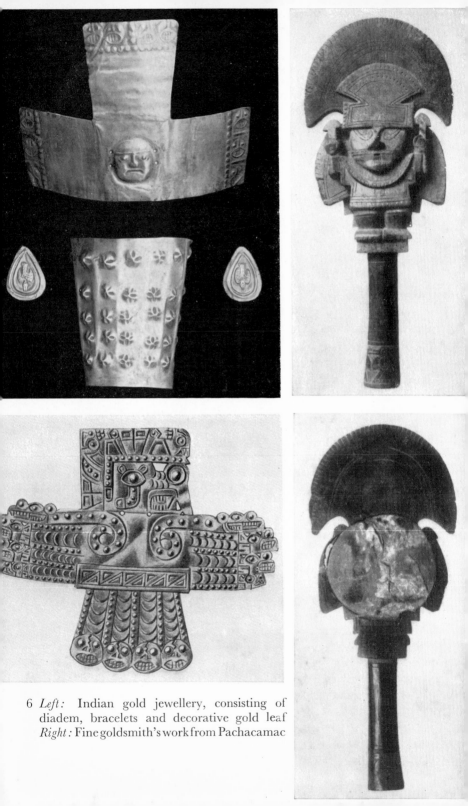

6 *Left:* Indian gold jewellery, consisting of
diadem, bracelets and decorative gold leaf
Right: Fine goldsmith's work from Pachacamac

Silverfish, sea shadows, flounders, rays, eels, sea perch, swordfish and tuna are to be found in incredible shoals.

It is little wonder, then, that fishing was one of the main occupations of the coastal peoples. Fishing was done mainly with a net or a hook, but narcotics and harpoons were not unknown. Usually a seine net was stretched, weighted with stones, between two balsas and lowered into the water. Many finds have brought

Mythical fishing scene from an early Chimu vessel

to light smaller sack-shaped nets. Fishing with a hook was done with the help of a long rope or a wand from the boat. Double hooks were frequently used, the rope being spliced in two with a hook on each end. The hooks were of copper, without barbs.

A particularly original mode of fishing was the use of huge bundles of reeds or bamboo bound in pairs and raised in front in the shape of a beak. One can still occasionally see today these craft which the Spaniards call *caballitos*. The fisherman sits or kneels on them, and on account of their great buoyancy, due to the air being enclosed between the knots of the bamboo, with the use of a small rudder can steer the vessel with great safety through the waves. After long use the 'sea-horses' were simply beached and dried in the sun.

One of the most interesting customs, however, which we see in many Chimu pictures as well as in China, was the age-old cormorant fishing. The patterns of old textiles show this bird helping to fish, and one sees him with the fisherman on a big raft with a cord tied round his neck, sitting there in great dignity as though fully aware of his importance. The cormorant, whose name is a mutilation of the Latin *corvus marinus*, has nothing in common with the raven except its black plumage, which, in the case of adult birds, assumes a metallic sheen on the breast and back. These sea-ravens do not fly in big flocks but in small coveys in Indian file with neck and head outstretched and a very swift wing action. They can rise high into the air but usually skim over the water. They are not divers, but fish by swimming and diving, can remain for very long periods under the water and swim there with incredible speed. The sea off the Peruvian coast is often dotted with their yellow-beaked heads, and when frightened they can be seen paddling away and disappearing beneath the surface.

While the nutritious vegetable diet of the Chimu was augmented by all these marine creatures, on land they also had the meat of various species of birds, one of which was a kind of duck called *nunuma*. According to Garcilaso it was larger than a European duck but smaller than a goose. Cieza de Leon also mentions these tame ducks and describes their plumage as black. Pictures of duck-like birds on Chimu ceramics, carvings and textiles are very common (Plates 18 and 20).

Among the reptiles, lizards were very common on the coast; some of them grew to a length of three feet. The iguana can reach four feet six inches and is usually leaf green but in places bluish-green or greyish-brown. It has a comb on its back, a scaly skin and a little pouch beneath the chin. When driven into a corner it defends itself bravely and is particularly vicious and sly. The females lay white eggs the size of a dove's in the sand, and in these breeding-holes one occasionally finds large clutches of eggs which have been laid by several beasts. The flesh and the eggs of the iguana are still relished today by the Indians.

As a true domesticated animal the guinea-pig was very widely bred in addition to the dog and the llama. According to the different colours of its dappled hide, found in the mummies, it must have been used at a very early period for sacrificial purposes as well as food. It is very seldom portrayed. Heavily peppered it is today in many regions one of the favourite dishes of the natives.

As regards the dog, the examination of a large quantity of animal bones furnished one more proof that Peru was populated from Central America. Man's truest companion, who has certainly accompanied him since the beginning, does not stem from South America and we must seek his closest ancestors, significantly enough, in Texas and Central America in the form of the *rufa* and *Mexicana* breeds.[58]

On account of the outstanding role which the dog played in the worship and in the whole religious conception of the coastal inhabitants, it must be noted that according to the shape of skulls and bones found in ancient Peru three distinct races can be distinguished—a type of sheepdog, a kind of dachshund and a fairly squat bulldog. These presumably represent the most ancient strains of the American domestic dog. These beasts were usually short-haired, but long-haired examples have been found among the dog mummies. Drawings of a realistic and a mythological nature are very common on both the earliest and the latest vessels and textiles throughout the country.

The llama, as a typical beast of the highlands, did not thrive on the coast, but it must often have been kept as a domestic animal, as is to be seen in the decorations on utensils and pottery. It was presumably always brought down to the plains from the upper valleys. To my mind its presence among the Chimu is a proof that since the earliest ages the latter had cultural relations with the inhabitants of the upper valleys and thus with the so-called Chavín culture.

According to the latest researches, the llama has been classified as a species bred from the wild guanaco. The alpaca stands in a similar relationship to the wild vicuña, so that it probably represents a hybrid species between the llama and the vicuña. The clearly defined results of this artificial breeding, namely the authenticated albinism and melanism in the llama and the alpaca, prove that they are both true domesticated animals and not tamed wild beasts.

The long, coarse wool of the llama on the coast, where the cotton plant grew and the climate demanded lighter clothing, did not play such a great part as among the inhabitants of the highlands, while the much finer and considerably longer wool of the alpaca and vicuña could be used for the silkiest materials. The colour of the llama, corresponding to the nature of true, domesticated animals, was very varied; some were completely white, others black, light and dark brown, the most usual colour being piebald.

The significance of these beasts, which stand midway between the Old World sheep and the camel, must be considered as being very high for the cultural development of Peru. With the dog and, in this respect, the insignificant guinea-pig they were the only domesticated animals. The llama, in particular, had an unmistakably ennobling influence in the Andes region, and the reason why the gruesome human sacrifices which took place in Mexico did not occur here is perhaps because a large animal could be sacrificed in place of a man. Countless pictures show a fine relationship between man and beast, although we cannot conceal the fact that in lonely regions the llama often served the young shepherds as a subject for sodomitic practices.

However much was accomplished in ancient Peru by vast expenditure of human energy, it is very questionable as to whether the enormous work entailed in the building of the ter-races would have been possible without the llama. Admittedly it can only carry a load of about 100 pounds on its back and cannot travel more than twelve miles a day; on the other hand it is extremely self-sufficient and, like the camel, can cross deserts for an incredibly long time, several weeks in fact, without needing water. If the fact that on the arrival of the whites the Indians had no knowledge of the wheel and many other amenities and that they did not use their beasts for milking aroused surprise it is easily explained in the case of the llama because the latter refused all attempts to milk it. An obstinate and self-opinionated beast, it goes berserk at any such attempt; it bites, kicks and makes use of its special defence weapon—spitting out a jet of evil-smelling cud. The meat of the llama kids is good and tasty. It was always much appreciated and in later ages was served almost exclusively at the ruler's table.

Hunting took place primarily in the upper valleys for the Andean stag and roe known as *taruca*, which lived singly or in herds in the bush. These beasts were caught for preference with the aid of nets and then killed with a club, rather in the way the fisherfolk operated.

Hunting with bow and arrow hardly seems to have been known among the Chimu, but in hunting, as in war, a catapult was used, a kind of hook on a board from which a spear was hurled. The meat obtained on the hunt was preserved by drying, brought down in this state by the mountain Indians and bartered with the coastal-dwellers for other commodities.

Stag hunting with net and catapult—vase decoration from Chan-Chan

Both meat and fish were eaten either raw, when not dried in the sun, or cooked with a lot of pepper and spice. Roasting the meat in dog fat, so much appreciated by the Aztecs, was quite unknown in Peru. The meal used for their various pastries was procured in an original way from the trunk of the algaroba and the tubers of the mandioca, both of which were scaled and rubbed together, squeezed and washed through a strip of bamboo and roasted as a complete dish, while the meal remained behind in the press, just as sago is cooked in Europe. The maize on the other hand was only ground and baked into cakes for great feasts; normally it was cooked quite simply and enjoyed as porridge or cut up small and roasted.

The Chimu also knew how to prepare from the corn a light beer which they called *cocho* or *cuzio*. The modern *chicha* of the Indians is prepared by soaking the maize for eight days in water and then letting it lie covered with earth for another five or six days. After this the cobs are dried in the sun, pounded between stones and soaked for one more day in a big cauldron. This drink, which is similar to wheat beer, is sieved through a large cloth and poured into clay vessels. It tastes sweet, and after being carefully stored takes on after a long time the flavour of wine. For festive occasions the Chimu brewed a strong intoxicating drink from specially malted maize or from cabuya juice.

The potato was eaten either roasted or boiled and could be conserved for a very long time. All their food was strongly peppered, occasionally sweetened with honey or syrup of young corn stalks, but the salt acquired by evaporation was seldom used for food. We have a good knowledge of the food of the Chimu from the Spanish chroniclers and also from those dishes buried with dead men, the remains of which have often been preserved.

Few of the vessels used to prepare the food have survived, since most of these plain cookery utensils were despised by collectors. Here and there in museums can be seen simple round clay pots, easily distinguishable by their blackened bases, and from various sources one learns that towards the end of their supremacy the Chimu used clay ovens pierced with holes for their cooking.

Among the various eating and drinking utensils used by the Chimu, as opposed to most of the South American races, appears the spoon, usually made of wood with a simple handle sometimes elaborately carved. Spoons made from bones or clay are also known, whereas the majority of the metal types were obviously used for industrial purposes.

Luxuries were alcoholic drinks, pepper, salt, honey and other sweetenings. Their main pleasure derived from the leaves of the coca plant. It grew in the highlands, was chewed with chalk as a narcotic and today helps the inhabitants to overcome long periods of hunger and thirst. This coca-chewing corresponds to the chewing of betel nut (also laced with burnt chalk) which is practised by more than two hundred million people in Asia. The utensils employed by the coastal inhabitants, above all the variety of containers to hold the chalk and the little spoons with their figured ornaments, are a common feature among the tomb treasures.

Finally the Chimu also knew tobacco. In the early ages and above all among the neighbouring races in the south, basing our knowledge on finds and ceramic decoration (Plate 48), it was apparently smoked through pipes[59] like those used today, while later it served more as snuff for exorcising and healing purposes. At the time of the conquest the Spaniards saw no trace of pipe tobacco being used or else they would have related the fact. On the other hand one learns that the Indians were great takers of snuff[60] and that the priests, in addition to other medicaments, mostly used green tobacco to achieve a state of ecstasy.[61]

From all we have said so far, it can be seen that Nature not only bestowed on the inhabitants of this land plenty of food and luxuries but that it also gave them the necessary materials for clothing and the other amenities of life.

The decoration on Chimu pottery shows every imaginable variety of costume from almost complete nakedness to the richest apparel. In many battle scenes one sees an acute difference between the victors and the vanquished. While the latter wear nothing but a loin-cloth, the former are richly dressed and adorned. It is probable that in these battles with savage races the prisoners had been robbed of their clothes before worse atrocities were perpetrated on them (Plate 12).

The loin-cloth was the first and most generally used article of clothing for the men. It consisted of a cummerbund wrapped round the hips, fastened with a strip of material in front, carried under the crutch and then wound round from behind as a belt, allowing the end of the cloth to hang down like a scarf.[62]

The next article worn over the loin-cloth was a close-fitting shirt (Plate 8) that varied very much in design. Sometimes it reached only to the hips like a jacket, while in other cases it fell down as far as the knees like a tunic. Shirts with both long and half-length sleeves and even sleeveless are portrayed in pictures, the first of these being the most common.

Skirts for men reaching to the knee, lengthening the short, tunic-like shirt, as can be seen in the accompanying illustration, similar to pictures from the ancient Orient and to Scottish folk-costume, seem to have been fairly frequently worn. The main article of feminine attire consisted of a length of light cloth, artificially draped over the whole body, reaching down to the feet and fastened with a broad girdle and many or few costly pins of silver, gold or copper.

Men wearing skirts—on a clay vessel from
Chan-Chan

The cloak of the early Chimu also consisted mainly of a square blanket, considerably longer than broad, worn over the shoulders and held together on the chest, while at the back it reached down to the knees and sometimes to the ground. The later poncho, on the other hand, was unknown to the Chimu. These cloaks, as will be seen on many of the vessels, naturally gave the wearers an opportunity of arranging them in graceful ceremonial folds. Some of them were six feet long.[63] They were usually made of white cotton and, as a result of their length, could also be thrown over the head like a hood, to protect the whole body.[64]

This leads to the discussion of the head-dress. It was mostly divided into three parts, the first protecting the actual head like a cap, the protective neck-cloth and, but not always, a band to fasten it under the chin or on the nape of the neck. From this original form a host of magnificent head-adornments were designed both for peace and war. The head-dress for peacetime was particularly attractive and practical for that region. Since the basic material was cotton with a wool pattern, a light practical head-covering resulted, while the neck-cloth protected the wearer from the sun, giving him both coolness and dignity.

Another form of headgear was the bright-coloured feather

helmet with a beautiful feather mosaic of woollen stripes which hung down the back. For special occasions it was customary to wear a little wildcat skin, the head of the beast to the front above the brow and the tail hanging down the back. For war purposes the cap was reinforced by a helmet, often spiked but adorned with feathers or animal emblems. The totemistic tradition comes to light here. At feasts and dances the normal costumes were considerably embellished by animal and human masks, stout magic staves as well as wings and plumes of magnificent feather-work (Plate 48).

As regards footwear, countless finds have revealed that the wearing of sandals was almost general. In addition, however, real shoes from many of the coastal regions have been recovered. For lighter footgear straw was used as well as skins and leather and finally the most magnificent sandals made of pure silver have been found.

A difficult question but one which must finally be answered in the negative is whether the Chimu wore stockings or socks. Since nothing of this nature has so far been found, we must accept that many such foot-adornments to be seen on vases are no more than decoration in the traditional mode. Here we must recall Xam Muchec, the grand master of King Naymlap's wardrobe, with his dyes and unguents. Both the men and women of the Chimu painted their faces.

According to the discoveries of mummies and vessels (Plates 29–31), tattooing also, at least among certain classes, was undoubtedly widespread among the population. Of their actual practice of tattooing we know nothing. Probably small bone utensils with sharp points such as occasionally turn up in collections were used. In the north skulls have been found showing an obvious teeth decoration, the canines and molars of the upper jaw being inlaid with little gold discs on the front, showing little polished grooves to contain the gold leaf. Dentistry can hardly be suspected.

As to whether the many known skull deformations denote an adornment or whether they served for religious purposes or to differentiate between classes remains uncertain. In any case such class distinctions as we know from the sources were betrayed by the hair styles, which assumed a great variety of forms. The hairdresser's art was practised with great care, and we learn that in certain regions the women washed their hair in juice of aloes to heighten its gleam and blackness. Combs appear of all shapes, both single and double (Plate 7).

An important accessory for beauty treatment was the mirror. The Spaniards mention them of polished silver and of copper, while in the collections we can find examples in pyrites in the simple form of round discs with a smooth, polished surface. One occasionally finds a similar disc in a decorative carved wooden frame with a handle exactly like a modern hand mirror (Plate 6).

Ceramic decoration in early Chimu style

We must not forget the little pincers which have come to light in countless forms, made of copper, silver and gold, often richly chased, used by the ancient Chimu to pluck their beards. With the sparse growth of hair common to the Indian races, this instrument, a kind of pincers with a broad lower end and a long or short handle, was completely adequate (Plate 7). There are also circular types, without a handle, covered with figures. These pincers were hung on cords with a host of other trifles or worn in rows on necklaces, so that they can hardly be considered as utensils but rather as jewellery.

To end this chapter we shall now deal with the most important subject, the dwellings of the Chimu. It is characteristic that from the very start, they consisted less of individual houses than of large communal buildings in which whole clans lived. These enormous barracks will be described in greater detail when we speak of the conditions ruling in their society on page 85.

The few single dwelling-houses in the almost rainless coastal region were either built of clay tiles dried in the sun, known as adobe, or simply of bamboo. These houses, like the magnificent palaces, were roofed with a comparatively broad, very outjutting thatch. Peru in the past was subject more and more frequently to serious earthquakes, and this was undoubtedly the main reason for such light roof construction.

The typical dwelling of the later Inca age, a square, gabled house with an interior doorless wall rising to the coping, separated into two main compartments, reverts to the age-old communal dwelling of the Peruvian Indians, to a basic form of house which is clearly portrayed on Chimu ceramics (Plate 8). Mythological drawings on vases from the early period already show this typical design (page 131).

In addition to the square building with a gabled roof and the old round edifice, they built for daily use shed-like houses with a roof sloping only on one side resting on two upright poles, the top on forked piles.

As regards home comfort the coast seemed, in general, better provided for than the highlands. The Chimu beds had real mattresses of cotton and sometimes of wool. As many of the pictures show, the head was raised, presumably by cushions. We hear of wooden beds, in which the Chimu, as most of the primitive folk of South America do today, preferred to sleep on their bellies. This can be observed in countless pictures.

For seating purposes small low stools were available (Plate 8), or people sat tailor-fashion on the floor as they do in Asia. Occasionally one sees Indians resting in a position which is normal for them but difficult to understand for a European—leaning with their back against a wall, squatting on their heels with knees well bent and the elbows resting on the thighs. Of the use of litters and many other objects denoting a high material civilisation, details will be found in the following chapters.

CHAPTER FOUR

Religion and Myth

THE spiritual bond which unites the Chimu kingdom with the more southern coastal civilisations is moon worship. It differentiates the conceptual world of these races from that of the later Inca with their strongly marked sun worship. Not until the weapons of Tupac Yupanqui, at the beginning of the fifteenth century, destroyed the armies of the Chimo Capac did the hour come on the coast when the sun more and more ousted the moon and a solar view of the world triumphed over the lunar.

Before closer examination of the Chimu moon worship it is necessary to cast a glance at the general rise of religious concepts among the Indians. A development which applies more or less to every race can be followed in their case with particular ease. Religion is not the indelible imprint of a certain race; its concepts like morals and customs, social life, art and science go hand in hand with its contemporary stage of civilisation.

The origins of all Indian religions lie in the fear of the inexplicable powers of Nature. The lightning which could split a tree, the turbulent rising water, hot springs, the fire-spitting mountains, the volcanic earthquakes which in those days suddenly made the ground rock beneath their feet, comets, unexpected falling stars—all these inspired the Indians with terror and apprehension. At first they thought to see in them hidden enemy powers. The simplest Indian languages have no expression which suggests a trace of religion apart from demon and evil spirit.

Curiosity, however, certainly one of the oldest driving forces in man, led him constantly into the mysterious darkness of the forest and out on to the sea, filling him with amazement and encouraging him to interpret the many phenomena of these natural powers. Even in their first stages of civilisation the Indians, like all hunting and fishing races, were acute observers of Nature.

Thus they did not overlook the constant struggle for existence in the animal world—the eternal internecine war which was so similar to their own life. The Indian also observed that animals possessed certain useful characteristics which men lacked. The great beasts of prey displayed a strength, the marine fauna an art of swimming and diving, and the birds the power of flight which could but arouse envy in him.

Soon to these characteristics were joined others which in his imagination he endowed with supernatural powers. In the rustling leaves of the forests he sensed the breathing of a demonic creature, in the crash of the thunder he heard the powerful wing-beats of the mythical thunderbird. Thus in his imagination the beasts appeared superior to him. But then he noticed that they too needed food, needed to breed and were subject to death, soon making him conclude that there was a certain affinity and alliance between the world of men and beasts. In the oldest Indian myths, men and beasts meet each other on equal footing, communicate in the same speech and approach each other on friendly or hostile terms. An alliance often results between men and beasts, the fruit of which appears as the visible union of two creatures.

This attitude towards the animal considered as a relative or a good friend from which the most varied magical powers can be transferred to man is generally called totemism. Since religious concepts are never of sudden birth and never entirely die but, as history shows, continue to bear for centuries the barely visible traces of their predecessors, one finds in the whole late religion of the Chimu, and even more in the art of the more southern regions, a series of totemistic traits.

The universal idea of totemism, based on the premise that man is a member of the animal kingdom, cannot be termed a religion in its narrower sense. Because it affords the thinking man a basis for his conception of existence, because it gives him a standard for his behaviour towards the world and the inexplicable, it is both useful and essential to be on good terms with the remaining natural phenomena, thus in a broader sense it comes within the orbit of religious experience.

In order not to speed on too far ahead with this thesis, I must mention here that the above-mentioned feeling of fear of the unknown powers was soon reinforced by a sense of gratitude to the benevolent powers of Nature. As they grew more civilised, the Indians gradually began to worship fire, heat, the waters and springs and the sea which gave them food, and to elaborate this worship into a simple cult. The desire to repay gifts, to placate the powers and make them bestow more favours led them from a highly comprehensible feeling of gratitude to the greatest variety of *quid pro quo*. These were the first sacrifices.

In all ages, men have considered the sun, moon and stars as something divine. In an earlier stage of civilisation, however, the overpowering significance of the sun for mankind was not nearly as obvious as one would imagine today. That the light of day stemmed from it had first to be discovered; for when the sun during the winter remained hidden for weeks on end behind the clouds, there was still light and the days continued their progress as usual. The path of the earth round the sun which determined the seasons could not be recognised in the sky.

The stars in the lonely hours of the night, however, in their gentle mystery and remoteness, must have aroused the kindest thoughts of man more than anything else. Around the moon and the resplendent constellations of the southern hemisphere, a host of the most beautiful myths were born, also among the Chimu. In the valley of Pacasmayo, according to the accounts of Calancha,[13] they told of man's origin from four stars, two of which were the parents of the kings and nobles, and the other two, no less brilliant, of the poor and working classes. The year was calculated neither by the path of the sun nor by the changing moon, but by a bright constellation which the Chimu called *Fur* and the Spaniards *Las Cabrillas*. It announced in the sky the arrival of spring, and the constellation in question was the Pleiades; its seven stars are repeatedly to be found on their ceramics and they played a similar role in Greek mythology.

Three stars which the Chimu called *Pata* and the Spaniards at a later date christened *Las tres Marias* appear in a charming Indian fairy story as one miscreant caught and held prisoner by two good stars. This refers to the magnificent constellation of Orion with his belt. The moon had dispatched the two stars to catch the third and to hand it over to the condors of the Andes as avengers. These vultures were portrayed by the four brilliant stars beneath the belt. There was no traditional story of Venus, but many symbolical designs on pottery can be attributed to her.

The role of the moon as lord of the sky was uncontested. Moon worship usually precedes sun worship in most of the older races. As opposed to the sun, the moon can be measured comparatively easily by its number of days. As the mysterious illuminator of the night it was also king of the dead and formed a spiritual bridge to the age-old cult of ancestor worship. The coastal region in particular called for a moon religion. The sun, with its burning

Canines on a crescent moon with stars, snakes and terraced symbols

rays, brought nothing but heat, drought and aridity. But at night the moon powdered the grass and plants with its soft mild light and covered the mountain slopes with dew. The influence of the moon on the tides and on women could not remain long hidden from the Indians, and its constant changes must have exercised their imagination.

Already in the earliest temples and on the oldest Chimu ceramics the moon is the focal point of a well-defined worship. The priests declared it to be the highest deity and still maintained this at the time when the new sun worship threatened the land, since the latter only stood in the sky during the day while the moon could often be seen by day as well as by night. Another ground for their opinion was the fact, which they had observed quite correctly, that the moon at times eclipsed the sun but that the reverse never happened. Solar eclipses even in the latest age of the Chimu were celebrated with great pomp in honour of the

moon as victor. But when the shadows of the earth fell on the
moon, causing its eclipse, it was a period of general mourning,
and as long as its face was covered specific ceremonies and dances
were performed. This recalls the early Christian era when, as
Hrabanus Maurus of Hesse in the middle of the ninth century
relates, the missionaries complained that the Germans still greeted
'Herr Mond' and during the eclipses hurried to his aid with a
great tumult and shouting.

To return to our main theme, it can be maintained that the
older and newer stages run parallel with each other throughout
the religious concepts of the Chimu. The moment a regular
priesthood collected the fruits of a religious thought, creating
and developing from a simple worship of the inexplicable an
actual religion with a ritual and dogma, the old totemistic concepts of the beasts had to be brought into the service of the deity.

As beasts of the moon the wolf, the dog and the fox must
rank above all. The previously mentioned acute talent for
observation among the Indians allowed them to see from the start
the character of these canines as night prowlers. They recognised
the dog in particular, man's first domesticated animal, as a true
and devoted servant. Why should they not look upon him then
as a servant of the moon since they saw often enough how the
beast held conversations with it in long-drawn-out howls. This
position of the canines as vassals of the moon can be observed,
as among all the ancient peoples of the world, throughout
America, and if in a later era—as in Mexico—the fire god was
given the calendar description 'triple hound' with the dog as
the symbol of the all-devouring fire, this is no more than the
adoption of vestiges of an old moon religion which ruled there
long before the cult of the sun.

In Tlaxcala, when the summer rain failed to fall at the usual
time, the Mexicans collected a number of their hairless dogs and
brought them to be sacrificed in the temple of Xoloteopan, believ-
ing it would soon start to rain with thunder and lightning.[65] The
rain, however, is connected with the moon, and the latter with
fertility, the night and the underworld—the last two concepts
being ambivalent.

It is significant that in Mexico, too, a dog appears as a guide
for the dead. The Greek Cerberus, the three-headed dog with

7 *Top left:* Pins and various articles of Chimu adornment in bronze and silver *Top right:* Gold beard pluckers of various styles *Below:* various double and single combs

8
Left: The Chimu
house *Centre:*
Carved wooden
box and wooden
stool *Bottom left:*
Embroidered
shirt *Bottom right:*
Shoes of leather
silver and bast

9 Canine heads in Chimu worship *Above and below right:* Chimbote vessels *Below left:* Mask in copper-gold alloy with moon decoration from the Huaca de la Luna at Moche

10

Top left: The Mexican Flowe
prince Xochipilli *Top righ*
Enthroned Chimu figure. D
sign detail on page 141 *Lef*
Spouted vessel in mature Chim
style

the serpent scales which guarded the underworld, admitting everyone but never releasing them again, was represented in the Aztec belief by the god Xolotl, who, as a dog-headed figure, led the dead and also the sun into the underworld—the latter, of course, as it sank into the night. According to the Aztec concept, a nine-branched river, Chicunauhmictlan, like the Greek Styx, surrounded the underworld and the souls of the dead had to cross it with the aid of a red dog. This ninefold river was merely a symbol of the western ocean into which the sun sank.

Thus the dog in Mexico was a moon beast, and in the land of Chimu it was no different. This is corroborated by various chroniclers,[66] in particular Cieza de León.[67] Countless finds of

decorative canine heads used in the cult prove this (Plate 9)— above all the metal head from the moon pyramid at Moche— as does the accompanying illustration. This reproduction of a mythical Chimu vase design shows two dog-like creatures dressed as men carrying a litter, on the stepped chair of which sits a figure with a bird-like face portraying, of course, the moon divinity. Sitting on the steps of the pyramid it can be distinguished as Lord of the Night by the crescent moon worn as an adornment behind its head, and a disc on a ray above its brow which, as in many similar pictures, signifies the accompanying evening star. The dogs in this illustration do not have natural tails but artificial ones tied to their waist. From what we know of the myths of the Chimu there is no explanation for this strange picture, but we do find something similar in the general present-day Indian conceptions of creation. Many tribes of the Haida and Tlincit, the autochthonous inhabitants of the west coast of Canada, have especially worshipped the dog with a strong tinge of totemistic thought, and often made it the focal point of their cult. The voyages of discovery by Captain Cook and George Vancouver in the last quarter of the eighteenth century opened up these regions, and Captain Cook brought home a magnificent collection of North-west American works of art. The merit and value of these were immediately recognised and most of them are today in the British Museum.

In the creation legends the dog played a main role not only with these particular Indian tribes but with many others. The Tinneh and the Coniagas of Catiac Island actually believed that they had originated from dogs. They were very proud of this origin and even today refuse to eat the flesh of this animal, having the greatest contempt for those tribes which do so.

The Tinneh relate that when the world emerged from chaos a beautiful woman lived in a cave and fed on berries. Doubtless this picture is also connected with a mythological concept. In this myth the cave obviously signified the bowels of the earth and it is probable that the berries depict the stars. While this woman languished among her berries, continues the Tinneh legend, she met one day a beast like a hound who followed her to her abode. He had the power of changing himself into a handsome young man and in this form became the father of the first normal human being. In this female figure we can see Venus, who, on instructions from the moon, was fertilised by the canine, and also the old Peruvian idea that mankind originated from the stars or, as in olden days, we can consider the moon as female and the role of the dog remains constant.

The dog's outstanding mythological status not only holds good for countless Indian races but extends from the Eskimos through the north-eastern Asiatics across China to South-east Asia. The myth embraces the idea of the dog as custodian of the dead and watchman in Hell and also the belief that the human race originated from a dog and a woman. Naturally one must base the coincidence of cultural phenomena in various localities purely upon cultural relations. But when similarities are repeated in sundry characteristics, allowing us to presume a continual link, then their relationship becomes more than a mere probability. This dog-myth complex is an example and it furnishes a further, by no means contemptible, proof of the view expressed in this book that the Indians were of Asiatic origin.

Wilhelm Koppers[4] in a most convincing pamphlet has shown that this creation myth extends over the whole Pacific area, making it appear that an ancient matriarchal civilisation was brought across the Bering Straits to America by Asiatic nomads.

Such widely distributed concepts must never be forgotten where and whenever Indian civilisations are in question, and the most surprising conclusions can result from them. Thus the Potoyants in California believed that there was an age when there were no men living but only dogs. They credited them with great wisdom and they were believed to have gradually assumed human form. At first they displayed many imperfections, possessed neither hands nor ears like the front canine on page 65. Soon, according to this Indian creation myth, limb after limb was elaborated, until in time the perfect aspect of man was reached when he stood up on his hind legs and raised his eyes to the sky.

One object that they had not retained from their previous state distressed the Potoyants—man lost his handsome bushy tail. As soon as they had got used to sitting on their haunches this fine adornment gradually became superfluous and finally disappeared. What was once lost could never be recovered. But when the Potoyant went dancing or to a feast to banish his daily cares, he fastened on at the appropriate place an artificial, magnificent bushy tail, forgetting in those happy hours all the misery of the present, intoxicating himself in the magic of a magnificent past.

This custom of the Californian Indians reappears on the Chimu ceramics and is in consequence particularly significant because the custom of fastening on a dog's tail at certain festivities is not confined to the Ancient American, but appears in many Egyptian records and also on many of the old Swedish rock drawings.

This analogy is not confined to this charming custom of tying on a dog's tail, for we must remember what the fox's brush still means today in hunting. The whole representation of the moon divinity is repeated on a multi-coloured large clay vessel (Plate 12) from the Maya civilisation, discovered at Ratinlixul in Guatemala and now in the Philadelphia University Museum. The description of the figure as 'a nobleman on a journey', however, is very unsatisfactory, for it completely overlooks the entire nature of Indian art. When we examine the vessel in question it is obvious that it represents an enthroned figure carried on a litter by two bearers and accompanied by a dog; this cannot refer to some noble personality on a journey but is quite frankly a moon mythological scene. The litter in its crescent form signifies the nocturnal planet and the moon god, for the figure carries in his right hand a disc, possibly the symbol of Venus, his accompanying evening star.

Beneath him, however, we find once more the servant dog and on his back falls the round shadow of the moon. In the top right-hand corner can be seen the hieroglyph '*Ahua*', which in the Tzental dialect of the Maya means 'Lord and king', and '*Votau*', which in the same dialect means not only the scythe but the bowels of the earth. Thus this figure has been inscribed as the moon, the king of the night, and portrays the darkness which sweeps gently over the vault of heaven as in a litter.

In the complex thought of the early races with which we shall deal later in this book, it was only natural that the litter as a mode of transport should often replace the barque. Just as in Ancient Egypt we find a moon barque sailing on its own power we find it similarly in the world of imagination of the Peruvian coastal inhabitants.

Ceramic decoration from the Chicama Valley

The steering and propulsion of the ship, as will be seen in the illustrations on this and the preceding page is achieved by clearly recognisable human feet, while the water is symbolised by small hooks and scrolls. In both cases the barques are adorned with serpent heads and as the property of the moon carry pitchers which contain the night dew. The above picture illustrates the comparison I made on page 18 with the 'blade' of modern sailing craft designed to give extra balance to the balsas. In this picture they are combined in a curious way with the legs. Finally the fish, which in this mythical drawing can be easily recognised as rays, appertained to the fish cult of the Indians. As I shall explain in a later chapter, this cult is bound up with the creation myths, and is to be found among the most disparate races. The oldest example is the Babylonian god Marduk, who caught in his gigantic net the monster Tiamat; it was depicted in the sky as the whale or Cretos which he split in two with his terrifying weapon. The Nordic saga of Thor who from a boat fished up the Midgard serpent belongs in this category (page 72).

As to how far we can regard as an ancient moon god the figure with the radiant halo and the scaled armour on its back in the ship to the left of the picture will be discussed to some purpose later in the book on page 151. It is also uncertain whether the smaller and less radiant figure on the right portrays Venus and whether in the larger ship in the illustration below she appears in her dual role of morning and evening star.

In Greek mythology Cerberus is not portrayed as scaled like a serpent by accident, for, next to the dog, the snake is considered a typical nocturnal beast. Among the Indians it is one of the most

Moon mythological pattern on a Chimu vase

important ambassadors of the underworld, just as the dragon is in China and the griffin in Europe. It comes from the centre of the earth and is far more mysterious than the fox, the relation of the dog, and already in the earliest ages, since religious portrayals were primarily dictated by fear, it was one of the most incomprehensible and terrifying creatures : it moved without feet, preyed on its fellow creatures and could mesmerise them with its glances and consume them in the most hideous manner.

In South America, where are to be found sixteen species of reptiles, many of them poisonous, and in the north and east of the continent the monstrous boa-constrictor and the anaconda, it is not surprising if from the very beginning they fired the imagination of the Indians. Soon in the creation of their myths the licking, hissing, biting flame and the jagged lightning were metamorphosed into serpents. Just as the snake appears in the portrayal of the Indian, Egyptian, Persian and Greek gods of fire, so among the Chimu it is often found as a ray and fire symbol.

The ancient gods on the collapse of a religious system often become the principle of evil; this applied throughout the world to the snake. This also accounts for the portrayal of the Indian Ahi, the Persian Ahriman, the Greek Titans, the ancient Nordic Loki, and the biblical Lucifer as the ancient serpent, and why so many heroes of antiquity and even Christian saints appear as slayers of dragons. As to how far the snake, which is connected with the apple of the Garden of Eden or the golden apples guarded by the daughters of the Hesperides, is bound up with the old lunar concepts, symbolising no more than the moon, cannot be elaborated here. In any case the Hesperides were portrayed in company with a snake, namely the dragon Ladon. The sacred ball game in Mexico undoubtedly represented the movements of the heavenly bodies. It is not surprising, then, that the god Xolotl with its hundred canine heads is also the god of the ball game.

Ultimately in Ancient America when the snake reared its head from the ground and became the plumed serpent, it was connected with an idea of the world readily attainable for that age. The feathers rose into the sky like a bird, from which it originated and which it symbolised. In the plumed serpent one has the age-old motif of the eagle and the snake, which in a host of guises appears in all the civilisations of the world. Spiritual man is no more than the poor earth-worm crawling in the dust; he recognises the laws of good and evil. Snake and bird become a principle; the plumed serpent symbolises a divine duality. Or in the words of the great Chinese mystic, Lao-tze : 'Ying and Yang are united in the Tao'.

But in Ancient America the eagle[68] is already a sun beast. Together with him the puma and jaguar, common enough in Peru—like the lion and the tiger in other parts of the world— were mythically bound up with the sun. Wherever one meets these beasts as symbols and they are not portrayed in a purely naturalistic or totemistic manner, one strikes the border of the Chimu kingdom.

At some point, before the invasion of sun worship, thought appears to have developed into pure monotheism and the concept of an impersonal god, if not in the mass of people, then in individual cases of priests and seers. In no other way can we interpret Calancha's remarkable creation legend which the good monk has handed down to us in a very distorted form, seen through the spectacles of his own fanatical belief.[69]

It is a question here of the god Conn, envisaged as pure spirit hurrying at great speed through the world pregnant with divinity, levelling the countryside and making it fertile.[70] To arrive at such a concept of unity, the best thinkers among the Indians, like those of other races, had to emerge from plurality. It is no wonder, therefore, that even the bloodstained Aztec polytheists occasionally attained the same level of knowledge.

The mass of the people, however, remained polytheistic. Since the desire for the fertility of their fields lay nearest to their hearts, we find, in the pantheon of the Peruvian coast, the mythological figure of fertility portrayed on innumerable vessels of different kinds. Its association with the moon and the night divulges itself by a snake wound round its head, while in its association with death the thought of arrival and departure is suggested by the Pan pipes which surround the figure, when it is not actually blowing the syrinx. The connection between death and becoming, as a religious concept among ancient races, was never paradoxical as it is in many modern instances.

The individual gods with specific names such as Wotan described by the Spaniard Corzo and written by Oviedo[71] as Guatan,[72] recalling Teutonic mythology and the Maya hieroglyph Votan for the bowels of the earth; the divinity Pachacamac whose cult exercised an exceedingly strong influence along the coast, like the creator of the world Viracocha, will be treated together with the actual worship at various periods and in various places in our evaluation of the individual shrines in the regional chapters. In this present chapter, however, we are mainly concerned with general premises in order to arrive at an understanding of Indian belief, Indian civilisation and art; for in their expression they are irrevocably bound up with each other.

The Nordic god, Thor, fishing for the Midgard serpent. Scandinavian wall drawing
A.D. 1000

One learns from Calancha that the Chimu of Pacasmayo called their shrine Si-An 'The house of the Moon'[73] and he goes on to tell us that five-year-old children were sacrificed there on couches of coloured wool and bamboo rods together with offerings of maize beer to the moon. We should remember that similar sacrifices took place among the Indians and the Romans at the time of the new and full moons.

The modern reader who hears of human sacrifices must consider how these arose before making a judgment. To the first fear of the divine was soon added the longing to possess and in gratitude for the wish granted to give something in return. From this exceedingly human trait were born the first sacrifices. When great favours were to be asked human sacrifices were the order of the day. This has been the case in almost every age and among almost every race. From various tombs we have proof of it in prehistoric Europe.

The knowledge we possess of the whole cycle of civilisation in the Mediterranean is very substantial. Apart from the Old Testament peoples, red-headed men were sacrificed in Egypt to Busiris, and in Greece, during the Persian Wars, the nephews of King Xerxes were immolated. The Germans sacrificed prisoners of war to Ziu and to their god of the dead, Wotan; the north Germanic kings offered their own children to ensure longevity for themselves. This must be remembered before we express horror at the gruesome human sacrifices in Mexico, or form too hasty a judgment on the whole of Ancient American civilisation.

In the land of the Chimu, as far as we know today, such appalling holocausts as took place among the Aztecs never occurred. The actual sacrifices of which we have proof seem to have been extremely limited and to have been effected only during especially important rites of the cult.

This ritual was just as much the actual goal of human life in Chimu-land as it was in ancient Babylon, where Marduk created men 'so that the gods could live in a state of happiness'. In human sacrifice, these ages experienced their death and rebirth exactly as the world does today in each great war. Religions have different aspects. To the dogmatic and metaphysical must be added not only a symbolical and ritual but above all a moral and a social side. Only in association with the whole civilisation do they begin to shine, to become transparent and to allow a glimpse of things behind the scene. That is why the century-old changing picture of the coast cannot possibly be taken from the highly coloured tales of the chroniclers, who, as children of their age,

G*

were bound to consider all alien symbols as the work of the Devil. It would be quite pointless here to expound their versions of individual creation legends. The faith of the Chimu can be assessed far better from the countless artistic drawings, by sinking oneself in the psyche of this people, by obtaining a glimpse into its history, from the numerous finds and excavations. Its dead will perhaps forgive modern science for disturbing the peace of their tombs and bringing to light all the utensils they once held so dear, for as a result they will begin to rise again before the critical eye of the present as they lived many centuries ago and relate their own early history.

The veneration shown to the dead is the most ancient and universal form of worship in the world, and we can trace it back far into prehistoric times. To give the dead man not only food and weapons but also his favourite possessions and even the company of his wife, servants and pets by putting them to death and burying them with him to make his life agreeable in the beyond was such a universal custom, that it is not surprising we meet it again in the land of the Chimu. It is only natural that, apart from their own family ancestors, the ancestors of the race, its kings and nobles, should be greatly revered, assuming more and more the nature of a cult the farther the hero himself receded into the darkness of the past. He was often raised to the position of a tribal hero to whom the whole people owed its origin, and the names of the deified ancestors in question some-times meant no more than a simple lord and king, such as the first legendary Inca, Capac Manco, chieftain of the race. It is likely that in the Indian word Capac lies the root of the Latin *caput*, the head, and in Manco or Manso the archaic word for many benefactors of humanity from Mannus to Menes.

Apart from the burial ceremonies, the dances of the dead and innumerable rites of the cult, the ancestral worship in the land expressed itself most vividly in the veneration of the so-called Huacas, a word which signifies not only the large temples and pyramids but a host of small and insignificant objects sacred to the Indians. A great deal of nonsense about them has been written in the contemporary literature of art history and folklore, ignoring the deeper connections and based on casual ignorant tales of the Spaniards.[74] The Huacas are not only closely bound up with ancestor worship, they also go back to the first primitive religious feelings aroused in the imagination of the simple man by some strangely shaped stone or object. When it is said the Chimu worshipped stones we hope that after what we have said so far of Indian mythology the reader will now be able to distinguish between an apparently meaningless idolatry and rites which represented piety and general universal concepts. These stones were called *Alec Pong* and were no more than ancestral images, as the word denotes. *Alec* means a prince, identical with *Aleph*, in the old oriental language.[75] *Pong* means not only a stone, but also a spirit, in which latter sense one finds it again as *Wong* among many negro races.[76]

The same criticism applies when Garcilaso[77] relates[78] that the inhabitants of the region of Jauja, the Huancas,[79] were dog-worshippers. This account can be explained by the role that was attributed to the dog in the Indian imagination.

To sum up : all these things which, like the great Huaca temples—literally 'I from here' or 'sacred'—are closely connected with ancestor worship and the worship of the dead and are no more than the shallow but widely distributed stream of the religious feelings of simple people closely bound up with their daily lives, desires and hopes.

In a narrow sense the Huacas were portrayed and worshipped partly as humans and partly as animals. Most of them were figures as illustrated below with plant, moon and other symbols and above all with animal attributes. This betrays an age-old connection with totemism, and José de Arriaga,[80] who was a fanatical opponent of the Indians' belief but at the same time one of the greatest experts on their ancient traditional religious outlooks and customs, has written very shrewdly and at great length on these Huacas. He maintains that they gradually became pastoral gods and protectors of the fields and must be distinguished from the Canopas, represented in human or animal form, the adoration and conjuration of which were not public but confined to the families and the household servants, comparable with the Roman *lares* and *penates*. According to Arriaga the veneration of the Canopas was identical with that of the Huacas except that it was performed in narrower circles. They were also handed down as heirlooms by the family. When the father died they were bequeathed to the eldest son or some competent relative.[81]

The Chimu, like the Inca, believed in a kind of protective angel, who was known as Huauquey (brother). This did not signify a human brother but a good friend and companion. This conformed to the religious concept of the vengeful spirits of the dead. The Indians believed that the spirit of a man, Illa[82] (the gleaming), on his death left the body as an invisible figure of light and then wandered aimlessly on earth. For the most part they believed that these spirits of the dead remained in close

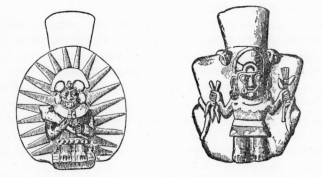

Huacas of Chimu pottery

contact with their relatives, protecting each of them from disaster. On the other hand the Indians also believed that the spirits of the departed would often take their revenge on those who had ill-treated them during their lifetime.

To protect them from such a revenge they not only had the above-mentioned protective guardian angel but also an amulet to frighten off or abjure the evil spirit. Each Indian possessed one and not infrequently several. They usually consisted of curiously shaped stones or pieces of metal as are often found today in the tombs, but parts of the totem animals were also used, such as claws, teeth, feathers, etc.

Everything connected with the ancestors or which had been in contact with them appears to have been endowed with supernatural powers; thus their forbears were always called upon to help when any important decisions or precautions had to be taken. The gayest feasts were laid on to this effect, and must be considered as ancestor worship and anniversaries. In this the mummies played an important role. This cult was greatly favoured by the climate, since the dry air protected the corpses from decomposition and enabled them, apart from the State mummies, to become a natural object of especial care. In many regions among the best-respected families the departed members were lined up in a row against the walls, often in the same rooms where the living ate and slept.

As Las Casas, corroborated by the archaeological finds, relates,[83] the nobles sometimes appointed the largest room of their house as a personal crypt and ossuary for their dead. In normal times the mummies of the rulers stood in the temple niches and their eye sockets—particularly on the south coast—were often filled with glittering eyes of octopus and occasionally, according to the chroniclers, with gold leaf. When the larger festivities approached, the mummies were brought out by the priests, cleaned, adorned and placed in the temple squares or carried around in gay procession on display as the sacred bodies of their ancestors. Archbishop Pedro de Villagomez of Lima confirmed this in his *Carta Pastorale* and translated the Indian word for such a mummy, *paccariscuna*,[84] as *Cuerpo de Sus progenitores*.

Father Juan Anello Oliva,[85] referring to this cult, relates that the Chimu mummies were known as *muñaos*, were housed in small shrines, adorned with feathers and covered with curtains of precious material.[86] This material was not merely cut at random from a length but related pictorially the deeds of the dead man, thus incorporating him in the ranks of the living. Special priests were enrolled in their service and sacrifices were made before them as in the case of the Huacas. The departed were surrounded by the objects they had used in their daily lives. They did not rank as actual deities but as ancestors worthy of reverence to whom the living owed a debt of gratitude and whose spirits could watch over their future. Details as to the burial of the dead with reference to the mummies will be discussed when we deal with the regional practices.

Ancestor worship as a whole was by no means the outward sign of religious practice but was most deeply connected with the outlook of the Chimu. As religion in its broadest sense represents the relationship of man to god, embracing the inexplicable, so also it rules the behaviour of man to man, in other words society, which for its part creates and transforms the religious forms of expression. Rather than end this chapter with a description of the dead I have preferred to start a new one with a study of the society and economy, in other words the institutions of the living.

CHAPTER FIVE

Society and Economy

THE coast had been politically subjugated by the Inca a bare hundred years when the first Spaniards arrived. Throughout the kingdom, which the Indians called Tahua-ntinsuyu, the invaders found the mythical number four. When Garcilaso translated this word as the 'four quarters of the world'[87] he was philologically inaccurate because the word merely means 'the four associated regions' or the four united provinces.[88] But the chronicler had judged correctly that the number four, which is still inherent in the present-day term 'living quarters' had some connection with an earlier religious concept of the world and heaven.

The conquerors were very surprised to find the inhabitants separated into groups of thousands, hundreds or tens. This separation had been devised by the ancient Italian and Germanic tribes, of whom the Spaniards were almost ignorant. The Peruvian races had much in common with the ancient Roman tribe, since they usually put ten thousand active warriors in the field, a hundred times a hundred, known as Hunu. The tribe was at the same time a well-organised army division which went to war under the leadership of its prince, the Curaca. It is interesting to note that in various tribes this Curaca was really educated for war since they needed the most capable man to take over command of the army, while the heir as the peacetime leader remained at home.

Each race normally comprised ten main tribes or groups of a thousand commanded by native chieftains as subordinate army corps and then split up further into hundreds and tens. The foundation stone of this whole social and military ramification was the Ayllu. At the time of the Spanish usurpation this word was used by the Indians to signify the family group and also the military hundred. Normally the complement of such an Ayllu could be reckoned as between six and seven hundred men, women and children. Based on the Viceroy Francisco de Toledo's census, it appears in fact that out of every six or seven members of the population at least one completely fit warrior was produced, so that for the troops the concept of the hundred was quite logical. In practice, however, there were naturally considerable fluctuations so that many groups of a thousand consisted of only eight to nine hundred and many a hundred comprised only seventy to eighty men, while elsewhere there was a surplus.

This distribution of the population endured to a large extent until the end of the sixteenth century, and we are well informed on this subject because the Spaniards were forced to use this reckoning to administer the land. Many of the tribes at that time, despite the declining birth-rate, still numbered fifty to sixty thousand souls.[89]

A few chroniclers and later writers who accepted their figures have attributed this distribution of the native population to the Inca, who were anxious to be kept closely informed about their subjects. This theory is quite understandable but historically false. The ancient distribution of Mongolian tribes was just as unknown to the Spaniards as was that of the Germans, the ancient Romans and many other races; like so many other organisations of this new wonderland, Peru, they were inclined to attribute this to the administrative prowess of the Inca. In actual fact the splitting into thousands and hundreds was far older than the Inca kingdom, and it is also clear that this system was by no means an anomaly developed historically. Small tribes, decimated in earlier wars, also possessed their five hundreds and fifties, and the terminology for the different groups was as varied as the position of the chiefs, their jurisdiction, choice and nomination.

There is no doubt that the basis of Chimu social life long before the Inca rule was a tribal and family organisation on the ancient Roman Gentile pattern. The most important chroniclers prove this. Bernabé Cobo[90] insists that from the chiefs of ten thousands downwards all the subordinate leaders were Caciques who had previously held the power in that particular region[91] and did not owe their position to the Inca. Las Casas also informs us[92] that the natives had long since possessed princes

11 Ancient Peruvian corn deity with crescent moon as head-dress

12

Top: Maya vessel
with moon mythological
design *Right:*
Chimu dish with warriors
and prisoners.
Brown design on a
white ground

13 'One-eye'

14
Left: Maya corn goddess *Below:* Two heads from the Chican Valley

from the chief of the ten thousand downwards before the Inca made them vassals. Francisco Falcón[93] and others corroborate this.

Just as the Roman tribes were divided into ten *curia* and then further in ten *gentes or centuriæ*, the individual races in old Peru were split up into ten main tribes and each of these into ten under-tribes.

The Spanish chroniclers recognised the relationship nature of this whole distribution. Santo Thomas remarks[94] that the Indians, like the ancient Romans and the modern Spaniards, used patronymics, which means that the names were handed down from grandfathers, fathers and brothers to the sons and further issue or taken from the country by its resident family members.

The ancient Peruvian Ayllu is of great cultural-historical significance not only as a form of social organisation; it admirably explains, when compared with its ancient Roman and German counterparts, the rise and development of different prehistoric economic organisations and the land ownership of the early agricultural peoples. By comparing the ancient Roman and the Indian edifice of society, one continually comes upon similar outlooks and customs. The Peruvian organisations are at a slightly lower stage of development and can be compared more or less with conditions reigning at the time of the first Roman kings.

To sum up: we know that the Chimu, like the ancient Romans and at a later date the Inca, had their particular clan names, which were handed down in the male line from father to son. In view of the totemistic concepts of the Indians, which we have already mentioned, it is not surprising that these names were constantly related to the beasts. Each clan had its own domicile, communal ploughland and fields, its particular deities, Huacas and Canopas, with their appropriate religious family feasts. The Roman ban on consanguinity ties was also applied by the Indians. Marriage with a woman from his own Ayllu was strictly forbidden.

Large families, therefore, developed because the sons not only remained with their parents until their marriage but settled down later with their young wives in the family house, which as a result constantly expanded. Similarly, the grandchildren later brought their wives to the grandparents' house to swell the numbers of those members of the family who had failed to marry or who had preferred to remain at home.

As we shall describe in greater detail when dealing with agriculture, everyone was allotted a certain job and even the children were occupied according to their strength and capacity.

For youth and age respectively, five stages of life were recognised, making in all ten spans of life. We give here the names in the later speech of the kingdom Quechua, as the Spaniards quite correctly recorded them.

(1) *Mosoc caparic:* The new-born babe still suckling its mother's breast.

(2) *Saya huamrac:* Toddler until the age of twelve months.

(3) *Macta puric:* The small child once it could walk until the age of five to six.

(4) *Ttanta raquizic:* The 'receiver of bread,' the school-child, as one would say today, who could not yet earn its own daily bread.

(5) *Pucllac huamrac:* 'The happy playtime' from eight to fifteen, during which time it performed light work under supervision, such as weeding and fruit-picking.

(6) *Coca pallac:* From sixteen to twenty, the age of 'the plucking of the coca leaf'. This task demanded a certain skill if the plant were to preserve its already mentioned narcotic property.

(7) *Ima huayna:* The 'almost youthful age' until the twenty-fifth year, when a young man was deemed to be an adult.

(8) *Hatum runa:* The man as full citizen and warrior with a right to his own home and a part of the community fields. This lasted until the age of fifty.

(9) *Chaupi rucu:* The 'half old'; this lasted until the sixtieth year when light work was still obligatory, and finally

(10) *Punuc rucu:* The 'frail, somnolent age' of dotage, when all tribute-paying ceased and he was no longer called upon for war service.

This well-determined distribution is as interesting as it is logical, since owing to the size of the families a good working order was essential. The elders were very insistent that no one should shirk his duty and the routine was carried out in a patriarchal manner. No young man could leave home without his father's permission, marry according to the dictates of his heart or treat his children as he wished. Although at the age of twenty-five the man was an independent adult he still had to obtain permission to marry from the head of the family, since the young couple had to be accepted into the larger household. The father, however, very seldom refused his permission except on special grounds. It was considered quite natural that a man who had reached the age of marriage should look round for a companion to increase the clan and provide more hands to help. A dowry, the Toma, was customary, and the community had to provide part of this. When several young people wished to marry the ceremony took place on the same day. A so-called 'lucky day' was chosen, and Calancha describes a quaint marriage ceremony of the Chimu in the valley of Pacasmayo. A new pitcher was filled with maize flour and a bonfire kindled with the fat of a young llama was lit in front of the engaged couple, which they had to tend until only the ashes remained. Then the marriage was consummated, the representative of the Ayllu joined the hands of the couple and to the joyous cries of the spectators announced that they were man and wife.

In certain tribes the young man could have a trial marriage, but if he left the woman he forfeited the dowry and had to provide a sum of alimony. On the arrival of the Spaniards this custom was soon suppressed at the insistence of the monks and was ultimately strictly forbidden.[95]

As is usual among ancient peoples the ordinary Indian possessed only one wife, while the princes and nobles constantly had more than one and sometimes a large harem. Only the head wife lived with her husband, but he had to support his concubines, who could not have led a very leisurely existence since they were usually occupied with weaving, plaiting and other household duties. When the head wife died, she could not be replaced by one of the concubines. The husband could only look for a new wife outside his own Ayllu. This was a wise and intelligent precaution because it excluded jealousy of the head wife and among the concubines themselves.

★ ★ ★

In the coastal valleys the Chimu settled by the fertile streams in several adjacent clans, whereby a more urban culture developed, while on the way up to the highlands because of sparser crops a single clan was the general rule. In this way village communities were born but which in turn consisted of related family groups. In the cases where several clans of the Chimu had created an urban settlement, each possessed its own confined quarter. On the north coast this was known to the Spaniards as a Cancha, a word which they translated as *patio* for an enclosed courtyard or *barrio* for a town district and with the word *'corral'* for a small courtyard.

As a result of the Indian custom of giving names, the chroniclers usually found this word coupled with the names of beasts, and such places as Cuntur-Cancha or Puma-Cancha confused them because they could not see the connection between a dwelling and the condor or a puma. They immediately insisted in their accounts that the Chimu kept various wild beasts as pets in their towns and that the doors of some of the buildings were adorned with pictures of them. These beasts, however, were merely the nameplates of the Chimu over their doors.

The clan quarters usually consisted of a large, rectangular cluster of buildings, surrounded by very thick, high walls with a single exit door leading into the open, as can be seen in the plan below. According to the area of the settlement, the interior was divided into several large enclosed squares with their own courtyards.

On entering such a dwelling-place by the main door, as the ruins of Chan-Chan clearly show, one was faced with a raised terrace backed by the rear wall of the courtyard. This was the sacred square, the Huaca-Pata, on which stood the temple. In one corner of the tetragon was usually a large cistern and in another corner a tumulus with walled chambers for the burial of the dead. In cases where the space was insufficient, the mausoleum was built outside the walls on the terrain owned by the clan.[96] The picture afforded today by the most disparate coastal ruins may change in its outward form but it is always basically the same. It is invariably an urban district clearly separated from the next, each self-contained and housing its own clan. Among the Chimu, members of the family, as a result of their urban civilisations, often totalled some sixty to seventy, who formed subdivisions in the large clan quarters we have just described. But even the minor apartments consisted of a rectangular building round an inner courtyard, on a more modest scale.

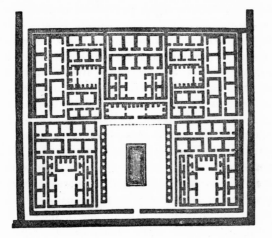

Part of a clan quarter in Chan-Chan. Thirty-nine separate buildings with 111 living-rooms and twenty-two small booths or chambers of the cult on the main square with the cistern

These Ayllu settlements became real fortresses with high massive walls which served not only for segregation purposes but at the same time as a well-contrived defence organisation on the part of the individual clans which insisted upon turning their dwellings into independent fortresses. These Chimu citadels were then often split up into small groups of buildings designed for the individual groups of ten and thus into real family quarters. They appear to have served as true casemates for the defenders.

The entire members of a clan were united even in death by irrevocable ties of friendship and kin. They were blood brothers. In their opinion they were all descendants of the same ancestral pair and as such they stood under the protection of the same clan god, their Huaca. This deity, signifying 'I from here', suited the ancestral worship of the Indians and illuminated their entire social order.

Since both the male and female members of an Ayllu ranked as blood relations any sexual intercourse between them was strictly forbidden. A man, however, could marry his brother's widow, for by her origin she invariably belonged to another clan than that of her husband and consequently of his brother. It was incest to choose a wife from your own clan, and this taboo was more strongly enforced than in ancient Rome, where in certain circumstances exceptions to the rule were tolerated—for example, when marriage within the same *gens* ensured the retention of the fortune of a rich heiress. Incidentally, in this connection we must mention that it was from lack of knowledge of the whole ancient Peruvian social order and on the grounds of a false interpretation of the traditional word 'sister' the chroniclers maintained that the ruling Inca always married incestuously. The words 'sister' and 'brother' just as 'father' and 'mother' had a far more all-embracing relationship significance. While in modern systems of relationship only the brothers born of the same mother are recognised as such, the Indian calls all male relations who should have been known as the father's brother's sons his brothers, and in fact all the males of the clan born in his own generation. In the same way he considered as father not only his real sire but also all the latter's male relations in the branch of the same clan and the same generation.

The names of the grandparents and all the female relations were just as generous in their interpretation. The Indian called 'mother' not only the woman who had borne him but all the women of the same generation and of the same clan as his own true mother.[97] It was always the ancestral chain which held good, and logically the man needed for his children other designations than the wife. When it was said that the Inca married their sisters, the Indian story-tellers of this tradition did not mean their actual flesh-and-blood sisters but women who belonged to the same race as the ruler. Having clarified this misunderstanding, a host of pseudo-scientific theories on the marriage choice of the Inca are dispelled.[98]

The Chimu had a similar classified system of relationship as is to be found not only in the Inca but in many North American Indian races, among the inhabitants of the South Sea Islands and the Indian Dravidas.[99] As opposed to the individual relationships between persons a whole sequence of similar connections in the same clan was expressed.

It is difficult to obtain a clear picture of the distribution and farming of the lands belonging to the individual clan communities. The first reports date from Inca days. This fact need not appear too disheartening, since it was a question of age-old tradition and custom which the Inca did not introduce but took over more or less ready made. The building up of their vast kingdom was only possible by being wise enough not to disturb the ancient order and only changing it when it was absolutely essential for their purposes.

Although the later Spanish officials paid little heed to the original distribution of the land in the provinces inhabited by the Chimu, we fortunately have fairly reliable information. Each clan tilled its own land according to its own ideas; it was the freehold property of the tribe. Although they could not do with it exactly as they pleased, above all not sell it or lease it to a foreigner, there were no State or age-old clan rights such as existed in Europe until the twentieth century in the so-called entailed properties where the heir succeeded *ex pacto et providentia*.

Apart from this family property there was also community ground which was normally left fallow or untilled, the remainder being wasteland. The sowing was done communally and the overseer of the parish with his elders of his village stipulated the time when work in the fields had to begin. On the appointed day all the fit men and women with their grown-up children went out into the fields and began their work after a small celebration ending with songs.

The individual families helped under the leadership of a paterfamilias, and when one plot was finished they went on to the next. Usually a prescribed sequence was followed. The first to be sown were the tribute fields, the harvest of which was intended for the princes and the priesthood, then the fields of the villagers and finally the land which was to be harvested for reserve in case of famine or provide for any villagers who had suffered some misfortune. This sequence was subject to change, and according to the accounts of Cieza de León[100] and

Zárate[101] the main work in the fields and gardens was usually done by women.

The unit of 100 with its attendant land was later known by the general term 'marca', a word which not only in its sound but also in its meaning corresponds perfectly to the old German noun 'Mark'. Since this word with the same meaning also appears in Spanish one might imagine that it would later have been introduced into Quechua, but this is not the case. Here we are faced with one of those strange language analogies. The word appears in the earliest age combined with Indian Christian names, and the countless place names originating from it are without doubt of ancient Indian origin. The connection of the word 'marca' with various names of beasts with totemistic significance astonished the Spanish officials, and when they heard of a llama mark, a falcon mark or a bee mark, they came to the conclusion that in the old days these places were noted for the particular animals. They persisted in this error for a very long time. Bertonio,[102] however, in his vocabulary as early as 1612 translated the word 'marca' as 'pueblo' and added quite correctly that 'marcani' meant villager and Julimarcani, a native born in Juli, the well-known Jesuit centre.

There is nothing very reliable that can be told about the size of individual properties. Garcilaso's[103] improbable theories can be dismissed out of hand, and agriculture was so very different in individual sectors both in manner and extent that a standard allotment to the landless can hardly be maintained. After the Conquest the age-old appropriation of the land was soon forgotten in favour of the amalgamation into administrative parishes, introduced in 1575 by the Viceroy Francisco de Toledo.[95] The replacement of the old clan chiefs by Alcaldes, the introduction of the Spanish tax system and the creation of large livings, the notorious encomiendas, almost completely destroyed the old mark and parish distribution, which nevertheless in remote parts of the north endured until the nineteenth century.[104]

It is also completely false, as many of the old and new writers on Peru maintain, to say that there was no private ownership and that all land was communal property. The sites on which the Indian houses stood, together with their gardens, in ancient Peru, were never the property either of the village community or of the State. They belonged everywhere the Indians lived together in large clans to the individual families. A similar unit composed of courtyard, house, barns and gardens in the Chimu kingdom was called Moya, and the Spanish officials in their reports referred to it either as hereditary estate or private property; Bertonio alone translated it as 'garden'. The idea of enclosure is inherent in the Indian word and it is used today in this sense in the word 'muya'. It has the same meaning as the English word 'hide', which is synonymous with the German Hufe, Huba or Hoba, i.e. something *taken out* of the land as a whole and separated into a plot.

Much nonsense has been talked about the ancient Peruvian economy, usually in complete contradiction to the reports of such well-informed and educated jurists as Polo de Ondegardo,[105] Fernando de Santillán,[106] Ortega Morejón,[4] Cristóbal de Castro[4] and others. Domián de la Bandera,[107] Polo de Ondegardo[108] and Santillán[109] state categorically that the fields and real estate, even when farmed for others, remained the property of the family.

Equally false is the denial that the Indians had no sense of private property. We shall deal later (page 135) with the Tumbes merchants, who were constantly away from home on private business and were by no means emissaries of the Government; a picture that can be elaborated by what we learn from the chroniclers about the trade and itineraries of the Chimu on land and sea. The fact that this trade primarily developed as barter has little connection with the matter. Money tokens consisted of small copper, silver or gold discs, the value of which was acceptable to the purchaser and cannot be considered as a governmental coinage. At times a consignment of easily distributable wares such as pepper, copper, cotton, maize and salt were used as currency.[110] The beginnings of a long-distance trade can be traced far back in time, llamas or porters being used for land and balsas for sea transport.

How far the social conditions of the coastal inhabitants apart from agriculture, marca and land distribution influenced the rest of the economy cannot, unfortunately, be stated scientifically but only arrived at by guesswork. It is possible that the production of manufactured goods was divided among the clans.

Various details with which we shall deal in Chapter Seven on the subject of artistic production would lead us to believe this.

And finally we must take a short glimpse at the legal conditions and certain ancient customs of the Chimu kingdom which again to a large extent are identical with those reigning on the coast, in the uplands and in principle with the entire Indian law and concept of life. We must discard out of hand the bright-coloured fairy-tale which was furbished in the Middle Ages trying to show the Inca kingdom as an ideal state, and not be misled by the later Inca laws, the single purpose of which was to hold the land together and nip in the bud any possibility of a rising.

We must base our findings far more on the age-old common law which the subjected Chimu continued to observe in its unabased form and with which the Incas never tried to interfere. According to ancient custom, the Chimu regulated their own internal matters themselves, and the Inca never tried to interfere with their family, property and succession rights or to disturb their deep-rooted common law. Obviously the Incas never entertained the idea of introducing a codified law for their gigantic kingdom, knowing perfectly well that this could never have been achieved. The individual chiefs of the Chimu ruled over their own subjects before and after their defeat.

In accordance with their clan law they could only arraign and judge those criminals who belonged to their own community and thus came under their jurisdiction. A Chimu judge could not punish a malefactor who did not belong to his marca, even when the crime or misdemeanour had been committed within his sphere of jurisdiction. He could hold the guilty person in custody but had to hand him over to his own clan for punishment. In cases of doubt the decision rested with the chief of the thousand or the ten thousand. Among the Chimu there was no judicial difference between individual crimes and therefore no professional judges. When a citizen contravened the ancient common law, he was arraigned before his Ayllu.[111]

An actual class of judges which even modern Americanists have tried to derive from a remark made by Garcilaso[112] never existed anywhere in the country. An independent judge would have been completely alien to the spirit of the whole clan and family organisation. Passing judgment was a very natural function to be carried out by the family and clan chiefs. If we read Garcilaso carefully we find that he mentions various judicial activities but never mentions an actual body of judges.

The whole of their justice was a matter of swift judgment, and long periods of custody or prison sentences were completely unknown to the Chimu, just as there was no appeal and no complaint against a sentence once it had been pronounced, since it was presumed to be just. The Spaniards regarded this Indian procedure as enlightened when they compared it with their own court cases which sometimes dragged on for many years.

Execution followed the sentence on the spot. The mildest punishment consisted of the miscreant having to carry a shameful burden through the streets under the mocking gaze of the crowd, or to stand for a certain time in the stocks. More serious crimes were punished by lashes with a truncheon or with stones on the back and shoulders of the condemned man. He was usually given either five or ten strokes. Since these were carried out with sharp-edged stones, considerable injuries were caused.

The death penalty was normally carried out by strangling or hanging. In particularly serious cases public stoning and decapitation were known, the latter being reserved exclusively for treachery in wartime. The form of death considered least shameful was the plunging by the condemned man from a high cliff. Guilty chiefs in this way could make their exit into the next world without being arrested.

Adulterers were often flung from the cliffs into the sea, but intercourse between unmarried people was given great latitude. On the other hand, unnatural vice was severely punished, as was abortion, since both the crimes in question damaged the strength of the individual clan. The reader who is interested in this subject scientifically will find the necessary references in note 113.

The punishments for all types of theft were very severe; a thief would be hanged even for petty larceny, and when the culprit could not be found immediately, a stake with green branches was planted in the middle of the road and the entire population ordered to catch him. Anyone harbouring a thief was punished in the same way as the thief himself; for a peccadillo he was strung up by his feet until he was half dead. As a result among the Chimu there were no locked doors or bolts.

Members of the tribe who were guilty of blasphemy—this naturally could often be no more than political rivalry—were buried alive beneath the remains of common criminals and dead animals. A particularly severe punishment was occasionally meted out to the Chimu physicians, the Oquetlupucs, who were very skilled in herbal remedies and the concoction of all manner of potions. These doctors were well rewarded for their efforts when they proved successful, but were mercilessly thrashed to death when their patients died under the treatment. According to Calancha, an Indian doctor whose patient died was bound to the corpse; this was buried in the normal manner, whereas the body of the doctor was left above ground until the vultures devoured him. This particularly stringent rule for doctors recalls the Babylonian laws of Hammurabi. When one thinks of the terrible punishments administered in Europe, not only during the so-called Dark Ages but far into the nineteenth century, the practices of these earlier peoples should not arouse undue surprise.

Finally, regarding the capabilities of the Chimu doctors we must mention that in addition to the use of numerous healing plants they also had recourse to blood-letting, small obsidian splinters set in hook-shaped wooden sticks serving as lancets. These instruments were inserted either in the painful spot or in the veins between the eyebrows. Emetics and purges equalled in their powerful doses those of any horse-doctor.

All that has been written on the occasional trepannings on living human beings cannot be taken without reservation. The condition of the several skulls found in various places, with rectangular or polygonal pieces removed with the aid of a sharp instrument, show by the unhealed edges round the aperture that the patient did not survive the operation very long, even if it had been practised on the living man at all. These trepannings are particularly common in Peru in the region of Tiahuanaco, where we must reckon with a highly evolved priesthood and where such skulls show every possibility that the patients may have survived the operation.

Apart from the question as to what malady the patient had suffered from, the presence of the above-mentioned priesthood gives rise to another thought. These Indian priests were, for their age—but in a different way from popular physicians—the advance guard of science. They had the necessary leisure to devote themselves to this subject. They studied not only man as an individual but meditated upon God and the world and were in quest of the soul. The word 'Illa' (see page 76), which doubtless means 'the gleaming' and describes the soul, was used also by the Indians for the large gall-stones they sometimes found in the bellies of llamas and other animals. Acosta deals with these at great length.[114] Apart from the fact that these stones were

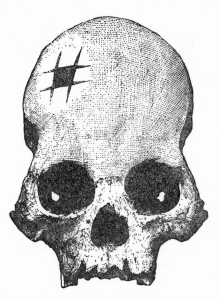

Trepanned Indian skull

valued on account of their beauty and their strong phosphorous content, which justified the name, we can assume that they were bound up with religious concepts among the Indians—concepts common to other prehistoric peoples which led to trepanning, either with a view to healing a real or supposed madman or to help people who were considered to be possessed by demons. Trepanning, therefore, must not be regarded in the modern medical sense by anyone wishing to understand the practice from a cultural-historical point of view.

Magic formulas, conjurations and the power of prayer in this healing art have precisely the same significance as all purely empirical efforts. Chimu medicine was on the same level as had been reached throughout the whole world in the course of many centuries.

Not until the end of the last century did the learned doctor come almost completely under the spell of natural history. Often enough he sat alone in his study as a research worker, while outside the people sought help from other sources, from quacks or real faith healers, who in their opinion had access to greater and more mysterious powers. Inherent in the creed of the faith healer, apart from the form his actual practice may take, there is something irrational—that faith that can move mountains, and which so often makes the modern psychologist the magician of the modern age.

In the knowledge of the eternal connection throughout history between the material and the spiritual it will not be difficult to follow the path in the subsequent chapter from society and economy to the nature of Indian art.

CHAPTER SIX

The Nature of Indian Art

ANCIENT American art has always intrigued receptive minds. No less an artist than Albrecht Dürer, returning to Brussels at the end of his Dutch journey, and seeing the first treasures from the New World destined for the Emperor Charles V, wrote the following simple words in his diary for the 27 August 1520 :[115] 'Throughout my life I have never seen anything that gladdened my heart so much as these objects. I have seen amazing art treasures and have admired the subtle genius of men in foreign lands and yet I cannot express the beauty of these in particular.'

Even at the sober Age of Reason Clavigero[4] reproached Robertson[4] for ascribing the enthusiastic reports of the conquerors to an overheated imagination, and defended Ancient American art which he genuinely admired, although he was unable to fully appreciate it. Then at the beginning of the nineteenth century the writings of Alexander von Humboldt appeared. In 1831 Lord Kingsborough[4] published his monumental work and towards the middle of the century William Prescott's[4] books received the widest publicity, were translated into many languages and kept in print; and the time was ripe for a completely new evaluation of Indian creative art.

John Lloyd Stephens,[4] an amiable, though unfortunately neglected, writer and sensitive critic of Ancient American art, explored the Maya region in 1839 and 1842 and wrote two fine books on the subject. Frederick Catherwood,[4] the English painter and engraver, who accompanied him, produced the first valuable sketches of the architecture and sculpture of the Maya cities. The sight of Copan in Honduras convinced Stephens that the American antiquities were significant 'not only as the remains of an unknown people but also as works of art'.

Since 1868 archaeologists, spade in hand, have given ample

proof that the accounts of the old chroniclers were not exaggerated and in fact lagged far behind reality. It lay in the nature of things that these first scientific workers should pay more attention to the historical than to the artistic aspect of the objects discovered. This picture did not change until the Romantic Movement spread throughout Europe. In its cradle a completely new interpretation was born. Here too, however, the interest in foreign races aroused by Herder and Goethe was purely literary in origin.

The example of Romantic literature with its preference for the past, its longing for distant lands and wondrous experiences, starting in France with Prosper Mérimée, was soon followed by painters like his contemporary, Delacroix, who turned their gaze out into the world, first to the Far East, then to the Greeks and Romans and later to Japan. Gauguin finally proved unfaithful to his peasant canvases of Brittany and not only spiritually but physically fled to the isle of Martinique on the American coast whence his longing drove him even farther to Tahiti in the South Seas. 'The savages,' he said, 'these innocents, have taught the ancient civilised man much—in art, how to live and how to be happy. And above all they have taught me to know myself better and I have learned from them nothing but the profoundest truth.'[116]

As though the age had demanded it peremptorily, artistic effort, with Cézanne as with Van Gogh, was directed towards finding the bases of phenomena concealed in the myth and the hidden life which flourishes and influences beneath the physical perceptible surface of things. While in France the lucidity of a spiritual balance ruled, gaily recognising the harmony of creation, the Dutchman Van Gogh transformed the whole reality into a sequence of fermenting visions. This would appear to be a reflection of the artistic forms of expression which can be observed among the Chimu on the Peruvian coast and the well-balanced art of the Incas in the highlands, as opposed to the savage tortured faces of the Aztec world in Mexico.

When expressionism made its appearance, discussions arose on the subject of exotic art. Not only in Indian, Persian and Chinese but also in Peruvian art a stimulus was found for the bolder treatment of colour. Taking American examples all these

Above: Indian woman's work basket. Tomb artifact with original contents *Below:* Woven bag in white and red with stylised pattern of llamas

16
Above: White cotton blanket with red and brown pattern.
Acón *Below*: Indian cloak in feather work. Ñazca

17 Bright coloured weave with a cotton ground. Paracas art

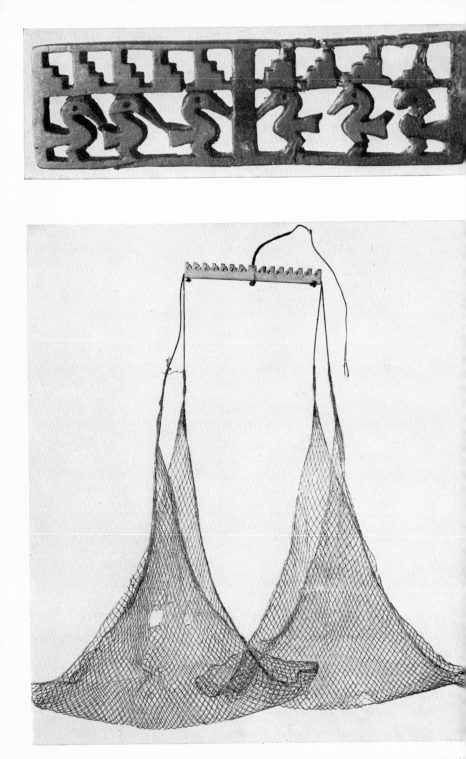

18 *Above:* A carved scale beam with stepped pattern and birds *Below:* Ind[ian]
scales with nets

artists learned the taming of forms and from 1907 onwards they experienced, in the Trocadéro collections, the compulsive power of primitive gestures. The Fauves and the Cubists were well acquainted with Peruvian, Mexican and Central American art. The sculpture of the Zapotecs had influenced them deeply. With admiration they perceived the bold contrasts and the subtle colour harmony in the textiles and featherwork of the Chimu and the art of Nazca. But above all they were astounded by solutions completely new to them in the interrelation of form and content, realism and abstraction.

About 1909 American painters returned home from Paris and began to immerse themselves in the collections of Mexican and Peruvian art which included many pieces from the Chimu kingdom in the American Museum of Natural History. Between 1912 and 1920 under the aegis of Wissler, Spinden, Mead and Crawford, the motives of Peruvian art penetrated more and more into North American creations, as they had done in Europe.

In Latin America the influences of the ancient art had never died. In this context one must not forget that it was imperial Spain, the leading world power of its age, which first met with that alien culture. It was the artistic Spain of El Greco and Velasquez which, with the aid of Indian architects and in the tradition of Ancient American art, created the Mexican baroque style, compared with whose thousand gleaming palaces and brilliant churches the whole of North American colonial art seems pale and lustreless. It is not within the scope of this book, which deals with Ancient American civilisations, to go deeper into this post-Columbian development. The reader must be content with a glance at the growth of an aesthetic understanding for Indian creative art.

In its best periods and stages the art of these old races can never be called primitive, although all their objects were produced with primitive tools. It is characteristic of Indian culture that the material creation of their works of art, as well as their works as a powerful state organisation, was produced with the tools of a primitive technique. With no knowledge of the wheel and with no beast of burden, the Indians solved the problem of transporting colossal loads. With no knowledge of the potter's

D

wheel they produced vessels of the most perfect form and on extremely simple looms wove those Peruvian textiles which compare favourably with any other textiles in the world.

★ ★ ★

Ancient American art has often been termed demonic. This, however, tells little of its innermost nature. On closer examination there is no such thing as demonic art but only occasionally a demonic pictorial world. Art itself has always been human. Those who do not understand it are pleased to call it demonic even today, just as over 400 years ago the Spaniards described the unknown Indian symbols as devilish.

Ancient American art is fraught with symbols to an extent most surprising to the European. This should only surprise him on first acquaintanceship and should not prove incomprehensible when he considers that in the last analysis all art is symbolical and in no country a mere copy of Nature. For the Indians who had no fluid script the literary expression of letters was replaced by the symbol. Many Indian works of art are the perfect counterpart of those of the early Middle Ages in Europe—no more than stories in pictures or interpretations in clay of history and myth. An understanding of the frequently used symbols needs not only knowledge and hard work; it is also a pleasure and a constant enjoyment, as we shall demonstrate on page 114 and have already mentioned in this book.

Anyone who delves enthusiastically into Indian art and is able to overcome the first feeling of strangeness will, upon familiarity with these objects, rarely ever discover such demonism, particularly when he handles the light vessels of the Chimu which have survived the ravages of time. They echo like far-off music and a southern race immediately comes to mind.

If one can use the concept demonic for the expression of Aztec art with its wealth of compelling forms, its frequently automatic symbolism, one must remember that even the figure of the flower prince, Xochipilli (Plate 10), today the pride of the National Museum in Mexico, once emerged as a human element from the cogs of the savage apparatus of a powerful compulsive religious philosophy. The same human trait is repeated in the high art of the Maya, expressed in that trachyte head of the maize goddess from Copan (Plate 14) in forms that immediately remind one of Ancient Greece and the Far East.

In the land of the Chimu and later with a faint echo throughout the whole vast kingdom of the Incas, Ancient American art and the genius of the Indian race created forms which can claim to be timeless. Without resorting to superlatives we can say that many of the Chimu portrait heads can be numbered among the most noble memorials of humanity—and they were created by Indian artists.

When one surveys the north and south continents of America, there is a striking difference between the intellectual and formal mobility of the north continent, between the gruesome masks of North-west America[117] and the far more peaceful and consoling balanced art of the Andean lands. It was a strange, cultural decree of history that the Nordic peoples of Europe were awarded the North American continent while the Southern European nations, on the contrary, settled in South America. The gaze of many Europeans has been too surfeited by the exotic blooms of late Mexican art, if the Ancient American creations as a whole are to be identified with the concept of the gruesome and the terrifying. Our knowledge of the appalling holocausts of the Aztecs lie behind this. Cortez and his companions counted 136,000 skulls in one single place.[118]

The Chimu, one might almost say, were the Greeks of the New World. I make this comparison of course with great reservations, for such analogies are often trivial. But to pursue the comparison, in order to combine in imagination the alien with the familiar we might say that the Incas with their outstanding state organisation, their practical architecture and, to a certain extent, stylistic sobriety were the Romans of Ancient America; while in the hotter regions, in the lands of the Maya and in Mexico where life was not entirely confined to the high valleys, the heat of the tropics forged the art into forms which one rediscovers only in India or in the sun-kissed lands of South-east Asia. The reason why the Chimu over a wide area succeeded in producing such a well-balanced art must be partly attributed to the happy external conditions of life reigning in their country. If a demonic pictorial world appears in South America it is only exceptionally in Chimu art and is hardly ever found in the art of the Incas. It was other races and other cultures which produced this tinge. The art of the Chimu is incredibly easy to recognise by its characteristic style.

This is not the place to debate questions of art philosophy as to how the phenomenon of style arose and why art as something formed—even when the artist himself believes that it is merely the personal expression of his ego or of a passing whim—is always characterised by an ordained style. So much is certain : the presence of a general age and folk style exceeding the individual artist and his individuality is by no means the prerogative of Western art. Style, derived from the Latin word *stylus,* is the unmistakable artistic script of a people or a particular age.

Each powerful style is exclusive and compelling. When a living art accepts something alien, the latter is not grafted on as something fortuitous but is absorbed into the organic whole. In general the true style pays little heed to the foreign element; it does not disturb it. Without a qualm and with complete self-assurance the designers of Western baroque incorporated their altars in the Gothic churches. Without hesitation, then, the builders of Mexican baroque expressed their own ideas of the world in many ancient forms. Insecurity or confusion in style are phenomena of lame static periods in history. But even these have style and one cannot call them styleless just as there is no such thing as a handwriting devoid of character. In order to acquire some understanding of Indian art it may perhaps be advisable to cast a glance at Europe.

Anyone who thought that the modern age with its rapidly changing art fashions is not subject to these momentary currents of ordained style would be vastly mistaken. To recognise the style of our age we are not far enough removed from it in time : it is still veiled by the personal. In years to come, however, here too the main trend which characterised this period and its artists will also become visible. The change from the Romanesque art of the West to Gothic took place without contemporaries being aware of it. The written sources of those momentous years, although very numerous, are almost silent even when they mention the new architecture which in an unbelievably short time covered the country with the brilliance of Gothic cathedrals. That generation was completely unaware that really new

architectural ideas and forms had taken shape. In 1137 when
Abbot Suger, an outstanding figure of his age, began to build the
Abbey of St. Denis, he recorded the smallest and most unimportant details of his work, but in no single line did he express his
awareness that he had created an entirely new style which we
call Gothic.

External art forms are invariably connected with their age;
art is never independent but intimately bound up with the
religious, intellectual and economic life of the people, irrespective
of their race, past history and social order. That, however, is only
one verdict. Style has twin roots. Independent of its connection
with the whole life of an age, which it reflects, it also consists of
an independent life of forms. Available possibilities are evaluated
in their own field, developed and often ruthlessly corrupted; new
possibilities arise and run their course. In this case the style
becomes independent of the culture, at least to outward appear-
ances. Nevertheless it always remains an expression of the intellect. This magnificent interplay of all the forces then forms that
style in which for a time everything that motivated it will be
expressed.

On these grounds a change of style need not invariably be
bound up with a change of the outward culture. Inversely a style
can change, undergo a complete rebirth while the outward culture remains the same. Then a basic revolution in the world of
form which was not apparent at the first upheaval has taken
place. Such statements that the art of hunting and fisherfolk is
always realistic, imitating Nature, and that with the transition to
a settled life and to agriculture a geometrical style constantly
appears, cannot be postulated as the natural laws of art. It is
more conceivable that not until a race becomes settled has it time
for peaceful work and that geometrical forms simply resulted
from the transfer of patterns from textiles to ceramics, which
could easily be manufactured in permanent dwellings, whereas
nomadic races for the decoration of their vessels confined themselves to forms of fruit and plants taken from Nature.

It is easy to realise that in all weaving geometrical forms
should be the first to be created, since these forms so often appear
in plants and crystals. Primitive races, however, did not look
upon this miracle as purely mathematical form but as filled with

incomprehensible life like the dark shadows of the wood, like the mysterious influences of Nature which inspired their religious ideas.

Real style in Indian art—and this was inevitable—was expressed in their pottery, architecture, textiles, jewellery and in the working of stone, metal and wood, embracing as a whole the artistic creation of a period. That the most perfect heads in Chimu portrait ceramics under the influence of Tiahuanaco art about the ninth century were adorned with geometrical patterns does not mean that a new geometrical style was born, or that the continuity of a magnificent plastic sense of form was disrupted, any more than that the human shortcomings and even incapacity in art could cause the collapse of the main stream of development.

In our general discussion of American Indian art within this limited region we have adhered to the following basic plan : that first we must examine the art of the Chimu, i.e. that of the northern coast, and trace its development from this point of departure in order to obtain an understanding of the art of the coast farther south. When we examine the creations of the Chimu as a whole over a period of more than a thousand years three style periods of great purity emerge. Between these there are naturally a number of transitions and retrogressions which allow us clearly to recognise each particular stage of development they expressed. The easiest way to read these styles is from the pottery available : because it is more typical and characteristic it must therefore take first place.

Naturally in such an exposé dealing with styles, the life and the finds as a whole will suffer diminution. Reality is always richer than all intellectual categories, concepts and descriptions. They are, however, indispensable if we aim for clarity and an understanding of the significant. The details and departure from the norm will then be comprehensible. We shall deal with these in the regional description of the art in the later chapters. With this reservation the three Chimu style periods will be described as follows.

The Early Style of the Chimu is the style of a still archaic period in which the linear, the purely graphic dominates, though a certain desire for plastic expression is still present. Examples

of this style are a distinguished series of simple vessels in which
the shape for practical purposes is only slightly stylised. In this
earliest Chimu pottery, as in the associated textiles, will be found
that ancient element of all Indian art, rhythmic repetition, [119] the
curve of the squat vessel being repeated in the bold arch of the
handle which runs upwards and ends in a single spout (Plate 27).

In these vessels a rather dull light colouring is the rule. Most
of the vases from the early period are of white or yellowish clay,
the pattern drawn, rather than painted, with a fine brush in
brown or black. The subjects, historical battles, scenes from
everyday life or hunting, are always in some way connected with
the myths of the people, often with different interpretations of
the creation with which we have already dealt. In these drawings
primitive blitheness as well as a keen sense of observation combine
in the archaic posture of the figures, giving them the kind of
awkwardness found in early Gothic or early Romanesque art,
which is of course one of their great charms. The decoration is
still thin and not carried out broadly as later, nor is it intentionally decorative but self-contained without undue rigidity, on
occasions approaching an almost Grecian purity of drawing.

The Mature Style. This is the classic art of the Chimu. A
decisive change-over to the plastic has taken place. In the most
beautiful examples of this art, the magnificent heads from the
various valleys of the coast, man is now the focal point. They
are still vessels but their handles have become purposeless and are
often lacking. Here we have the most incomparable sculpture in
the whole domain of Peruvian art. The forms have now become
articulated and the limbs in the many life-size portraits are often
suddenly detached. The surface comes to life and is well par-
titioned. There is no trace of that fear of empty space which one
so often meets in Central American art. Even the geometrical
forms sparkle with secret life. This art at the height of its power
gives the impression that in the portrayal of the human face
nothing is now impossible; the mythical scenes of the earlier
period have been replaced by pictures of everyday life. Naturally
it is not the life of the white man and his ideals, nor is it that
rationalism which has never been shed since the days of the
Greek. It has no connection with materialism but to a certain
extent with transcendental naturalism, for even in the apparently

most faithfully realistic representations, a vestige of the conceivable in addition to a breath of the incomprehensible remains, which is the secret of these Indian works of art even if to European eyes they seem to swing between the coarsest realism and the purest abstraction.

The Late Style of the Chimu shows a fatigue in the line drawing. The great stream has dried up and much that was original has been lost. Now the clumsy and the purely frivolous appear. The bright colours of the Early Style have been replaced by dull blackish tones. The effect is often insipid. On the other hand this late art often pleases by its greater wealth of shapes more than does the peak period. Occasionally a type of photographic, almost documentary realism replaces the vivid effect. Now it is a quest for material, often a boring repetition, a loss of brilliance and fullness which cannot be balanced by a mere piling up of material. The sculpture no longer appeals to the sense of touch but lapses into the picturesque, as so often happens in a late style.

This then is the natural history of the main style of the Chimu. In its natural development it must be realised that a domain of art and culture, extending over such a vast area and lasting for such a long period, fulfilling the laws and regulations of repetition, was inevitably subjected from time to time to stylistic undercurrents resulting from the influence of alien cultures and the existence of an archaic and primitive population. The frontier of the Cordilleras was in spite of everything no insuperable wall and to the south the kingdom lay open to a host of the most powerful influences.

Everywhere among the Chimu, therefore, one finds an art of association. It radiates from a region which the Spaniards so aptly called the *Cejas de la Costa*, the 'eyebrows of the coast'. The Chimu did not live in a wilderness. As they spread out into the valleys, they followed the watercourses up into the mountains where they either met with earlier arrivals of their own or other races which at these altitudes lived under completely different conditions and possessed culture more rural than urban.

The heads of the valleys could not feed as large a population as the broad oases on the coast. It is also possible that in the Andean valleys an archaic people had settled, as in the uplands

THE NATURE OF INDIAN ART 105

of Mexico, who were also in possession of a similar culture. Although earlier in this book it has been maintained that the Chimu arrived as nomads from Central America, it must not be presumed that they were the sole bringers of culture to the vast region of the Andes.

In any case from their contact with the races on the mountain slopes and their cultures, influences appeared in the Chimu kingdom which manifest themselves in a kind of provincial style. Two clearly disparate styles at least can be distinguished. The first of these styles which deserves its name only in Chimu country has assumed its place in scientific literature under the unfortunate term *Chavín Style*. Now Chavín de Huantar lies in a rocky wilderness and could never have been the capital of a large kingdom or a widespread culture. Since there is nothing more difficult than changing a generally accepted terminology we shall be obliged to use this description in the course of this book.

The second provincial style in the Chimu kingdom bears the names of the various excavation sites—particularly *Recuay* and *Huarás*. It is in the nature of such provincial styles that they change far less than the main style of a period since they are more subject to local influences and that above all they have a very much longer past. To a certain extent the lower stratum upon which a new culture is built is inherent in them: this continues to survive and constantly comes to light again.

The names Recuay and Huarás lead us to the valley of the Upper Santa. In its lower reaches it cleaves the mountain near the coast and here, as well as farther south in the powerful knot which the Cordilleras form near Serro de Pasco, the gigantic Andean chain can be crossed with comparative ease. In the latter spot on the coast, foreign influences are easy to trace and finds have been made in Huacho, Chancay and Ancón which have nothing to do with Chimu art and very little with the art of the more southerly population, but present a contact with a more primitive culture beyond the Andes such as spread along the Amazon reaches. Those curious large egg-shaped urns, which we shall describe on page 200, must be ruled out when we discuss the specific art of the Chimu and the other coastal tribes.

In such a study it is imperative never to lose sight of the cultural and geographical data. Only by constantly consulting the map and examining the main conditions, the clearly confined coastal valleys and the plateaus of the mountain and by comparing it with a cultural map can one understand how these developments are correlated. It would be pointless here to go into greater detail on Chimu culture before we reach our regional survey. I shall merely say, therefore, in this connection that the art styles we have mentioned are reflected in all the aspects of art. This also applies to architecture, where we find five different types of masonry and five kinds of brick, with variants, i.e. simple cones used in the earliest buildings; followed by square, laid and polished cast bricks used as the style approached maturity; thick alternating bricks; and with the late period once more smooth, smaller examples eventually developing into rounded types almost like cobble-stones. I have intentionally avoided confusing the reader by dealing with these provincial styles at this juncture so as not to risk losing sight of the main theme. The art of Pachacamac, therefore, strongly influenced by the style of Tiahuanaco and the art of Nazca, will be dealt with in a different chapter since they must both be dissociated from that of the Chimu.

CHAPTER SEVEN

Material and Form

ALL artistic creation is the ennoblement of material and the spiritualisation of the physical through the mystery of form. In the inspired hands of the artist the physically conceivable is transformed into the purely comprehensible ideal. Here, however, we meet with the profoundest difference in the nature of Indian art from all that Europe and the white man has created down the centuries. The ideas of abstraction and realism could be used in the traditional sense and it would be pointless in this work to contrast an outer and an inner form, although this concept is implicit in the entelechy of Aristotle, is to be found in the eighteenth century in Shaftesbury's[120] 'inward form' and since Kant[121] has disappeared for ever from aesthetics. In this book when we refer in future to form, the outward, visible and tangible, the visual form is meant, whereas for the inner form expressions such as figure, meaning, significance, etc., will be used with the necessary elucidations.

Visual forms cannot stand alone. Their essential prerequisite remains the material. Where a feeling for the ultimate miracle of the material—in which all the possibilities of form slumber—is lacking, the spiritual content of a work of art is never apparent. A sympathy with the malleable matter is inherent in all good form, and primitive man always began with the craftsmanship in order to revert to the conceivable via the heights of the intellect. Nature itself provides the material for the work of art in mineral and vegetable dyes, wood, stone, silver, gold and last but not least in clay—the fundamental soil of the earth on which everything rests.

Therefore it is perhaps appropriate to begin our observations with pottery, for ceramics go back to the earliest cultures. In the dawn of history the myths tell of men being created from dust. At a very early age the idea of the figure formed out of clay was born. We find it in the biblical story of the Creation as well as in the saga of Prometheus, and in a particularly beautiful manner the Greek myth locates the discovery of painting and sculpture in the workshop of a potter in Corinth.

Even the hardest wood decomposes. Copper, bronze and iron can be destroyed under the influence of damp and the acid content of the air and the soil. Precious metals, too, are powerless against the twin enemies of their plasticity and human greed, which invariably recasts some old statue in a new form or leaves its imprint to conform to new aims and thoughts. The fired clay, however, is virtually immortal. It is also unchangeable and man alone can destroy its form. Thus there is no material worked by human hands, the form development of which—whether it be only in potsherds and fragments—can be traced with continuity so far back in time. Clay tablets today record the faith, creation and knowledge of the Assyrian and Babylonian races,[122] and one can safely call ceramics as a whole the earliest signposts of prehistory.

Indian pottery, in common with the whole of European Stone Age art, had no knowledge of the potter's wheel; in every other respect it was of a far higher standard. The portrait urns which housed the ashes of the dead in Northern Europe may sometimes have been made with the idea of clothing the unworked clay once more with the living form, but the examples that Schliemann found in the lowest strata of Troy were not burial urns, and it must always remain in doubt whether the underlying thought of the urn in the form of a house was not the wish to give a familiar home to the remains of the dead man. All these vessel shapes which can be seen today in museums are characterised far more by their natural formations, and one also speaks today—without necessarily thinking of portraits—of the neck, the belly and the foot of this or that vessel. Fruits and above all the hollowed-out gourds were presumably the first natural prototypes.

This explains the remarkable fact of the constant lack of solidity, both in the Indian ceramics and in the vases of most of the ancient cultures throughout the world. That these vessels with their conical or rounded bases served exclusively for suspension is by no means incontestable or the ultimate explanation.

Even if we accept this, we must always recall the different types of fruit.[123]

Of the conical bases of the vessels which have caused such difficulty to modern museums as regards display that stands usually have had to be made for them, it has occasionally been maintained that they were originally perfectly suited to give the vessels a good purchase in the sand. On the other hand it could be said that in this way many beautiful parts of the painting would have been hidden and that this particular form has been found in every conceivable part of the world, including countries where the soil is rocky. In countless niches of the Peruvian buildings, where these vessels often stood, one can hardly presume a sandy foundation. In actual fact level ground had nothing to do with the appearance of many vessels.

To the original forms of fruit was added another, that of the animal's udder or bag, which like the entrails or the gullet represents one of the oldest natural forms of container. The feet of certain bowls from Pachacamac (Plate 25) are strangely reminiscent of the dugs on a cow's udder.[124] European words such as the German *bocksbeutel*, or the French and English words *bouteille* and *bottle* respectively for a flask, still recall their ancient meaning.

Modern, rational-thinking man realises that early art was never intended to be purely symbolical although it was so in its deepest and innermost nature. The ancient American vessels are the forms of expression of a specific creative circle. If in them, as in the royal tombs of Ancient Egypt and Greece, we find the same intention of giving the dead man all his favourite earthly possessions, it sprang from the religious conviction that these objects would be used by the dead man in the beyond as he had used them during his lifetime.

Individually, however, various pieces of this pottery represent, within the main stream, both the general historical development and artistic technique as well as the outward expression of the pure creative urge which often, despite all ties, and when necessary, broke with the old forms and unexpectedly managed to create a new pictorial expression. Thus one day these vessels were given an even and solid base not only because it was practical but because it was beautiful.

The enforced splitting of the free and related arts as a whole into individual branches is as alien to Indian art as it was to the great cultures of the European Middle Ages and the Far East. This divorce was far more the result of social and economical development towards the end of the last century which itself finally degenerated and became confused. Throughout the whole Age of Reason all artistic creations were considered as a great and indivisible unit and a concept such as the so-called handicraft was completely unknown.

Whether, as so often happens, one accepts that the most beautiful examples of Indian pottery were made solely as burial objects, or whether one believes that they were designed for purposes of worship for the living, by the liberation from practical purposes so typical of the more simple commonplace utensil, the resultant untrammelled form reaches the borderline between freedom and the demands of the design. In all household utensils made by sensitive, artistic hands, wherever there is an element of freedom that points to something more than material aims, then those symbolical burial objects take flight into a spiritual world which, for those early human beings, was in unbroken harmony with reality.

As long as a work of art is observed merely as a pure phenomenon of form it bears the stamp of the ageless and needs no further significance or explanation. No work of art exhausts itself completely in this way: the form can never be separated from the content and in their creation both are joined to outward conditions by a host of ties. In this context we must now deal with the technique of manufacture.

At the outset, on the Peruvian coast, as with most early races, the utensils were produced by the so-called coil technique. Starting from below, rope-like strips of clay were superimposed spirally, the outer and inner sides of the built-up walls being moulded later. At an early age followed the firing of the ceramics, after moulding, at the open fire, and later in actual kilns. These were not unknown to the early Chimu because of their knowledge of smelting.

Clay and wood forms, stamps and patterns were soon employed, as proved by the many models for a variety of vessels, which have been discovered. Such aids were popular since they

allowed a kind of mass production; they were also employed
for all manner of relief figures and friezes on the black ware of
the later age, while on the vessels of the early style, natural
models, such as the corn-cob or the mussel-shell, were pressed
into the soft clay and thus used as forms. Not only the decoration, but complete figures, and even the best-known and most
beautiful portrait heads of the Chimu were constantly repeated
from their clay moulds and only the head attire was occasionally
altered; so that in the great museums of the world which possess
examples of this pottery one often comes across the same faces,
the only difference being the adornment and the painting. All
this points quite clearly to the fact that in the big cities a regular
trade existed; it was probably in the hands of whole clans
and families.

In the vessels with a broad opening, the formation of the head
in a double mould involved no difficulties since it was possible
to insert the hand and press the clay against the outer wall. For
the closed vessels, however, the base had to be removed so that
the potter's hand could be inserted. The pitchers with the carved
handles were worked in the same way, the body being shaped
from outside and the base added later. The reason one finds these
handles on heads where they seem to serve no useful purpose,
nor to satisfy any aesthetic sense, was because in the old days
when the sculpture was being fired in a kiln it had to have an
opening to prevent it from cracking in the heat.

On the other hand the question arises : were all these vessels
created merely to disappear for ever in the eternal night of the
grave as all previous literature on the subject maintains? Taking
into account our remarks on ancestor worship and in view of the
countless proofs of a very active water worship, both in the land
of the Chimu and farther south along the coast, one wonders
whether many of these ceramics, when they adorned the houses
of the living as huacas, did not contain water considered as
sacred. If we accept this premise the symbolical representations
are far easier to understand. If in many of these pitchers water
was really preserved in connection with the general coastal
worship, then these narrow spouts become comprehensible, since
they are a natural precaution against evaporation.

Nearly all the vessels possess a fine patchy, presumably silted undercoat applied in different colours to the clay—in Chimu country, usually white and yellow and, in the region of Nazca, black and red. The vessels with the dark background, however, are rarer than those with light, the latter appearing in their greatest beauty in Nazca, where it is often hardly distinguishable from a smooth coloured glaze. In the Chimu region a smooth yellow background is typical of the early style, while the black tints of the later ceramics lie in the clay itself, which is fired to the hardness of firestone.

The rarest examples show a smooth, gleaming surface which sometimes reflects the light in a soft, white shimmer reminiscent of the silky brilliance of Greek vases, due to a fine wash similar to the porcelain of the Far East. It is a question here of a very resistant but not entirely impermeable 'slip' which under heavy application gives a kind of varnish, forming outwardly a thin layer and to a large extent absorbed by the undercoat. This overcoat cannot be compared with the so-called coloured glazes of antiquity because it does not, as in the case of Greek vases, have a different effect according to the different colours but covers uniformly the whole piece, sometimes extending to the base or in the case of beakers and bowls to the inside surfaces. All these vessels, as closer inspection has revealed, were carefully modelled before the fine layer of paint was applied to the clay and on this once more the drawing; over the whole the soft gleaming varnish.[125]

In the course of world history the art of clay has often been related to architecture in the twin figures of plastic adornment and surface coating. This occurred to a great extent throughout the whole cultural area of Islam, in early Grecian and Etruscan architecture as well as in the masonry of the Nordic Middle Ages and the Renaissance. Ancient American Indian art with its Cyclopean relief-adorned walls adds a further interesting chapter on simple technique used with great effect.

Even the basic form of Indian architecture, the pyramid, is more a work of sculpture than of construction. From whichever side the observer sees it, his eye always takes in the constantly fleeing plane surface. That the Indian stepped pyramids have a trapezoid platform on top instead of rising in equilateral triangles like those of Egypt does not alter the fact that in both cases a

19 Illustrations of Indian music *Above left:* Tambourine player with Dance of Death relief *Above right:* Flute player *Below left:* Death's head with Pan pipes *Below right:* Mythical musical scene on a spouted jug

20
Above left: Indian loom with work in progress *Above right:* Gay Chimu weaving with stepped pattern and wild beasts *Left:* Ancient Peruvian quipus *Below:* Blue cotton weave from Pachacamac with canines bearing sceptres

21
Three
Chimbote
vessels *Left:*
Black double
jug with rays
and birds
in relief
Below left:
Prisoner
Below right:
Two monkeys

22
Above: The sleeping bird. Chimbote *Below:*
Two beakers from Pachacamac with symbolical
design in Tiahuanaco style. The faces bear
traces of tears

clearly defined boundary of the base is missing and with it the
actual element of space. The pyramid solves itself in its incline
and does not crown a specific space like the top of a tower, but
acts far more as a symbol and memorial or, very often, simply
resembles the natural prototype of the mountain, which really
protects but bears within it nothing of the tension of true space.

The simplest system of surfaces and lines raises these monstrous
creations, which seem to grow out of the soil like a piece of
stylised Nature. It would be a fatal mistake on the basis of the
simplicity of form elements to regard Indian architecture as
being more simple than it really is. Apart from the buildings for
specific purposes, the terraced fields with their artificial irrigation
channels, the mighty main roads and huge fortresses, the large cities
of the Chimu such as Chan-Chan, with some 200,000 inhabitants
in its heyday, posed a number of complicated problems which
were admirably solved in spite of primitive technical aids, as a
glance at the temples and palaces will show. They will be discussed in the chapters dealing with the various regions.

Admittedly most of the ground plans typical of Indian architecture display a strongly schematic rectangular system, but to
break up this severity a harmonious treatment of space was
employed, apart from the circular buildings and the picturesque
terracing. Nor can it be maintained that the column, the beamed
roof or the arch were unknown in Ancient American art.
Although the latter only appears in the form of the so-called
pseudo-arch, achieved by the use of protruding stones, this
limitation similar to the arrangement of pillars and roofs is
related to the extensive area of the Indian buildings, and light
roof construction is the ideal solution in a land which is subject
to constant earthquakes.

When considering the overall picture we must remember that
the present-day ruins give us only a very incomplete picture. No
less than 450 plinths have been found in the ruins of Chichen
Itza in Yucatan, and on the Peruvian coast with its large population conditions could not have been very different. Ancient
American art actually shows particular beauty of unity and
harmony. We begin gradually to understand these buildings with
their decorative system in which their beauty was based on the
actual living nerve.

Indian wall decoration is not incorporated into the architectural scaffolding but bears the marks of a highly original surface
decoration. With instinctive confidence each building section is
captured within the framework of the design and represented as
a surface contour. Thus each individual form serves only as a
fleeting support and a transition to the next until eternally new
repetitive or contrasting tints are added, producing that breath-
taking line in which plants and animal shapes mingle or run in
sequence. Nevertheless at various intervals in this play of lines
appears a symbol which achieves its magical effect solely by its
rhythmic repetition. By this expression we do not mean the
futile, mechanical repetition of something that has once been,
but a constantly renewed present evolved from the swift-flowing
stream of experience. Here we have a form of expression characteristic of the Indian cosmology which will be found again in his
speech.

The Indian's urge for symbolical expression was by no means
satisfied in the inexhaustible fantasy of the walls of his places of
worship covered with pictures, the effect of which was originally
heightened by bright-coloured ornament and later by gilding.
Often in the basic form a far deeper thought lay hidden which,
at least in Central America, supports the tradition that most of
the round buildings were dedicated to Quetzalcoatl, the God of
the Winds.[126]

★ ★ ★

Among primitive races the symbol was not born as the result of
abstract thought and theoretical simplification, but from natural
experience. In any interpretation of the Indian symbols we must
reject the hypothesis that it only deserves a hearing if it rests on
a scientific base and specifically that it must be based on the
complex thought and imagination of every race. When we
examine the Maya calendar system—where the orbits of the
planets Venus and Mars are developed in highly complicated
leap-year systems and which, in order to be effective, could not
have been evolved over several hundred years but had to be put
into practice, and further consider that in these systems the
intercalary days became the focal point of the religious cere-

monies and the great regulator of the symbols—we overlook in
such hypotheses the simplest psychological premises.

Although on the one hand we find that the overwhelming
terror of a world catastrophe on such days held the Indians in
thrall, we are forced to accept on the other hand—in view of the
complication of this calendar system—that it was the exclusive
property of the highest priestly caste and we cannot agree that
the masses ever understood it. How then in the simplest pottery
and the simplest textiles, which were often made by peasant
women, could such rare intercalary events be correctly denoted
by crosses, steps, etc., so that we can still decipher them today?
And finally, what material remained to the daily world of the
imagination during the many years that lay between these leap
years?

Chimu stepped ornament

It is certainly good practice also in science not to seek
deeper meanings where simple explanations suffice. One of the
ornaments shown in the accompanying illustration which often
appears in the early art of the coast—if we are to interpret it by
the Indian ideas which were so strongly dominated by astronom-
ical events—in the quadruple steps portrays not an imaginary
Mars intercalation[127] but the far more easily observed four phases
of the moon, which must have fired the imagination of the most
insignificant potter and were entirely in harmony with the age-
old cult of the coast. For in the above illustration it is unnecessary
to interpret the spirals as symbols of the wind but rather as the
movements of the nocturnal satellite; the waxing and waning as
well as the black and the white moon are depicted with perfect
symbolism. That this step motive is frequently connected with

moon worship is shown in the illustration below of designs from the north coast where the steps and other articles of worship are amalgamated with spiral masks and fishes. But these spirals, like the steps in Indian symbolism, are certainly not of single significance but are connected far more with the idea of movement, like the scrolls or hooks on pages 68 and 69 which undoubtedly represent flowing water. From this portrayal of movement, the spirals in other cases may represent the wind and its whirlwind movement, as in Plate 30 in the ear-ring of the upper figure, which, by its beard in the breeze and its complex character, recalls the Mexican deity Quetzalcoatl.

Patterns from Chimu vessels

For lack of written tradition the last word has not yet been said on the significance of Indian symbols, particularly in South America. Thus many signs today remain completely obscure and have been subject to more or less imaginative attempts at solution which are only mentioned in passing or questioned in this book. The deep symbolical content of Indian art as a whole cannot possibly be disputed and will be dealt with in a later chapter.

To sum up what we have already mentioned with regard to the connection between script and weaving, it is best to examine the many symbols from the textiles. Most hands were employed on these, and the wall ornamentations of the shrines and palaces were often no more than a repetition of the textile patterns. But few of the old materials have been preserved and on the excavation sites one usually finds only later hieratically developed forms which often obstinately resist any attempts at deciphering. To try to attribute these forms to technical grounds and to maintain that they were inevitable because of the Indians' simple tools is completely to misrepresent the facts.

In weaving, as in no other field, nothing was beyond the Indian creative capacity. There is hardly a method of execution in modern textiles which the Indians could not have achieved— although with different methods. Their textiles show a wealth of weaving forms which cannot fail to surprise and delight even the most blasé observer. To appreciate the connection between pattern and technique the whole gamut of experience and the tools at their disposal must be the first consideration for any understanding of the ancient Peruvian weaving types. Schmidt has dealt with this subject at great length.[128]

For the layman who has difficulty in following such a technical description it can be stated in brief that the looms of the old Peruvians were based mainly on the principle of mechanical alternation, by which the warp could be altered at will with a single grip so that the strands could lie alternately over and under the weft. With selector and plaiting bobbins the ordinary types of weaving could be produced without further difficulty. For the completion of richer patterns and materials the Indians also worked with a number of selectors and bobbins so that another group of strands could be introduced.

The so-called 'loader' of the modern loom was usually replaced in the Indian frame by a bamboo or wooden weaving staff which often reached a length of three yards and was adorned with heavily engraved patterns. The shuttle was a thin tube which led the unthreaded warp strands alternately from left and right through the weft. Occasionally beautifully carved wooden pins were used for this purpose. Before the start of work the larger looms had to be fastened to a kind of trestle which kept the bobbins free and the warp thread taut. These trestles were made of two light poles, stuck into the ground at a suitable distance from each other and attached at the top (Plate 20).

For minor tasks the weaver used two loom frames stretched between two battens, one end of which hung from the ceiling, while the other, as the illustration below shows, was fastened to the belt of the weaver, so that the strands could be kept taut by the position of his body.

We have little information as to how the Indians worked in

patterned weaving. These two-colour materials are of a comparatively late date. The highest artistic merit was achieved by those
textiles in which the pattern was worked later into the woven
background with bright strands. It can often be observed
immediately whether these pattern strands were woven at the
same time as the foundation or whether they were worked later
into the ready-made fabric with a needle, so that in actual fact
it was merely a kind of embroidery such as is often found in
knitting and other techniques. A very good overall picture of
these various techniques will be found in Raoul d'Harcourt's
copiously illustrated work.[129]

Indian weaver.
Drawing from Chan-Chan

As opposed to the other South American races sewing was very
widespread among the ancient Peruvians. As a result the most
variegated materials were pieced together with borders and trimmings attached. As a general rule metal or wooden needles with
an eye were used. Finally there were metal stencils with which
the pattern could be applied to the fabric. Dyeing was universal
and a variety of techniques were invented similar to those employed in batik and other special methods of dyeing. Both the
coastal and the highland peoples had a great quantity of plant
and mineral dyes at their disposal. In order to impregnate the
material efficiently they were first rendered coarse and absorbent
so that they could be steeped in silicates, particularly chalk and

aluminium but also with iron oxide. The red tints were obtained from cochineal while the blue dye was procured from the indigo plant. This is obviously a striking proof of progressive agriculture among the Chimu, but, in addition to white, Nature provided brown and blue wool which was used in great quantities.[130]

The most varied assortment of woollen yarn has been found in the tombs either rolled into round balls or wound round small spindles, usually made of clay, stone, mussel-shells or intricately worked metal. Distaffs are also of the greatest variety and are often loaded with silky llama or vicuña hair.

And finally, as a particular jewel of Indian textile art, we must mention their featherwork. This was a handicraft practised on the coast from the earliest times. In the neighbourhood of Pacha-camac and in regions farther south examples on a cotton back-ground with the feathers closely sewn together in rows have come to light. Each small single quill was carefully secured with twine to the backing and fastened with a safety knot.[131] With infinite patience the feathers were arranged into the most beautiful and delicate patterns until the most disparate articles of clothing were covered with them. A rich garment was the result—softer than silk or velvet. It is impossible to give even a faint idea of the brilliant colours in a black-and-white illustration. When straight fringes were required the feathers were often carefully cut. The bird world on the coast offered a fantastic choice of plumage, the favourite being the tiny gold and green metallic feathers of the quenti humming-bird. The feathers of the camantira, a charming song-bird about the size of a swallow, with a green head, blue wings with gleaming red tufts and beautiful black feathers, were very popular. The Chimu obtained yellow feathers from the chayna, while the parrotlike tandia produced the necessary white feathers. But we have by no means exhausted the list of the countless birds which provided feathers for this graceful work (Plate 16).

Enhancing the textile industry was the sophisticated plaiting of baskets, huts and mats, the techniques usually employed being the so-called stepped and double plaiting. It is hardly surprising that the former should go hand in hand with the geometrical orna-mentation on pottery, and apart from a running border we find zigzags, small squares or crosses but not the 'meander' pattern.

Nearly as admirable as the art techniques we have already mentioned was the ancient Peruvian skill in metalwork. In the earliest tombs of the Chimu metal was frequently used for weapons, tools and jewellery, and there can be no doubt that axes, knives and other implements as well as countless ornaments were manufactured in great numbers out of metal. Nordenskiöld has proved fairly conclusively[132] that a Copper Age preceded a Bronze Age and that the earliest Chimu apparently used only pure copper. Since this metal is comparatively easy to work it often comes to light in some of the very ancient American cultures. Silver and gold as easily malleable metals were also used from the very earliest times.

Strangely enough we know very little about their mining, which must have been done in grand style in view of the enormous wealth of metals found by the Spaniards on their arrival. Since the Conquistadors continued to exploit the mines the ancient traces today have almost entirely disappeared. While gold was recovered mainly by washing the river sand, silver and copper—according to the chroniclers—were mined. Tin, which is necessary in the making of bronze, was found only in the Bolivian plateau and, at the time of the Inca rule, won solely from the Carabuco Mine near Lake Titicaca. Its use on the coast casts a light on the age-old trade relationships that existed throughout the country. Lead and quicksilver were also found in the tombs, but the latter only in the shape of cinnabar, which, like cochineal, was a favourite dye.

Not only did the Indians practise the art of smelting from the earliest time but they also knew how to make beautiful gold and silver filigree. In making their articles of jewellery they seem to have preferred bronze to pure copper on account of its brighter gleam. The hardening of their simple tools was done by hammering, while the casting of the metals took place in small conical smelting-pots made of a mixture of clay and chalk; into these the air was blown through copper pipes with very narrow nozzles.

Silver headdresses played a great role among the Chimu, and most of them were in the shape of a crescent moon. However, silver headdresses are also known, hung with little silver discs or silver rings in connection with the Pachacamac cult. Plates 6 and 7 give some idea of the great variety of jewellery in bronze,

silver and gold designed to adorn the breasts, arms and legs; per-
colated brims of metal, pearl necklaces, rings worn in great
numbers and often of the most artistic filigree work and different
types of brooches.

★   ★   ★

To close this chapter we should like to say a few words about
Indian music, in which the problem of material and form once
more appears in a completely new and individual guise. Unfortunately we have so far learned comparatively little about their
practice of music. On the other hand countless instruments—
particularly wind instruments—have been found in Peru : the
Pan pipes or syrinx (Plates 28 and 40), later known to the Inca
as Quena, flutes made of clay, silver and bamboo as well as
trumpets of the same material. Drums, too, usually of the tambourine type (Plate 19), and bells have come to light in various
forms, while it seems almost certain that string instruments were
completely unknown throughout America before the Conquest.

Furthermore, we can only surmise the character of the old
music from what the surviving practice of the natives has taught
us.[133] But since European music has exercised its influence for
centuries many false or at least unsound conclusions have been
drawn. Any attempt to elucidate Indian harmonics is made
difficult by a striking peculiarity of their music—an obvious preference for the soaring note, like the tremolo of the voice or the
vibrato of the violin. This can hardly be notated in the present-
day scale.

In addition a special characteristic of Indian music is the lack
of harmony between the dancing and instrumental rhythm and
the rhythm of the song. In so far as they have remained untouched by European influences one still finds today the natives
sing and dance to a drum accompaniment wherein three different
rhythms can be used—for the beat, the step and the voice. Thus
the Indians' sense of form once more in this field contravenes the
ordinary canons of Western art.

CHAPTER EIGHT

Regional Survey and Chronology

THE many artistic treasures which have been excavated on the Peruvian coast owe their preservation to the fortunate circumstance that the Indians buried their dead, together with their most valued and favourite possessions, in the spirit of ancestor worship.

The nature of the climate and soil is such that the testimonies of those lost cultures have been preserved almost undamaged, even when they were made of the most perishable material. The ground, rich in saltpetre, and the dry air produced conditions similar to those to be found in Egypt. The most fragile feather-wear, delicate wood carving and bright-coloured fabrics have survived in such a magnificent state of preservation that they often give the impression of having been made a few days ago.

Unfortunately many of these new-looking objects really are modern, since in fact they are fakes. This holds good particularly for pottery, but also for reproduced tissues, weapons, etc., which are very common. The frenzied hunt of the first Spanish diggers for treasure was followed in the nineteenth century by the collectors of art treasures, and it was obvious that their demands were often satisfied from very dubious sources. Not far from Piura at the beginning of the '80s was a large pottery which imitated exclusively the old vessels, dispatching them to the harbour cities. Clever dealers approached foreigners who bought these antiquities with great enthusiasm and distributed them throughout the world. Finds which are reported to have been dug up from under an age-old algaroba tree must always arouse a certain distrust, although such details often tend to make really old and valuable objects even more interesting and valuable. As a pathetic testimony to ignorance, to lack of connoisseurship, many fake cloths are on display today in our museums. The same collections of course also possess undoubtedly genuine work which, having just been started on the loom, is yet in such a good state of preservation that the weaving could be continued without the slightest difficulty.

The architecture has been more protected than damaged by the shifting sands. Its greatest enemy was the rare but often exceedingly destructive hailstorms. The rainy year of 1925 caused irreparable damage to the ruins of Chan-Chan and along the whole coast and we must be content that photography had already reached a sufficiently high standard for much to be preserved in pictorial form. As a rule human hands have only caused damage to the buildings in places where the Spaniards suspected treasure. In such cases they shrank from nothing; they would divert a river towards the temple to undermine it and would rummage ruthlessly among the stones and the graves. Occasionally destruction was caused when material was needed for building churches and houses. The natives who have remained untouched by European culture feel even to-day an awe which forbids them desecrating the old shrines.

★ ★ ★

In our description of the different regions in the following chapters we shall mention about twenty larger and several smaller rivers[134] in actual Chimu-land, as well as fourteen further main valleys in the domains of the southern cultures to the south. For the purposes of this book and on general, historical, archaeological and stylistic grounds we have separated these into the following cultural regions:

THE NORTHERN COAST: THE KINGDOM OF THE CHIMU

1. *The equatorial frontier region.* The country round the Gulf of Guayaquil to the Sechura Desert with the Rio Tumbes, the Rio de la Chira and the Rio Piura (Chapter Nine, Map page 138).

2. *The northern part of the kingdom.* The neighbourhood between Sechura Desert and the Pampa de Paján with the Rio de la Leche, the Rio Chancay, the Rio Zana and the Rio Jequetepeque (Chapter Ten, Map page 182).

3. *The heart of Chimu-land.* The ancient cultural region between the Pampa de Paján and the lower reaches of the Rio

Santa with the Rio Chicama, the Rio Moche and the Rio Viru (Chapter Eleven, Map page 182).

4. *The mountain pocket.* The Upper Santa valley between the White and Black Cordilleras with the Cordillera de Conchucos and the Rio Toblacha (Chapter Twelve, Map page 182).

5. *The transitional region.* The hot, dry country between the lower reaches of the Rio Santa and the Rio Pativilca with the three bays Chimbote, Samanco and Casma and in addition the Rio Nepeña, the Rio Huarmey and the Rio Casma (Chapter Thirteen, Map page 182).

THE CENTRAL COAST: PACHACAMAC

6. *The kingdom of the Cuismancu.* The shrines of the central coast from the Rio Pativilca to the promontory of Chilca with the river courses of the Rio Huara, the Rio Huaral, the Rio Chillon, the Rimac and the Lurin (Chapter Fourteen, Map page 196).

THE SOUTHERN COAST: THE WORLD OF NAZCA

7. *The kingdom of the Chuquimancu.* Extends from the promontory of Chilca across the Rio Mala, the Rio Omas and the Rio Cañete (Chapter Fifteen, Map page 196).

8. *The land of the Chincha.* Embraces the Rio de San Juan, the Rio Chincha, the Rio Pisco, the Paracas Peninsula, the Rio Ica and the Rio Grande de Nazca (Chapter Fifteen, Map page 196).

In this extensive area many of the names today well known in literature call for a certain clarification. Old and more modern cities, rivers, valleys and provinces are constantly being confused, since for one and the same feature a modern or an archaic Spanish word is often used in addition to terminology from some Indian dialect, making distinction very difficult when trying to pinpoint a certain place.

For the description of the place, river and district names in this book we have followed the official text in the latest maps and publications of the Ministerio de Relaciones Exteriores, the Ministerio de Fomento, the Dirección de Obras Publicas y Vias de Comunicación as well as the Dirección nacional de Estadistica in the Ministerio de Hacienda y Comercio of the Peruvian Government, while the ancient Spanish and Indian names, when they are frequently used, are added in parenthesis. When the spelling in the official documents or elsewhere in Peru fails, the general South American version has been followed. Double descriptions have been avoided and the possibilities of change have been noted wherever necessary in order to achieve unity as far as possible in this survey.

For the scientific exploration of the land the motoring roads built in recent years and above all modern air travel with its unsuspected possibilities have been of considerable help, whereas the railways play only a very minor role. From an aircraft the old city sites can be recognised with astonishing accuracy down to their smallest detail, whereas on the ground one spends weeks of effort trying to achieve the same result. From a bird's-eye view the sand of the dunes often seems to lie like a gentle veil over the ruins and the foundations fit together into huge ground plans, as can be seen in the aerial photographs (Plate 33).

The railways serving the regions in question were nearly all built during the second half of the nineteenth century. The most important are the Central Andean line, opened in 1870 and today equipped with modern diesel engines, which runs from Lima across the mountains to Oroya and from there to Cerro de Pasco and Huancavelica, and the second line on the coast running north from Lima to Pativilca before turning inland. Independent local connections run from Chimbote to the lower Santa Valley, from Trujillo to the Chicama Valley, the Jequetepeque Valley, Chiclayo and Piura.

The whole country, however, is criss-crossed with beautiful modern motor roads which allow communication between the individual valleys, often following the ancient Chimu routes. The great north-south road leads from Tumbes along the coast to Paita and Piura, forking many time until two branches cross the desert via Sechura and Motupe until at their junction, Lambayeque, they hug the coast southwards to Pisco. From there a short stretch of railway leads inland to Ica and from that city in a straight line to Nazca, the southernmost point of this survey.

Before examining the individual regions in the following chapters in an attempt to portray the general art and culture of the coast, it is necessary in the next few pages to put a certain amount of chronological order into the survey and also to elaborate the terrain under discussion. In recent years the following scholars in particular have busied themselves with Peruvian chronology: Kroeber,[135] Means,[136] Olson,[137] Tello,[138] Tozzer[139] and Uhle.[140] On page 34 we have mentioned the sources to be consulted for the comparison and complementing of the relative Central American chronology. Naturally the different scholars vary in the terminology they use and in the dating of sundry details. In judging the great sequences of ancient Peruvian cultures there is, however, a remarkable consensus of opinion. The combined results show that from the earliest times which come within reach of the spade along the whole coastal region dealt with, only two extensive cultures of more than merely local significance developed: Chavín and Chimu. Some scholars consider Chavín and others consider Chimu to be the elder. This is of little consequence since both the cultures in question were many times interwoven and above all travelled a part of their historical destiny together.

Not even for the lowest stratum of these ancient cultures can the term 'primitives' be employed, nor can we term them a purely Stone Age creation; for the most varied use of metals was known to the earliest Chimu as well as to the men of Chavín.

From the seventh to the tenth century, therefore, noticeable at least in the actual kingdom of the Chimu but more strongly marked in the parts of the country which came under the influence of Chavín, above all on the coast round Pachacamac, is the strong influence of Tiahuanaco art, which gradually dies away in the tenth century. After this era the coastal styles recover their indigenous form and the late style of the Chimu continues to live beyond the Inca supremacy far into the first Spanish age. On the basis of the above-mentioned works and according to our own opinion on the development of the Tiahuanco culture,[141] and with due consideration for the valuable results which have ensued from the tree ring calendar which we shall describe later, we have compiled the table on the opposite page.

This distribution of time covering the period of the ancient Peruvian development of style needs a short commentary on the main points and above all raises the interesting question as to how it fits in with a chronology for the whole of America.

As a general rule archaeologists in the very understandable joy

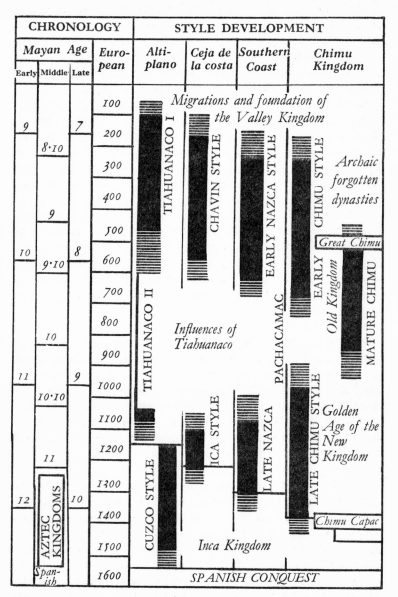

Diagram showing the chronology according to the Maya Calendar parallel with the style development of the Ancient Peruvian cultures

of exploration and the frequent discovery of such ancient things are inclined when dating their discoveries to go much too far back in time. This has been proved most clearly in the south-west of the United States, where as soon as the tree ring calendar was available all earlier dates had to be put forward considerably.

The tree ring calendar, first developed by Douglass,[142] is of particular significance for the entire American chronology, and with its astonishing simplicity has been a real Columbus's egg in the field of archaeological research. Above all it has confuted the long-held opinion that many geometrically patterned vessels were particularly old. It is no longer necessary to deal more closely with the polemics written on this subject. The tree ring calendar has solved the matter once and for all.

It is merely a question of sawing through old trees and comparing the varying curves of the yearly rings in the same way as one takes fingerprints. In rainy years, as a result of increased growth and additional rising of the sap, broad rings are formed, whereas in periods of drought the rings are smaller; they differ not only in their width but by the nature of the intercellular veins of resin and oil of the relative pines.

On sawing through trees in the same neighbourhood some particularly striking rings will be found in different positions. If on the second tree they are near the bark but towards the centre in the first, it follows that the tree with the similar outer ring must be the older : it has developed a structure characteristic for a certain year because it already had x number of years behind it which the other tree lacked. If such comparisons and contrasts are made with sufficient care and patience, trees or wood will always be found with inner rings matching outer rings which have previously been discovered.

When a living tree is felled its outermost ring represents the year of the search, while somewhere farther inside a ring will appear which corresponds to another perhaps long since dead trunk, as trees grow to a very old age. In this way, starting from the present, we reach a perfectly reliable date in the past. An incontrovertible chronological sequence of rings and their corresponding years result until we have a real calendar which can be used in a variety of ways and which today already reaches back to the beginning of the Christian era.

23 Late style types of Chimu art *Above:* Parrot as double gourd in reddish-brown clay *Below:* Fish and fruit in relief work. Black clay

24 Chimu late style *Above and below right:* Typical composite vessels in reddish-brown clay *Below left:* Black vase from Lambayeque

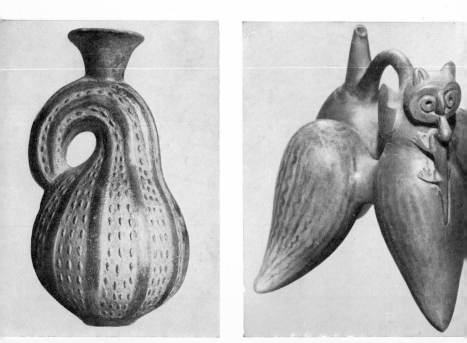

25 *Above and below left:* Typical early forms in broad wash design *Below right:* Polychrome dish from Pachacamac with udder-like feet

26 *Above:* The flat beach at Huanchaco. In the foreground left the sparse-
flowing Rio Seco and the abandoned fields *Below:* The steep coast of
the barren frontier district south of Huarmey

Since it is perfectly easy to check the grain of wood found in buildings or graves with this unusual calendar, in order to verify at what period some particular piece of wood grew and when it could have been used, so in favourable conditions it is possible today—where earlier one dated to the nearest half-century— often to date it within ten years. The only condition for a success- ful use of this calendar is that the wood from which it is cal- culated must come from a region where the yearly rainfall was constant over a large district. Irregular rainful must naturally result in different ring pictures. This fact limits the use of the calendar but its great significance is unimpaired. By slow and patient work great progress is possible and perhaps new aspects of the subject will soon be discovered.

The present-day starting-point for measuring time by the tree ring calendar is in the area of Arizona and New Mexico together with the bordering states of Colorado, Utah, California and Nevada. Here, as on the Peruvian coast, we have a desert but by no means uninhabitable region with a hot, dry climate. It has been inhabited for at least two thousand years by Indians whose descendants still live there today. In Europe they are known usually as the Pueblo and they appeared in that region at the beginning of the Christian era as a hunting people with no know- ledge of the plough, slowly developing an interesting urban cul- ture which reached its peak in the fourteenth and fifteenth cen- turies. It is characterised by many-storeyed and also by round buildings, and a clan settlement can easily be recognised. The invention of pottery among this people must be dated some- where in the fourth century A.D. On the lower-lying desert stretch of South Arizona, living a more urban life on the flat river banks, the Hokoham dwelt in single houses built of clay tiles. Agricul- ture and large artificial irrigation canals characterise their culture.

These two and a few smaller races related to them were all keen potters and a mass of finds can be dated accurately by the tree ring calendar since clay wares and wood were often dis- covered together. The results show that a specific geometric style evolved here at a very late age, a parallel which can be found again in the art of Ica and its transition to Inca style. The reliable method of dating by the tree ring calendar has given one more irrefutable proof that the geometrical pattern in Indian art need not necessarily have originated as a result of the influence of weaving or plaiting techniques. They provide the general style comparison with an all-embracing and accurately dated material from which the whole development of the Indian sense of art can be read in all its purity. It is very gratifying to recognise in these Central American creations the great difference between the early geometrical form and the later highly decorative patterns.

When this form world is carefully compared with that of Tiahuanaco the latter loses much of its mystery and can be grasped as a more or less natural stage of development.[143] It is therefore no longer necessary to consider this style as a beginning and its whole appearance on the Peruvian coast becomes easier to understand. It is clear that a rich, powerful culture with magnificent buildings and colossal transport achievements, with an art that created for itself a perfectly stylised hieratic picture language which must have needed an enormous span of time to develop, could not possibly have developed out of nothing.

But since a more primitive lower layer cannot be found or proved in the ancient Peruvian cultural regions this first development must be looked for elsewhere. If we follow our thesis that the Chimu and their southern relations from Pachacamac and Nazca invaded the land from the north, a more urgent task awaits us: from which part of the great Central American area did these nomads come? This task is made more difficult since a controversy still rages as to the final correspondence between the ancient Maya calendar and the European. The problem has reached a point today when it will have to be solved by astronomers rather than archaeologists.

From the standpoint of Peruvian research it is highly probable that we must set the whole of Maya culture far further forward in time than Spinden thought, approaching in this way the theories of Seler and Lehmann.[39] The cogent arguments of these scholars based entirely on the state of preservation of the ruins demand further attention. If the Chimu invaded the land from the north it is clear that these intruders must either have arrived in a pre-Maya calendar age or have been members of some Central American races with no knowledge of hieroglyphics or who for some reason had completely lost or forgotten them. The last supposition is hardly feasible since it cannot be disproved that on the overthrow of the priesthood by discontented chieftains or from some religious or political causes an old script and calendar tradition could have been suppressed. Far more significant is the whole cultural condition reigning on the Peruvian coast. The presence of moon worship alone before the later sun religion provides such a weighty argument that the scales must fall

Moon mythological scene with canines and serpent beams. Pottery designs from Chan-Chan

decisively and the cultures in Peru as a whole must be considered as much earlier and those in Maya country on the contrary much later than has hitherto been maintained.

Thus a whole American concept has arisen, based on historical observation and possessing an inner logic which cannot be seriously disputed by the finds: one day, perhaps, after the solution of the riddle posed by the Maya calendar, new and empirical viewpoints may result. For the bonds between Central American and Peruvian cultures today speaks a host of material which is augmented by almost every new excavation. The cities and buildings of the Chimu were in their age the greatest ever created by Indians and it is quite impossible to study this culture on its own without a glance at the entire evolution of Ancient America.

When one studies the conscientious excavations of recent years in the old Maya cities of Cahal Cunil, Copan, Hatzcap Ceel, Holmul, Lubaantun, Piedras Negras, Pusilha, Quiriga and Uaxactun it is obvious that these races used neither gold, silver nor copper as a general rule. A few finds made in Palenque and Tikal are questionable and one is justified in accepting that on the collapse of the old Maya kingdom comparatively few metal objects existed. A stylistic comparison between the art of Chavín, in which perhaps one must see the very first cultural import of the Chimu on the Peruvian coast and in the Andean region, and that of the old Maya kingdom shows a striking similarity in the lines, so that it cannot be incorrect to maintain that the traits of Nazca art reappear in Oaxaca, as Joyce has already suggested.[144]

The curious proof of these ancient connections was suppressed for many years by the statement which appeared so often in literature, that even the more modern Aztecs knew nothing of the rise of the Inca kingdom in South America, and people came to the very unsound conclusion that hundreds if not thousands of years before no such connection could have existed. In actual fact, however, even the assertions of the Aztecs cannot be taken in all good faith. When at the Court of Montezuma the white intruders were told that no such connections existed it was certainly not the first political white lie in world history. That the merchants and ambassadors of Montezuma travelled as far as Panama is today no longer in doubt.[145] There, however, they must have at least had some knowledge of South America even if they did not have any actual connection with that country.

Against the Aztec assertion that they had no idea of Peruvian culture also speaks the report of Las Casas.[146] This describes the llama, which lives only in the Andes, and the balsa, from information furnished by South American chiefs many years before the Spaniards had conquered Mexico or even arrived in South America. But even if such communication in later ages could not be proved and if the age-old trade relationship of earlier ages did not produce countless finds, nevertheless from the art point of view a genuine relationship existed between the two regions, although this is difficult to describe with accuracy.

Hrdlicka, in a very old huaca in the Chicama Valley found two vessels next to some skulls of clearly Central American type: two bowls, one of which was a tripod and in its shape and decoration characteristic of what had long been recognised as the artistic creation of Costa Rica, Nicaragua and Panama. It is therefore understandable that Lothrop should conclude that all the art objects previously catalogued as Peruvian resembled those of Ecuador.[147]

Allowing sufficient time for the development of the individual cultures to bring them into line with the discoveries we must accept that after the first great migration of the archaic races and people in Central America, as on the Peruvian coast, there was a certain balance. As the result of the founding of larger kingdoms or alliances, settled conditions reigned over the years, giving an upward thrust to the whole economical development, resulting in the erection of gigantic buildings and the creation of esoteric religious systems.

It is more difficult, however, to say why these individual cultural renaissances ended—whether lack of land in the case of over-population, climatic changes or strife between rival powers were the outward causes. The collapse of the high culture in Central America may have been caused by the invasion of more barbaric races from the northern regions, producing conditions such as occurred in Europe at the time of the folk migrations, when the powerful but inwardly corrupt Roman Empire succumbed to the onslaught of comparatively smaller hordes and culture disappeared for many years.

Among the wild races of America, too, there were small and comparatively insignificant groups who were determined to fight for better things with all their might. The Aztecs underwent a complete transformation in Mexico in less than 200 years, from the time they founded their capital, Tenochtitlan, the present-day Mexico City, in 1324, until it was destroyed in 1521 by the Spaniards, from a small nomadic tribe into a ruling power such as the Europeans found, a power that made the kings and rulers from the Gulf of Mexico to the Pacific Ocean tremble.

Very much the same applies to the Inca in Peru. Although opinion as to their founder differs, everyone agrees that even in the second and third century after the capitulation of Cuzco the Inca kingdom was only a kind of city state, extending not much farther than its own valley, before it assumed the gigantic proportions found by the Europeans on their arrival.

Nothing could be more incorrect than to try to ascribe the great Indian culture to the most recent and best-known races. When we speak of Ancient American art and culture we must not forget that we are speaking of at least 2,000 years and that within this long span of time the most disparate races, cultures and art styles were born, blossomed and died. It would be basically false to look upon Ancient American art merely as the art of the Aztecs in Mexico or of the Incas in Peru. This widespread idea is as false as its antithesis, that the whole art of the West was expressed by the Nordic-Gothic and subsequently by the Italian Renaissance.

The Aztecs and the Incas were the most important races which the Spaniards met at the Conquest, but they were not the only great nations in the vast country of America, nor did they represent an original art or culture. Our chronology therefore may give a general survey where on individual points great accuracy of facts cannot be reached, an accuracy which is for the most part unnecessary since history never stands still and one is constantly engaged with the eternal flux of things.

CHAPTER NINE

The Equatorial Frontier Region

THE region of the Gulf of Guayaquil together with the district round the Bay of Sechura and the valleys of the Rio de Piura, Rio de la Chira and Rio Tumbes represent the most advanced outpost of the Chimu empire whose northern borderline must be taken as the last-named river or in the Cordillera del Chilla (Map page 138).

The city of Tumbes opposite the Isle of Puña was also the gate by which Pizarro and the Spanish Conquistadors entered. Here the white men made their first acquaintance with the land of the Chimu, and it is perhaps not amiss to pause for a moment and examine this remarkable historical meeting on the basis of the chroniclers' accounts. Even if their accounts differ on various points, we can, by and large, obtain a fairly clear picture.

When in 1526 Ruiz, Pizarro's pilot, sighted that first Indian craft with the large rectangular sail (page 18) and drew alongside, he entered into relations with the Indians on board. They were men and women from the neighbourhood of Tumbes, to which city the balsa itself belonged. Some of them were wearing rich jewellery and their cargo consisted of artistically worked objects in gold and silver which they bartered with the coastal dwellers. The attention of the Spaniards was mainly aroused by their strange garments made of magnificently fine material embroidered in the brightest colours with pictures of animals and flowers. These garments were actually made of alpaca or of the even softer vicuña wool, both of which in their softness surpassed the wool of the llama and was so brilliant and flexible that when it reached the Spanish Court it was often mistaken for silk.

The merchants had a pair of scales to weigh the precious metals, utensils which the Europeans had never seen before in Indian country—not even in Mexico. In the museums today there are plenty of well-preserved and very beautiful scale beams

of ivory or wood, some of them decorated with silver. These finds
from Chimu country are often embellished with carvings and
usually have holes in the centre and at both ends. The inner holes
were for the suspension of the scale while the side ones were
designed for the ropes which carried either two small nets (Plate
18) or metal bowls to receive the objects to be weighed against
stone weights. Other scale beams are bored throughout their
entire length and carry in this groove a rope with a net on one
side and the weight secured to the other. Scales specially designed
for precision weighing have been found and these have two small
discs in the ring allowing horizontal control. None of the so-called
Roman scales, which many of the later chroniclers describe, has
as yet been found in Chimu country.

The Indian merchants from Tumbes gave Ruiz to understand
that in their country great herds of cattle grazed in the fields and
that in the palaces of their ruler gold and silver were almost as
common as wood. Naturally the Spanish listened greedily to this
information, which corresponded so perfectly with their hearts'
desires, and the pilot, although he thought they were exaggera-
ting, decided to detain a couple of these Indians so that they
could learn Castilian and later act as interpreters.

More than a year went by until the Spaniards, after great
effort and suffering, once more under the leadership of Pizarro,
arrived in the region, but this time more as cautious and peaceful
explorers than as violent conquerors. The nearer they approached
the Gulf of Guayaquil the more impressed they became with the
coasts of Panama and Colombia—these men who had met real
savages and even cannibals—with the signs of a higher culture
which the general aspect of the land and its inhabitants afforded.
Everywhere they could see the fruits of agriculture, and the coast
looked particularly inviting. Algarobas grew on the flat beaches
and their fragrant branches pervaded the air with sweet scent.
On the heights between lay huge built-up terraces planted with
maize and potatoes and in the hollows cocoa bushes thrived.[148]

The region became more densely populated and settlements
could be seen on each new foothill past which the Spaniards
sailed. Balsas, sporting a gold mask as a flag and heavily laden
with Indian warriors, occasionally circled Pizarro's ship, which
soon reached the Gulf of Guayaquil. Here the river valleys

appeared to be unusually fertile and beautiful while the white huts on the coast gleamed and smoke rose from the thick settlements among the hills. The Europeans were now level with the 18,000-feet giants of this particularly magnificent Andean chain. They could see Chimborazo with its broad round peak which rises like a dome from the Cordilleras and then Cotopaxi with its dazzling white cone, at that time the wildest and still today the most active volcano in the world.

In 1527, from the sea Tumbes appeared a reasonably large city with many stone houses in an enchanting setting. At some distance from the shore Pizarro saw huge balsas full of warriors making towards them. They were attacking the nearby island of Puña, as they soon discovered. When Pizarro drew close enough to the Indian flotilla he requested his two men from Tumbes, who in the meantime had become interpreters, to order one of the commanding officers to come aboard his ship. This order was carried out.

They stared in surprise at each object, and particularly at their own countrymen whom they had met here so unexpectedly. The latter explained how they had fallen into the hands of the foreigners and portrayed them as fabulous creatures who had not come to Tumbes with any evil intention but simply to learn about the country and its inhabitants. This was ceremoniously corroborated by Pizarro, who encouraged the Indians to return to their balsas and tell their fellow countrymen what they had seen and learned. Pizarro also stressed that he wished to engage in peaceful barter with the natives and asked them to send him provisions.

In the meantime a large part of the population had collected on the shore watching in surprise the swimming fortress that now lay so calmly at anchor in their bay. They listened eagerly to the tales of their countrymen and repeated everything to the elders of the city. It was not long before bananas, maize, sweet potatoes, cocoa beans and other products including game, fish and a few llamas were brought. Pizarro had seen rough sketches of the latter beasts but had never seen a living example. He examined this strange creature with the greatest interest. It was to be nicknamed the 'Indian's little camel'.

The following day Alonso de Molina, accompanied by a negro

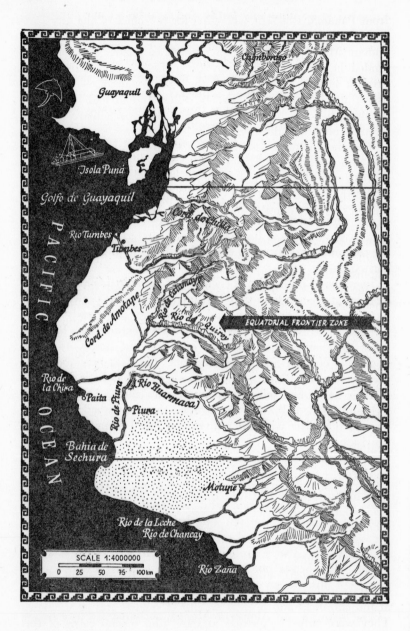

SCALE 1:4000000

0   25   50   75   100 km

from Panama, was sent with gifts for the chief of the city consisting of pigs and poultry, all of them unknown beasts to the Indian. Molina had a host of marvels to relate. As soon as he landed he was surrounded by the natives, who expressed the greatest surprise at his clothes, the light colour of his skin and above all his long beard. The beardless Indian had never seen anything like this before. The women were particularly curious about Molina and did not wish to let him go.

The Indians were just as astounded by the black skin of his companion. They could not believe that this was natural and tried to rub off what they thought was paint with their hands. When the African tolerated this with his usual good temper and flashed his white teeth their pleasure knew no bounds. The Indians were also curious about the strange animals which the Spaniards had brought. When the cock crowed and his cock-a-doodle-do rang out, these simple folk clapped their hands in astonishment and asked what he had said.[149]

One too easily forgets today what an effect these strange phenomena must have had on the Indians and how much they must have contributed to the easy conquest of their land. A no less significant event had been witnessed by the Spaniards on their voyage farther in the north, where after resting in an Indian village they had left behind a sick horse which the inhabitants of that neighbourhood regarded as a creature of a higher nature. They brought it into the house and offered it food which would presumably have delighted any man : roast fowl and all manner of meat delicacies. The poor beast starved to death.

To their amazement, on entering Quito, Pizarro's troops realised that when the Indians saw the Spanish horsemen on their mounts for the first time they did not realise that they were two separate entities. They looked upon them as two-headed monsters and the spell was only broken when one of the riders was thrown from his horse. At this moment the Spaniards were in mortal danger.[149]

Molina, Pizarro's envoy, was escorted to the dwelling of the chieftain in Tumbes. It was magnificently appointed with guards at the entrances and a great wealth of golden and silver plate. They were only too pleased to show him several parts of the

Indian city, including a fortress made of rough-hewn stones. Cieza de León reports that it was not particularly high but covered a very large area.[150] This was the rule in most of the Indian dwellings, which, even in the later Inca times, occasionally reached two and very seldom three storeys. Close to this fortress was a temple which according to Molina's description, glittered with gold and silver.

His description appeared to Pizarro so exaggerated that on the following day he decided to send a second emissary, who in his opinion would be more reliable. For this purpose he chose the Greek knight, Pedro de Candia.[151] The latter went ashore in full armour, as befitted a nobleman, with a sword at his belt and a blunderbuss. His appearance caused more amazement than Molina's had done, since the sun gleamed on his harness and radiated from his weapons. They had heard a great deal of this terrifying weapon from the interpreters and asked the ambassador to let it speak to them. The flash of the powder, the loud report of the gun and the splintering of a board which had been put up as target made a great impression on the Indians and the white man was immediately treated with the greatest respect.[152]

The reliable Pedro de Candia also described the temple as being virtually covered with gold and silver plates and reported that the fortress was surrounded by a triple ballium. He saw the convent of the Sun Maidens, an Inca innovation, and found many models of fruits which cannot have differed from those works of art in the late style of the Chimu to be seen in the museums today. It is important that on this visit Candia also maintains that the city was magnificently provided with water through a number of canals, thus conforming perfectly to our picture as a result of excavation of the other cities of late Chimu culture.

When the Spaniards visited Tumbes for the second time in 1532, now as conquerors, the city with the exception of a few houses had been completely destroyed. The great temple and the fortress had been very heavily damaged and the contents looted. The people of Tumbes had once more waged war on their particular enemies the inhabitants of the Island of Puña. The rulers of this island were the Tumpala, or Tumala, who as a result of the insignificance of their domain as well as their constant preparedness for war could remain independent—even in the time of the Spaniards—to a certain extent up to 1570. Salazar de Villasante names Don Diego Tumala in 1573 and his son as rulers and speaks of them as good Christians.[153]

In the whole region the current language was not Mochica but a dialect which Calancha in his rather confused account on this subject[13] called the *'lengua sec'*. *Sec* is obviously a word from the Tallan language which today has disappeared and does not signify any particular name but speech or language in general.

Pattern from a clay vessel, Plate 10

It is a common phenomenon that on asking a question of Indians one receives from them not a particular but a general termination, because they are often at a loss to know what the questioner actually wants. In the word *sec*, we apparently have an almost universal root word found in the most disparate languages. We meet it again in the German *sag-en* and also in *säg-en*; *sägen*—to saw—is no more than the transitive form of *sag-en*, meaning that the word is speaking from the noise caused. In a similar way *tränken* is the transitive form of *trinken* and *fällen* of *fallen*. Since only forty to forty-five words can be safely determined from this whole language it is not worth while going into the matter any more closely here.[154]

The people of Tumbes, as a buffer state between the warlike but rather uncultured people of the Ecuadorian coast in the

north and the no less warlike but more civilised vassals of the
Chimu in the south, always retained a certain independence even
when they became part of the Inca empire. They stuck grimly
to their old customs and uses and were a rather savage and
aggressive tropical people. The princes possessed a host of jesters,
singers and dancers at their courts. Unnatural vice was quite
common and human sacrifice far more prevalent than in the
actual kingdom of the Chimu. On the other hand these frontier
dwellers were industrious farmers and are famous for their skill
as weavers.

If the Chimu from Chan-Chan at its peak was the theoretical
overlord of Tumbes his real power began first in the more
southerly, thickly populated valleys of the deep-water river Chira
and the Piura,[56] which in its upper reaches is also called the Rio
Huarmaca and at its mouth the Rio de Sechura. Everywhere in
these valleys the archaeological finds show the powerful influence
of the Chan-Chan culture in its later phase.

In the Chira valley as in the valley of Piura stand the first
adobe pyramids so characteristic of Chimu architecture—unfired
clay tiles dried in the sun. The Rio de la Chira rises on Ecuadorian soil from the two lakes Mamayacu and Huaringas and joins
the sea some sixteen miles north of Paiti; it brings down so much
water that its lower reaches are navigable.

The Chira in its southern main stream is called the Rio de
Quiroz in the older literature and on the more modern maps the
Rio Quiroy, which is basically the same term as for the lower
reach, while a second northern upper reach after the fork of the
valleys is called the Rio Catamayo. Between these two sources
lies in the old valley of Quiroz the so-called Huaca de Chira,
near Sujo (Map page 138).

This was the focal point of the domain of one of the twelve
legendary rulers in the Chimu Valley. The basic length extends
about 120 yards from north to south and about ninety yards
from west to east. The upper terrace of this three-tiered pyramid
at the time of the Chimu must have afforded a fabulous view
over the broad fertile valley with the Cordillera of Amotape or
La Brea outlined against the distant sky.

The pyramid is built of adobe mixed with earth. On the third
platform are curious traces of wall remains which rise vertically

and repeat the trend of the whole building; they are three or four yards wide at the base but reach a bare five metres in height in places. Although these walls were originally covered with smooth mortar or fine clay, on which today, although very faded, can be seen traces of bluish paint, they were later covered with a host of rough tiles. Eventually the third terrace, too, like the rest of the huaca, became a solid unit outwardly formed from a mixture of earth and adobe.

This ruthless overbuilding of earlier architecture, which in itself was a substitute for the original tumulus, is to be found all along the coast. The new ruler never bothered to preserve the old but insisted upon imposing his own style and enforcing his will as he entered the scene at some new cultural epoch.

In the whole of the region we have described enough pottery has come to light belonging to the early style to confirm that in the oldest period it was still under the influence of the Chimu. The overwhelming majority of the finds, however, show clearly that the late style triumphed in the region of Lambayeque. Various private collections in Piura, the first settlement founded in Peru by the Spaniards, also contain certain vessels in red clay with a white neck found in the neighbourhood on which a so-called cursive ornament is painted in dark brown.[155] The other ceramics, however, all belong to the typical monochrome ware of the late style which in this particular case usually consists of highly fired dark red clay because the two watersheds in the last days of the kingdom were very thickly populated.

For the sake of completion we should mention that among these finds some display the so-called Chavín style which has caused much ink to be spilled in the literature on this subject.[156] This, however, need cause no surprise when the reader remembers what we have mentioned on page 105 about the significance of this style for the Chimu kingdom, and looks at Map page 138, which shows that the Rio Quiroy extends far into the mountains, offering a favourable opportunity for a settlement. A similar influence of style elements and the displacement of ceramics from Cejas de la Costa promptly recurs at the next river with its source deeper in the mountains, the Jequetepeque and its attendant valley of Pacasmayo (Map page 182).

Since in the frontier region the late style already appears on countless utensils we shall describe it here in great detail, since in its realistic significance and symbolical unpretentiousness it is better suited for study than the early style or the art of the mature period.

The pot-bellied flat-based form in the late art incontestably serves the purpose of holding as much liquid as possible. Furthermore, the delight expressed in decoration shows the end of a cultural epoch. The round walls are often decorated with a form system, which, with its strange conjunction of the contradictory naturalistic ornamentation and natural stylised pictures of plants and animals, is a vague reminder and a ghost of age-old symbols.

Everything appears ponderous and solid in comparison with the lightness and delicate sculpture of the earlier ceramics and is only loosely held together in a vague picturesque outline. It outweighs by far the protective enclosing forms. Open generous bowls offering their contents are almost entirely lacking. These belong exclusively to the art of the Inca and the completely different style of Cuzco. Their colours appear just as crude as their shapes are clumsy. The clay does not become a brightly painted object but merely a surface to carry colour like a coloured glaze. According to chemical tests this coat of paint consisted of a very constant mass of primary matter, the differences being achieved by increase in the amount of carbon whereby the whole process of oxidisation on the surface was perfected in these late objects.[157]

The reddish-brown vessels which have been found in the frontier region, with the exception of the colour, are very similar to the predominantly black examples in late style. They can best be appreciated when considered as single colour wares. Their character is so clearly expressed that they can immediately be recognised in any collection of Peruvian antiquities. The majority are of black clay with the ornament usually in relief (Plates 23 and 24).

The black, very dark grey or reddish-brown clay can support a great heat in firing because it usually contains a considerable amount of graphite or similar metallic substances. The proportion of silicate usually exceeds 60 per cent while the proportion of aluminium varies between 10 and 20 per cent. Iron content varies between 4 and 9 per cent while magnesium potash and

27
Brilliant
creations of the
early style.
The design
on the vessel
in the centre
below is
reproduced
on p. 68

28

Above: Indian mummy in its original garb.
The face is covered by a gilt copper mask and
the feathered head-dress is secured by a fillet.
The body swathed in bast is covered by a
tapestry-like fabric. A beard plucker hangs
on the breast and a reticule over each
shoulder *Left:* Two pan pipes players with
death's heads from Chan-Chan

29

Right: Unpainted clay head with tattooings incised. See text

Below: Spoutless heads from Moche and Chan-Chan

p. 57

30

Above: The Bearded God. 'In Mexico . . . also existed the myth of a culture-bringing God, Quetzalcoatl, portrayed as bearded and white-skinned. After bestowing the blessings of knowledge on his people he disappeared to the East . . . one day to reappear from there.' The myth of his return played an important part in the subjection of the Indians by the Spaniards; the conquistadors had beards and were light-skinned. See text page 204 *Left:* The happy sleeper

carbonates is less than 10 per cent, and there are only insignificant traces of manganese and nickel.

The single-colour vessels were already known to the early Chimu and produced for centuries along the northern coast. Of those that have survived only about 3 to 5 per cent are older vases, while the wares of the late period represent about 75 per cent. With this strongly disparate condition of the finds it is possible to recognise quite easily to which particular cultural epoch they belong.

Very characteristic of late Chimu are vessels joined together with a bar and whistling double flasks which the Spaniards knew as *chifladores*. These also crop up in the excavations of early sites and form a remarkable parallel to finds made in Central America, in the Zapotec area and in Guatemala.[158] In the centuries preceding the Conquest they were widespread along the whole Peruvian coast. In many different forms of ceramics, particularly in the heads of parrots and monkeys—in other words of mimicking beasts—we find holes and outlets which caused a piping or a comical gurgling noise when the water was poured out of one side and the air entered the other side of the vessel. It would be interesting to know what people who hold the view that these ceramics were originally intended for the tombs think of these entertaining objects, which, without some practical use in life, could hardly have developed in such a variety of forms.

The human figure is very seldom portrayed in the late sculpture. The potters used for preference animals, fruits and plants. As a whole the late style, as a result of the increasing coastal traffic, tends towards the more southern forms including a double gourd held together by a single bar adopted from the vessels of Nazca (Plates 45 and 47), whereas the tubes in the mixed region of the central coast retained their old harmonic forms, lengthening and changing them without managing to make them the less beautiful. The late style maintained the early delight in form repetition until it develops into double and manifold vessels arranged together or superimposed in every possible way; they no longer speak the imperative language of the old days but often merely chatter.

CHAPTER TEN

The Northern Part of the Kingdom

THE northern part of the Chimu kingdom was separated from its equatorial frontier zone by the vast dreary desert of Sechura. Near the Rio de la Leche on one of its upper reaches lies the ancient city of Motupe, Pizarro's next goal after Tumbes and San Miguel. The Rio de la Leche also forms the language frontier between the Sec spoken in the frontier region and the Mochica or Mochic, the official language of the Chimu.

We are now in the region described in Chapter One of this book which corresponds by and large today with the Peruvian department Lambayeque. In the valley of the Rio de la Leche lies Jayanca, which, according to the saga of King Naymlap, was beseiged by Llapchillulli's clan, and the other places referred to in that story, such as Tucume, much farther to the south, are also located in these valleys. The most powerful and deepest river in this region is the Lambayeque, today known as Chancay. It has its source in the Hualgayoc Cordillera and flows through a broad plain to the sea forming a large delta with many arms and canals. The whole landscape has greatly changed since in 1924 an ambitious plan to increase the water's flow was put into practice to lead it through a tunnel from the Huancabamba at the mouth of the Amazon beneath the Cordilleras.

The town of Lambayeque formerly stood in one of the best irrigated patches of land and was the capital of the eponymous province, until large parts of the old irrigation system were flooded. After the destruction caused by this, the desert threatened to engulf the settlement, which then took second place to the more important Chiclayo with its 20,000 inhabitants and its rail communication with the harbour of Etén, which, as a result of the prevailing south winds, is not a very favourable spot for shipping. The artificial irrigation of wide expanses of land well endowed by Nature has since the days of the Chimu, in many parts of the country, encouraged very large populations. The distance between Lambayeque and Chiclayo is a mere six miles and the whole region is strewn with ruins which provide the same monotonous picture of foundations, partly rectangular, partly square, walls of adobe and finally low man-made mounds which served as burial places.

Although most of these buildings have been partially destroyed or looted so that their interiors and the apportionment of the rooms can no longer be determined for certain, it is still apparent that the walls are frequently orientated in certain directions, mostly set at right angles, and must have been typical Ayllu settlements with their attendant temples. Around the huacas one finds slightly undulating or swelling soil, where the remains of older walls are visible, proving that a large city pulsating with life once stood here. The countless ceramics taken from its ruins in the characteristic late style of the Chimu, which we have dealt with in the previous chapter, fill the large museums of the world and are labelled Lambayeque, Chiclayo and Etén.

The various remains of pyramids are particularly interesting because a three-tiered huaca about two and a half miles from Etén, with a base of 70 to 100 yards, possessed—as the following sketch shows—a flight of steps leading straight to the upper platform, very similar to the buildings found in Central America. The cultural connection between the ancient art of the Chimu and the north from which they came is here once more clearly visible.

A few miles farther down the valley a second huaca was found. This is not pyramidal in form but more a fortress-like building which must originally have had vertical walls. The large burial place at the foot of this structure, some six yards above the valley-level terraces, shows that in the old days there must have been a fortress settlement here. The same ground plan recurs throughout the kingdom of the Chimu and we shall describe in detail the frontier fortress of Paramonga in Chapter Thirteen.

When one leaves the short watercourse of the Rio Zana and crosses a mountainous stretch of desert one enters a large valley which is generally known as Pacasmayo. It is, however, irrigated

by a river called the Jequetepeque. The word obviously originated from a mutilation of the original Jectepec. Since an important upper reach of this river is also called the Rio Puchu and
the chroniclers call the valley in which the site of Chepén lies
Guadalupe, because the eponymous shrine was located there,
obvious possibilities for confusion arose, and they have been
exploited in the literature of Peruvian antiquities.

From the frequently quoted Augustinian historian, Antonio
de la Calancha, we know a great deal about this region.[159]

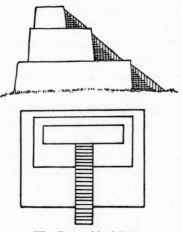

The Pyramid of Etén

Calancha reports that like Lambayeque it fell to the Chimu
chieftains and was conquered by one of their best generals. His
name was Pacatnamu, which merely means paterfamilias. After
his victorious campaign the Chimu set him up as vassal prince
over the conquered land, where he ruled wisely and with clem-
ency. As a result of this the whole valley and his capital were
called Pacatnamu in his honour, from which word the present
Pacasmayo is derived. The modern harbour of the same name,
however, does not lie in the main valley of the Jequetepeque but
on a southern tributary of the same stream separated from its
actual river bed by a sandy hill, such as so often appear in the
plain near the coast.

Calancha is a writer who is as remarkable as he is interesting. Like a mole from long confused blind alleys of scholastic observation and mystical obscurity he throws out cogent accounts and historical stories into the bright light of day, leaving behind him the whole molehill of scholarship. It is surprising how accurately he could occasionally report geographical details and how fundamentally he pursued details from the material he had collected and then quickly explained or discarded them in accordance with the knowledge of his age.

In the mass of material he handed down and which was evaluated in another part of this book, as a check to archaeological finds, he had only said a little more of what he observed— when, for example, he wrote that the Indians of Pacasmayo worshipped the sea—modern research would probably possess a key which would open many a door. Calancha merely relates that the Chimu called the sea 'Ni' and they made to it offerings of maize meal, red dye and other 'worthless' things. Nevertheless in the next chapter we shall try to explain the deeper meaning of this behaviour on a wider plane.

The chronicler describes the whole river irrigating the valley as springing from two sources; the one in the neighbourhood of Asunción and flowing to the valley from Condebamba, the other in the neighbourhood of San Miguel on the road to Cajamarca —two facts which are quite conclusive. This river, the waters of which he describes in detail as being clear, fresh and teeming with all manner of large and small fish, is without doubt the Jequetepeque. Near its bank, Calancha continues, and not far from the seashore was a treeless plateau three lenguas long. The part nearest the river was called Pacatnamu and contained a large number of buildings and ruins including those of the palace that had once housed its ruler and his household.

This description refers to a ruined city near the mouth of the Jequetepeque on a plateau between the northern border of the valley and the sea, which one can safely assume to be Pacatnamu. The huge ruined city affords a surprising sight from the air. In magnificent harmony rise seventy pyramids and terraces in rectangular order, wall after wall. All these pyramids have flattened tops like those of Etén, and above their steps from the north led the Central American ramp.

As centre of the town, lying nearer to the coast, rises the largest of the pyramids, which today still stands almost sixty feet above the sand. North of it opens out a huge empty space which was flanked by graded terraces, while behind it is a mighty tetragon which can be presumed to have been the seat of the ruler. The typical Chimu burial hill is not lacking in one corner of the palace plan and the whole can be presumed to have housed an ordinary hundred. The pyramid which in such cases normally stood near the terrace within the outer walls is turned outwards, giving the whole building its public character and at the same time producing a simple brilliant architectural solution.

The smaller living and temple citadels at Pacatnamu possess huacas which are often only six to twelve feet high with a base of fifteen to eighteen feet, while the main pyramid we have described measures over 180 feet at its base. These huacas are frequently placed outside the building as a result of the security which a large city like this obviously enjoyed.

The strangest fact, however, is that beyond the river outside the enclosed site of Pacatnamu stood a particularly noble pyramid similar to the pyramid group of Moche south of the river of the same name near the capital of Chan-Chan. South of the mouth of the Jequetepeque, near Pacatnamu, is a large artificial hill which rises from the verdant plain near the sea to twin peaks, earning it the name Huaca de dos Cabezas (the huaca of the two heads). The apparent splitting of this pyramid occurred because the treasure hunters once more did their fell work here with particular rage and persistence.

Excavations in the past years[160] have opened up tombs in Pacatnamu in which the dead lay in long, narrow tube-like coffins, facing north. This direction could hardly have been fortuitous, for the pyramids, with a few exceptions which face to the west, look to the north. It can no longer be proved, at best only suspected, that the knowledge of the Chimu as to their origin from the north is expressed in this, a knowledge which in those days was perhaps very vivid and also found expression in their worship.

Sun worship would have demanded orientation to the east, but this is nowhere to be found. On the other hand the dead who have been brought to light again after more than a thousand years afforded clear evidence of moon worship.

A great rarity was discovered twelve feet below the ground in the shape of woven materials dating from the early Chimu era. Today they are exhibited in the National Museum at Lima. The slashed effect of the weaving contains a serpent house and in addition to serpentine beams the so-called canine carrying a heavy sceptre. Other red-and-yellow embroidered veiling fabrics show the early style of the Chimu in their ornament with the stylised head of a ray, which is also connected with the coastal worship of the moon and the sea, like the ray on pages 49 and 68.

In such portrayals of the ray we must obviously see a convention, since it is seldom replaced by any other fish. A host of other motives such as the ray constantly recur in the art of the Chimu and demand an interpretation. The striking armouring of the tail which one finds in the curious creature in the picture on page 153 is repeated unmistakably on page 22, and a closer comparison of the two scenes reveals all manner of similarities which would point to a common mythological background.

A well-trained observer who examines Indian representations as a whole will undoubtedly be reminded by such drawings of Maya art. A younger and an older god often face each other. The younger god represents good and the older evil; the latter harasses mankind and is the lord of the five dead useless days at the close of the year. Mam, as he is called, appears in the pictorial art of the Maya with an empty snail-shell on his back. He is often arrayed in a kind of chequered shirt which occasionally appears in Nazca art and in Central America with the hieroglyph adorned with four circles. This shiftlike garment is no more than a tortoiseshell, or more specifically the shell of the alligator turtle, a snapping turtle which when captured immediately attacks the man—this particularly ill-tempered beast was naturally a very good representation of the treacherous old god. A remarkable Chimu snail-shell is illustrated in Plate 37.

Among the Maya the young god was a corn deity because of the great importance of this plant in the Indian's life—the God of Provisions in the broadest sense. All the Maya figures reminiscent of Buddha represent this Maize God. A beautiful maize and fertility deity from the Peruvian coast is illustrated in Plate 11.

Since the figure in the left boat on page 68 also wears a carapace on its back it is possible that it too had a place in the
mythological combination of an old god and a second, younger
one. In this category also fall the ray-like creatures on pages 68
and 153 in the pictorial world of the coast. In this art it is always
a question of a world of pictures and a whole range of appurt-
enances and it would be completely wrong to attempt to gauge
these ceramic designs by the light of modern rational thinking.
It often appears as though the Indian artist put all the magic
signs of his intellectual repertoire in his picture in order to use
their conjurative powers for the purpose of gratifying his own
desires.

The particular attraction of early Chimu art is that it pushes
the typical contrast between realism and abstraction in Indian
art to the limit, whereby a wonderful purity of drawing remains
compared with which the pictorial art of Central America lags
far behind. If the pictures, according to European ideas,
express abstract thoughts, if the figures appear to be fabulous
creatures, their existence is never transposed into the beyond but
live and exercise their influence in a completely real world and
constantly remain recognisable in their details. Most of them in
fact display keenly observed features of Nature. Thus the character of this art enables us to draw conclusions as to the dwellings
and clothing of those men, of their customs and organisations
such as we have done for both fishing and hunting (illustrations
on pages 49, 53 and 56).

In the picture on page 131, which represents a conjuration, a
prayer, or the questioning of a divine oracle, one can—despite all
the mythological trappings, the canines on the roof and the snake
beams—recognise the type of building and the typical central
support as the bearer of the roof. In the drawing on page 154 we
see a ray-like dragon above the quintuple stepped waves or the
outline of the Andes, and then once more serpents in various
guises the disc and the triangle with angles like dancing feet,
which recur far away in the north-west Argentine[161] in South
American art, the meaning of which no one has yet discovered.
On the other hand we can recognise a warrior figure and the
details of his costume and can confirm that the headdress conforms entirely with those found in graves.

When we try to account for this fascinating uninhibited inter-play of magic signs and images of reality the question is already answered: the frankly hieroglyphic nature of these signs, their general distribution and use, demanded that they should be com-prehensible to the men of those days. Therefore, they could only take their prototypes from reality, and today when we try to decipher them we must start from the premise that the abstract concept was to be both conceivable and portrayable. That this pictorial world was complex, as was the thought of primitive

Vase painting in Early Chimu Style. Viru Valley

peoples, cannot be often enough stressed today and we shall refer to this subject at greater length elsewhere in this book.

In its present connection and in order to round off and give a clear picture of the early art of the Chimu we must deal a little more closely with the actual ceramics on which these comprehen-sive and aesthetically often enchanting designs are to be found. They display, like those of the Later Age, a single style from the Gulf of Guayaquil on the northern frontier of the kingdom to its southernmost frontier fortress on the Rio Pativilca and must therefore be treated here as a single unit.

Most of the ceramics belonging to that period are of reddish clay, at least partially adorned with a tender white or yellowish white slip on which the pattern is painted black, brown or reddish brown in thin simple strokes, since all the power and form is concentrated on the lines and not on the colour. Only very seldom do we meet with finer tones than in the early Chimu ceramics and these are yellow, orange, deep red and in a few exceptional cases with bluish shading.

In the excavations made at Pacatnamu vessels were found in the characteristic early style of the Chimu, including many coarse

The Battle with the Dragon. Painting on a Chimu vessel

urns which also frequently appear farther south, and finally a vase was found in Chavín style with a coronet and a girdle of snakes, a proof of the fact we have mentioned for the region of Piura, i.e. that the so-called Chavín style for a long period ran parallel with early Chimu and always cropped up where the valleys, as in the case of the Jequetepeque, penetrated deeper into the mountains and at the same time into the region of Cejas de la Costa—the Eyebrows of the Coast.

Among the finds of Pacatnamu we must mention the burial of the dead in tubes, a common feature throughout the whole Chimu kingdom and suggesting that they were always at great pains not to bring the corpses into immediate contact with the earth. As regards the burial itself, the most disparate types come to light in individual regions, and we therefore propose to deal with them as a whole in this present connection.

Apart from particular cases of the cult, which we discussed in

Chapter Four, where the body of the dead man remained for a long time in its former surroundings in order to play its part to a certain extent in the daily life, it would appear at least among the simple people that they had to part with them merely for lack of space and the impossibility of tending them. The mummies were buried then in one form or another, according to the region and the standing of the dead man, but above all presumably according to the specific customs ruling in the particular clan.

As Calancha relates, burial normally took place five days after death, during which time there was keening and mourning. The body was carefully washed, the knees pressed up under the chin until it assumed the characteristic posture in which most of the mummies of a later age are today found. They were then garbed in their everyday clothes, to which a special wrap was added. Bamboo and basket-like weaving was mostly used, but garments and clothes have been found containing all manner of daily utensils besides the actual mummies. Among the Chimu the man was often dressed as in life, his favourite possessions sewn into a hide or a mat and in this way further protected by a bundle of leaves, grass or seaweed, the whole covered over with a huge piece of cotton material. This strange packing often served to make his transport to the burial place near the tribal shrine an easier matter. The dead were often carried to the most famous temples a great distance away, and this accounts for the variety of the finds at one and the same level.

Mummy bundles of the Late Age

Occasionally one also finds mummy bundles, inside which several corpses are tied together. This could have occurred in the case of people dying at the same time from a disease, but it is also possible that in this way the dead man was granted the company of his relatives. In the case of mummies in a squatting position the arms were mostly wound round the crossed thighs and the bowed head rested on the palms of the hands. At times, however, they crossed on the breast, a position which is often found in the rows of outstretched corpses. Sometimes with these mummy bundles the outer wrappings are simply tied together with thick ropes or enclosed in a coarse woven net.

As to how often burial, on account of pestilence or as the result of wars, took place rapidly and with a lack of care can no longer be determined today. When no true burial chambers with tiled walls were available, protective roofs of bamboo, wood, matting or clay were used, while in the simplest form the corpse was simply plunged head downwards in a large clay vessel. Before and around the mummies were laid the articles to be buried with him, including slings, fishing lines and hooks for the men, while the women were given spindles, distaffs, pins made of cactus thorns, cotton, yarn of every conceivable kind, work baskets and combs apart from pots (Plate 15). Next to the corpses of children were sometimes laid terracotta dolls.

Usually among these objects were placed little figures of stone or copper, or, as we have already mentioned, amulets which the living wore under their clothes to protect them from misfortune. Several corpses have been found with copper discs in their mouths like the oboles which the Greeks placed in the mouths of their dead as payment for Charon to row them over the Styx. And finally mummified pets were buried with their masters : dogs and parrots which were embalmed in the same way as human corpses. The dogs often had their ears cut for purposes of homoeopathic magic.

In whatever manner the mummies were packed the desire was always to preserve the aspect of a human figure, occasionally by a superimposed artificial skull and clothes adorned with jewellery. Special care was taken with the headdress, and thus we have discovered real masks of wood, clay, silver and gold. These masks were then given artificial eyes of mussel-shells with glued-on eye-lashes. Artificial hair has also been found, and the whole 'make-up' (Plate 28) varies a great deal according to time and space and the customs of the particular tribe. There is little art in them, but no less than in a modern cemetery. Death is ever present today as it always was, whereas art is a great rarity.

CHAPTER ELEVEN

The Heart of Chimu-land

WHEN the traveller leaves the region of Pacasmayo, turns south and crosses the Pampa de Paján, he enters the Chicama Valley—in other words, the first of the three estuaries which form the kernel of the kingdom.

The Chicama Valley is so extensive and fertile that at first sight it appears monotonous, since for miles on end nothing can be seen except light green patches broken only occasionally by some farm buildings. This valley is the larder and provision chamber of modern Trujillo, as it once was in the far distant past for Chan-Chan. The railway connects it with Huanchaco (Plate 26), which for three hundred years was the harbour that served both the Chicama Valley and Moche. As a result of the heavy seas this port has gradually lost its significance and ships use the more advantageous ports of Salaverry and Puerto Chicama. In the foreground of the aerial photograph can be seen the Rio Seco, one of those typical streams which dry up for six months of the year, and away to the right large regularly set-out fields which today are abandoned.

Since the ruins in the Chicama Valley are very similar to those we have described in the north we need only mention here a few of the best known, as for example the sixty-feet-high Huaca el Brujo covered by a late cloak of tiles. It lies on the coast north of the Chicama river estuary and has virtually been cleft in two by the treasure seekers. As a result the outer wall of an older subsequently overbuilt pyramid from the era of the Early Chimu styles was exposed, showing that geometrical ornament which recurs in Moche and vestiges of painting in white, yellow, red and blue. The plateau on which the huaca stands bears two more pyramids, Coa and Prieta, besides which in all directions will be found desecrated tombs.

About twenty miles inland up the valley the three-tiered pyramid of Facalá stands on a beautiful escarpment like a picturesque ruined citadel. The rectangular tiles of the foundations as well as the conical form of the settlement dates it from the earliest age of the Chimu. The pyramid of San José Bajo and a few other buildings, including the Huaca Chiquitey viejo, confirm that more than a thousand years ago this whole region was covered by Chimu buildings which changed their style very slowly.

The fame of the Chicama Valley does not lie in its pyramids but in the enormous fund of beautiful and noble ceramics which are still to be found today in this former capital of the kingdom. The plastic creations of the Mature style are often recognisable by the fact that in the case of the heads the face and in the figures other parts such as hands and feet are left without the coat of varnish, giving them a natural tone and a remarkable life-like-ness. Many of the faces have reached the peak of perfection because they were carefully worked over and polished with mussels or flat stones. The unglazed vessels, however, often have a fine piecemeal light or brownish-red background into which the sparse overlay colours are fired. Other faces again are coloured and the head and neck cloths are in vivid colours. The decoration of the headdress is frequently the step pattern of the earliest age showing its connection once more with the ornaments of Tia-huanaco style. Such details provide useful clues for their dating, and most of the most beautiful and mature of these figures must be ascribed to the Chimu golden age (Plates 13 and 14).

Nevertheless for the northern coast between the Early and Late Chimu style, in other words, at its maturity an over-whelming influence of Tiahuanaco art, can hardly be count-enanced, as has often been done. In that event we would have to back-date the mature art which bears, in particular, the features of the Chimu and could not possibly be classified as an imported article from the highlands to the early days of the coastal culture. It would be ridiculous to suppose that Chimu art originated with an almost fabulous plastic art which would be ill-suited to the drawing genius of that archaic art to be found in so many of the potters' designs.

In the ceramic masterpieces which have been found in such quantities it is a question of heads and other figures which despite all their realism of portraiture are by no means portraits of the dead man, for these same faces constantly reappear and in one instance we have even found the model from which they were almost mass produced. We must not misinterpret here the naturalistic character of Indian art. According to what we have already propounded on the religious concepts of the coastal inhabitants it is doubtless conceivable that we are dealing here with huacas and more specifically with the revered figures of ancestors, either tribal heroes or more closely related clan chieftains. They adorned the countless wall niches as well as the houses of the living, finally to be their companions in death. To the Indian mind death was not an end, and eternal sleep often appeared as something desirable, as in the legend of King Naymlap. To this circle belong those figures which in Plate 31 seem to sleep, reminiscent in their naturalism of the usual 'make-up' of the mummies, but at the time of the Renaissance ennobled by art and touched by the breath of eternity.

Not until the transition to the Late Style did a crass naturalism develop, which with the documentary fidelity of photography perpetuated the slightest features so that in those figures we can often read the story of their maladies, as in the many portraits of one-eyed men, victims of the brilliant light and the hot sand blown up by the desert whirlwind. Even though it is impossible and perhaps ridiculous to try to dam the many-branched flowing stream of development of Chimu art and separate the individual periods from each other, we may be permitted here in conclusion to hint at a particular characteristic of the Late Style: not until the last centuries with the expansion of travel, population and commerce on the coast did that surprising variety and wealth of forms appear in its final guise. The archaic art in its whole nature was far more simple and in ceramics confined to the ever more popular potbellied jug with the hollow spout, the surfaces of which lent themselves so magnificently to decoration. The mature art, however, halts between the strong simplicity and the uniqueness of Early Style and the overflowing forms of the late age; it is the wise sense of proportion of many classical ages.

★ ★ ★

Only a comparatively small chain of mountains separate the Chicama Valley from the river on whose banks the ancient

31 The Mummy

32 Huaca del Sol, the main pyramid of Moche. In the enlarged photograph below can be seen the ravages caused by the heavy rainfall on the clay surface down the centuries

33 Aerial photographs of the two large palaces at Chan-Chan *Above:* The first palace with a sunken garden in the foreground, the cistern in the centre and before it the prison. See plan on p. 163 *Below:* The second palace. See plan p. 164

34 Recuay style *Above:* Mythical bathing scene *Below:* Bath-houses *left* with canopy and *right* with stone steps

capital of the Chimu once stood. The stream in its lower
reaches, after passing the eponymous village of Rio de Moche on
its way to the mountains, arrives at a city called Rio de Otusco,
7,000 feet above a fertile cauldron. The whole valley can best
and most comfortably be seen from Trujillo, since this city in its
delta-like estuary stands on a gentle slope near the sea. Trujillo is
the second oldest Spanish city in Peru and was founded in the
same year as Lima, 1535, by Almagro. He christened it after the
birthplace of his fellow traveller, Pizarro—Trujillo, in the Spanish province of Estremadura.

In this region the mountain is not high as in the other parts
of the coast, although its outlines are surprisingly bold and varied.
Some of the spurs form sharp ridges which at first sight look
unassailable. Behind them like corridors rise ever-higher crests,
until above the dark ridges can be seen an occasional glitter of
snow. A reddish granite gives the whole mountain background
majesty in the slanting light.

★　★　★

Chan-Chan lay between the sea and present-day Trujillo, north
of the Rio Moche about five miles from its bank. In Mexican,
Chan meant 'snake', and Nachan signified the house of serpents.
Na, however, was also a Chimu noun. The word-picture Chan-
Chan in its striking rhythmical repetition alone almost proves
the nature of the worship that was practised here.

The ruined city covers the southern end of a large plain
picturesquely fringed in the east and north by the mountain
foothills, while the Moche Valley to the south and the Pacific
Ocean to the west form its confines. Today, thanks to a gradual
rise in the soil, the sea has retreated some hundred yards, as can
clearly be seen by the still visible Chimu harbour installations
which lie on dry land, comparable with the ancient city of Ostia
at the mouth of the Tiber. The harbour itself consisted of rectangular basins open to the sea in their full breadth. Behind them,
separated by small dams, were further excavations which with
the aid of weirs could in those days be brought into communication with the seaward basins. Lying somewhat higher a large
dock was obviously designed for collecting fresh water and to
allow a certain regulation of the river and the estuary. All these

F

harbour installations were enclosed by sloping walls facilitating the protection of the craft, since they could be hauled up the gentle slopes on to dry land without much difficulty.

Inland the whole plain is covered with the ruins of houses, streets, squares, bases of pyramids, further huge cisterns and aqueducts. The ruins of carefully planned canals leading to squares on which in the old days stood magnificent gardens, and countless other memorials of a lost culture, leave us with the impression of a most imposing urban region. The Moche River brings down water throughout the year. From the earliest age the whole plain must have been transformed into a green paradise, thanks to a well-planned system of large reservoirs and weirs.

The actual city area covers about eight square miles and was enclosed by a huge wall which, with the help of additional inner walls, ensured the safety of the various clan quarters. An outspoken tendency towards the rectangle is unmistakable in the whole layout of the city, but this could neither have been monotonous nor have had a tiring effect, thanks to the irregularity with which the pyramidal tumuli and shrines broke the picture, their impressive area and size being a pleasant relief to the eye.

In the ruins we can see quite clearly the traces of two huge palaces. The first and larger of these (Plate 33) forms a rectangle of over 500 yards long and 400 yards wide. Outside the rampart wall clearly visible in the aerial photograph we can notice in the foreground on the large raised surface those sunken gardens which were frequent on the coast. In the old days the sand was removed until firm soil was reached with enough moisture to encourage luxuriant vegetation. Towards the middle of the palace site at one angle is a second large rectangular raised embankment which in the old days was a cistern. Farther to the right in the foreground is the inner ballium, a powerful rectangular wall with a number of cell-like chambers; this has been termed the prison, an obvious misnomer according to what we know of the laws and punishments of the ancient Chimu. Warfare and religion may very well have had their own particular laws.

These cells are reached through the single entrance to the north in the high massive brick walls. The palace originally had a single entrance to the north, to be seen in the background of the illustration, whereas in the aerial photograph the various breaches in the outer walls were obviously made by force at a later date. The above-mentioned chambers are in five rows each of nine cells and were approached by special stairs which can be seen on the plan above. The theory that this site really represented a prison becomes credible because not only were the foundations built of heavy stone but the partitions were particularly thick.

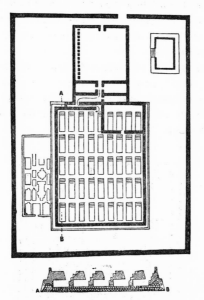

The 'Prison' in the first palace of
Chan-Chan

A very similar building in the second palace (Plate 33) opposes this theory. The latter is somewhat smaller, lies closer to the sea and is surrounded by two high walls, the outer one being of unfired bricks and the inner of superimposed clay, leaving a broad defence zone of about six feet. As can be seen in the aerial photograph this second palace contains no cistern. The latter lay outside the walls in the foreground of the aerial photograph. Inside the second palace, more or less at the same place where the so-called prison lies in the first, is a shapeless pile of rubble, the Huaca Misa, which has been burrowed into on all sides and in which the corridors and inner chambers are still visible. Rivero,[4] in the middle of the nineteenth century excavated here and reported that these cells were very stoutly built and that the walls were covered with hewn stone. At the same time he describes the many mummies found in this huaca, rich garments, metal figures of men and beasts, among others a wooden idol and many broken fragments of mother-of-pearl. This find makes one suspect that these chambers were used for purposes of a cult, perhaps in the service of some deity connected with the bowels of the earth and in particular with the snake which gave its name to Chan-Chan.

The two palaces, in addition to the countless installations which can be clearly recognised in the aerial photograph, contained many courtyards and gardens, long corridors leading to open squares on to which opened rows of halls followed by close-pressed small houses.

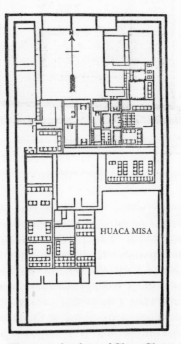

The second palace of Chan-Chan

The ground plan of the second palace on the previous page gives a closer view of the highly involved design employed in these buildings and the general order ruling in them.

Before the destructive influence of the heavy rainfall of 1925 wall ornamentation of a very high standard could still be recognised in several places. Many of the rooms had walls in which diagonal and crucifix-shaped bricks formed small niches; the inner surfaces of these were covered with a smooth layer of fine mortar obviously intended to receive the huacas. Remains of figures testify to both the Early and the Late Chimu styles.

The height of the walls fluctuate normally between twelve and twenty-four feet, most of them having a broad base and tapering upwards. This type is also to be found in the northern part of the kingdom and obviously represented the best safeguard against the frequent earthquakes. When sun-baked bricks were not used, the clay was often cemented with small pebbles from the river.

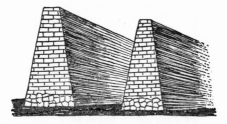

Reconstruction of the walls

A certain northern orientation can also be observed in Chan-Chan. The walls all run parallel to the coast or to the sea and there are no irregular walls. Narrow streets or alleys between the courtyards are characteristic and the quaternary number in this city plan is represented by four particularly large tumuli which were called by the Spanish treasure seekers or the earlier owners of the land Huaca del Obispo, Huaca de Toledo, Huaca de Concha and Huaca de la Rosa respectively. These huacas, with the exception of the Huaca de la Rosa, do not lie within the old city but on the outskirts of the ruins. Probably the tallest of the four, the Huaca del Obispo, was used for the purposes of the cult, the Huaca de Toledo being a burial ground for the notables, whereas the Huaca de la Rosa, where many particularly good wall ornamentations come to light, may have been a former royal palace built on a large mound of earth. No further details of the Huaca de Concha are available because it was completely destroyed in the middle of the last century by treasure seekers.[162]

Nowhere in Peru has the search for treasure been carried out so intensively as in Chan-Chan, where the Huaca de Toledo afforded the richest booty. Fifteen years after the founding of Trujillo the Spaniards heard the first reports of hidden treasure and opened the tombs in the above-named huaca until the fifth paid to the Crown alone amounted to more than 47,000 castellanos. The total value of the precious metals found in this single shrine could be assessed at about six million pounds sterling today. The treasures found in the royal tombs consisted of gold goblets, bowls, small figures and a wealth of jewellery. The most interesting object was a fish of solid gold. According to Indian reports its pair should have been found in a second pyramid, but it never came to light.

In the days of its brilliance the capital of the Chimu afforded a magnificent spectacle of green enchantment, of beautiful building sites with public gardens and palace courtyards the walls of which were covered with fine white plaster painted with vivid scenes such as one can still admire today on much of the pottery. Other walls were covered with geometrical arabesques (Plate 36), chequered and rhomboid patterns as well as complicated patterns in severely hieratic style, reminiscent not only of Tiahuanaco but above all of the inner courtyard of the Relief Chamber of the palace at Mitla, the burial city of the Zapotec kings.

In the old days all these pyramids looked completely different. They were built in terraces, the lowest of which had a base of more than 300 feet on one side and heights of 180 to 210 feet were no rarity. The grandeur of the ancient Mexican pyramid Cholula was never attained, but on the other hand the Chimu seemed to have built a great number of them. On their terraces stood noble buildings with well-constructed roofs and richly painted walls. Verandas supported by twined algaroba trunks cast cool shadows and many corridors communicated with the inner rooms. The doors had large, heavy, richly adorned curtains such as figure on some of the ceramics. These pyramids with their outbuildings and gardens must have been a magnificent sight.

Beyond the Moche River not far from Chan-Chan and about three miles south of Trujillo is a greyish-white mountain covered with drifting sand, the Cerro Blanco, at the foot of which on the left bank of the river are to be found two of the most venerable shrines in the Chimu kingdom. According to the later Inca custom the larger was termed by the Spaniards the Huaca del Sol, and the smaller the Huaca de la Luna. The first pyramid (Plate 32) with its height of 120 feet is the largest surviving edifice on the Peruvian coast, and seen from the water looks almost like a natural hill falling steeply towards the river, whose bed was originally farther away. According to Calancha's report the water was diverted by the first Spaniards up to the temple wall in order to make it collapse. Since then the rising waters of the river in summer down the ages have torn away huge parts of the old building, forming a deep gully in which the smooth solid bricks laid skilfully in alternate tiers, flat, upright and super-imposed, still have the power to impress us today.

After crossing the river one comes to the western foundations of the temple, a sixty feet high rectangular terrace, on the south side of which at the west corner the actual temple pyramid rises in steps almost as high as the base itself. This too once had smaller steps which in the course of time were washed away by the rain. Approach to the temple is easiest from the west, since here it leans against a natural hill and the walls have collapsed. On climbing the platform one finds that they have been burrowed into and the part towards the river is today but a shapeless mass. The pyramid has a rectangular base and in the old days must have possessed ten steps.

When Montalva and his companions in 1602 undermined the temple by diverting the water they discovered silver plate and dishes of gold and copper alloy and the figure of a bishop eighteen inches high which Calancha describes as being of pure gold from the waist upwards. These objects, which like so many fell to the insatiable smelting desires of the conquerors, have naturally disappeared for ever. On the other hand Manuel Pio Portugal[163] made just as important discoveries beneath the foundations of the western façade of the Huaca de la Luna, that stately, somewhat sixty feet higher shrine of the moon built with large flat-lying tiles often grooved at the edges. They were objects worked in the same gold alloy as Calancha mentions, which the Indians call *Anta cori*—Andean or copper gold. Radiating leaves of gold leaf, bells, disc-shaped breast-plates, a sling board and a flute also came to light.

The most valuable and important, however, were four masks of different sizes, one of which (Plate 41) is ten inches high with eyes of inlaid mussel-shell and circular openings in the ears which served the Indians as an adornment for the powerful and the well-born, who invariably wore ear-plugs. In addition to this mask with the impressively sober and dominating face another almost as large was found with unbored ears—a pasty insignificant round face wearing a coronet of movable leaves. This find was complemented by a smaller mask of an elderly-looking female face and finally by a very interesting mask of medium size portraying the head of a canine (Plate 9) whose teeth were made from mussels and richly adorned with crescent leaves.

When one questions the significance of these objects in the old days it is essential to cast a brief glance at another shrine on the coast which several of the Spanish chroniclers describe. This is the temple of Rimac, near Lima, which is only a distortion of that word. In Quechua language it was called Rimay, and Rimac means no more than the orator or speaker. Since this word is of Quechua origin it cannot be the original name of the god but merely an explanation given by the later Incas for what they saw. Obviously the priest used this mask in order to speak to the people in the name of the god.

This view was confirmed by Garcilaso, who, in common with other chroniclers, relates[164] that the inhabitants of that valley worshipped an image in the shape of a man which foretold the future like the Oracle of Delphi. This remark of Garcilaso's leaves us in no doubt as to the use made of the masks found in Moche.

We have already dealt in an earlier chapter with the role which the canines played in the cult. We must see in this round head adorned with a crown the embodiment of the moon god, whereas the ceremonial mask with the human features must have

belonged to the speaker himself. It is questionable whether the
small mask with the female face can be considered to be Mama
Cocha, the sea goddess.

One thing is certain : wherever the art and symbolism of the
Chimu has been studied it has been insufficiently realised how
very closely this race of coastal dwellers and fishermen in those
arid lands must have felt themselves bound to the water. We can
safely accept the premise that in addition to ancestor, moon and
star worship they also practised a very clearly defined water
worship. The gold fish found in the Huaca de Toledo in Chan-
Chan testifies to this. It cannot be regarded as a mere casual
ornament; it belongs to the whole cult of the coast. The snake
which plays such an important role in the same cult is both beast
of the underworld and of the water : a sea snake, and which
frequently symbolises the sporting of the waves.

Everything in the country was dependent upon water in good
and bad times alike. Violent rains were no less natural catas-
trophes than the drought which imperilled whole harvests and
lives. The sea offered them a large part of their fish diet and
ruled the entire economy of the people. Thus the kingdom of the
Chimu was predestined to have a formal water cult.

Water, which today still covers three parts of the earth's surface, in its superlative significance for all life occupied the minds
of the earliest thinkers. One of the four elements of Aristotle,
Thales of Miletus, 600 B.C., termed it the only true element from
which all living bodies evolved. According to Pliny the clouds
were formed by a thickening of the air, and even Newton considered steam to be very closely related to the air. This significance of water as an element of creation in the religious concepts
of various races was soon elaborated by the idea of cleansing,
both physical and spiritual. This applies to Indians and Persians,
Egyptians, Greeks, Romans and Mohammedans. Baptism in water
is not an exclusive Christian custom and it should be remembered
that the christening stones were earlier known as *piscinae*—fish
ponds.

Holy water blessed by the priests with salt added has since the
fourth century in the Roman and Greek Catholic Churches been
the sacred symbol of spiritual cleansing and preservation. It was
preserved in its own vessels, which, down the centuries, had

F*

taken on an infinite variety of forms—pitchers, beakers, bowls and ore and clay urns, portable or for hanging purposes, or again immured on plinths. This must all be taken into account when one inspects the vessels found in great quantities in Chimu country which bear the symbol of water and the fish, the significance of which was for so many years misunderstood.

We referred on page 149 to Calancha's account which tells that the Chimu prayed to the sea and offered it gifts of white maize meal and red ochre; this was obviously a symbolical ceremony in which colour symbolism was employed. To the white and the red in the account only the complementary black is missing. Calancha did not mention this because it was represented by the depths of the sea and its eternal night. In all the civilisations of the world we find a repetition of the coloured triad, white, red and black, in its strongest contrasts. White symbolised the light and the day; black darkness and night, and red blood. These colours have been perpetuated in the flags of the most disparate nations; blue, which very often appears in the tricolour, replaces the black and is also the colour of water. Its worship among the Chimu was not exhausted merely in the ceremonies mentioned by Calancha. We merely have to study their art and everything that the chroniclers have handed down in the way of Indian superstition, and accept the presence of various goddesses who have been associated with the water and the sea.

What further ideas were bound up with them cannot be discussed here, since the finds of Chan-Chan and Moche are inadequate in this respect. Not until we have exhausted the whole land of the Chimu will it be possible in our chapter on Pachacamac to return to this question and try to find a solution in the religious concepts of the Indians as a whole, including the figures of the gods of Pachacamac and Viracocha.

CHAPTER TWELVE

The Mountain Pocket

THE Valley of Trujillo, which we have dealt with at length in the previous chapter, is separated from the sandy desert stretch by the Rio de Viru—a short river, poor in water, on the banks of which many finds have been made, proving that this region also belonged to the heart of the Chimu country. Farther south, however, the cultural picture changes. Geographical features appear which must have basically influenced the art, the architecture and the whole life of this country.

Almost precisely at Latitude 9° S., the longest and deepest river on the Peruvian coast debouches into the sea. The Rio Santa, named after a town at its mouth, rises beyond the western chain of the Andes and is the only river to break through the mountain and reach the plain through a narrow gorge, while its upper reaches (also called the Rio de Huacas) form a large 120-mile pocket inside the mountains.

As can be seen on Map page 182 this mountain valley runs exactly parallel to the coast for about sixty miles and is bordered to the east by the main chain of the Andes, which in this section bears the proud name of the White Cordillera, since it offers here the most spectacular view of the whole Peruvian *altiplano* with a row of snowy peaks rising to an average height of 18,000 to 21,000 feet. Even the higher mountain chain by Lake Titicaca cannot vie with the impression that the mountains here make on the traveller.

In the west the upper Santa Valley is enclosed by the Black Cordillera, which derives its name from the fact that its peaks are black and not covered with eternal snow, although their crests seldom fall below 10,000 feet. The pass or the so-called Callejón of Huailas where the river changes its direction from south to north, suddenly turning sharply westwards to the coast, represents at the same time the end of the Black Cordillera as a range. At the spot where the gorge begins, the main chain suffers a further breach, made by two right-bank tributaries of the Santa; the smaller one is the Manta, and the slightly wider and longer one the Chuquicara, or, as it is called today, the Rio de Toblacha.

These two rivers also cut deeply into the Andes, and between them towers the Cordillera de Conchucos, a higher massif reaching to the snow level. Since the valleys are eminently habitable the multiple cleaving of the mountains must from earliest times have facilitated a constant communication, whether peaceful or hostile, between the Chimu on the coast and the settlers in these rich valleys, which are particularly famous for their ores, notably silver.

In pursuit of this theory we must take a short excursion into the South American Alps.

The Cordillera de Conchucos, to a height of 12,000 feet, is strewn with ruins, fortifications and tombs dating from very ancient times, particularly in the fertile region near the sulphur spring of Andamayo, the site of the fortress, Sitana Racay. Here tombs of a unique type were found, their presence being announced by single menhirs or complete circles of stones. Excavations brought to light about six feet below the soil enormous stone slabs sometimes more than nine feet long, six feet broad and eighteen inches thick which served to seal the tombs. In some were found mummies in a squatting position, in others empty vessels and hunting trophies, but often the tombs were empty without giving the impression that they had been ransacked in olden days.

Chulpas are a feature of Huarilca, in this region which is comparatively near the coast. These are strange round brochs about eight feet in diameter and eight feet high : these housed the mummies. The largest and best known of these monuments stand several hundred miles farther south of the mountains in the neighbourhood of Lake Titicaca, pointing to an age-old upland culture. Archaeologists have not yet found a satisfactory solution for this connection.

On entering the Huailas gorge formed by the Rio Santa in the

Cordillera de Conchucos further chulpas appear near Quilcotay. These are not circular like those of Huarilca but dice-shaped and rather smaller—a bare two feet square with a slightly protruding cornice round the flat roof. The walls of these small towers are comparatively strong and made of schist. Normally the visitor has to crawl inside through a small door where occasionally he will find a few skulls and bones.

The village of Huailas itself does not lie in the actual Callejón but high above it in a broad precipitous adjacent valley. The ruins of two old fortress sites stand higher up on the right bank of this tributary. The next settlement of importance in the narrowing main valley of the Upper Santa is Carás. At 6,750 feet, where the rainfall is regular and heavy, in a beautiful alpine setting are the remains of the Tumsacaica fortress. Beyond Yungay, which has become famous as the scene of the Battle of Ancash between the Bolivians and the Chileans in 1838, we reach the hot miner springs of Carhuás, which must not be confused with the previously mentioned Carás. Here we are 7,878 feet above sea level. The valley narrows still further, broadening out in places into larger coombs.

In Huarás, which lies at the confluence of the Quilcay and the Santa slightly above the latter on the right bank, we have reached 9,080 feet, with a far colder climate, where, however, water does not freeze and maize still grows. At the eastern end of the city at the foot of the mountain lies a low hill, Pumacayan, on which once stood the ruins of a huge building—probably a fortress or a temple. At the south-westerly end of the village is a second ancient settlement; many of its walls are made of sun-dried bricks, in accordance with the custom of the coastal inhabitants, despite the fact that stone was plentiful in the mountains. This is very striking and makes one think that at least for a time this settlement and its culture were influenced not from the mountains but from the coast.

Sculpture which has been found shows human figures and beasts which for the most part cannot be accurately deciphered today. The human figures like those of Tiahuanaco have exaggeratedly short legs and usually carry sceptre-like staffs. The influence of that remote culture is not only unmistakable in these finds but on many occasions obvious in the ornamentation.

Various features then in the older settlement point to the moon cult of the coast, in particular the serpent symbols once present in great quantities.[165] The two valuable pieces from Huarás illustrated in Plate 35 were fired in white clay and are very characteristic of this art. The mythical figure on the left side shows teeth typical of the art of Tiahuanaco, while the left hand holds a trophy head on its knee, a requisite which seldom comes to light in the north but is comparatively frequent on the south coast in the art of Nazca. The figure with the vicuña in the plate on the right is also of white clay and bears on its head the gleaming crescent moon of the Chimu.

The highest settlement in the valley is finally reached at about 9,900 feet above sea level at Recuay, while the Santa itself springs at a height of almost 12,000 feet from the small shallow mountain lake Conococha, which in turn obtains its water from the surrounding springs and from another small lake 600 metres higher up. On the slopes are veins of salt water which often cover the cliffs with a layer of crystalline salt, giving the illusion of snow.

About three miles up the valley from Recuay unique clay vessels have been found which often seem overloaded with figures and are painted alternatively with powerful red, white and black lines. Among the vast collection of Peruvian antiquities this is known as the Recuay style. Here the ingenuous naturalism of the Chimu joins with the strongly stylised sense of form reigning in Tiahuanaco in which one clearly senses that the native originality is born from the spirit of the coast, while the coarse nature of mountain art confines and frustrates, impressing it at the same time with a certain calm gaiety without succumbing to archaic rigidity. The most magnificent examples, in addition to the white and sparsely used gleaming red, sometimes display greenish tones and are characterised by particularly fine and careful modelling, and by the blending of their surfaces. Most of the coloured vessels were found in small rectangular walled tombs in which neither skulls nor the usual human remains were discovered. We can hardly presume, therefore, that these were tombs. It is very questionable whether these ceramics were associated at all with burial; they must have served for some water worship, more or less self-imposed by the countless mineral and healing springs which flow in the Upper Santa Valley. It is significant that vessels such as those in Plate 34 often portray bathing scenes with bath-houses or water-carriers in stylised treatment. The latter seen from the front often resemble a seated warrior figure, as we see in Plate 35, bottom right, whereas seen from the back their vessel form is obvious. As a general rule all these pitchers possess conical spouts which allow them to catch the beneficent liquid. In their decoration the idea of water in its most varied aspects is portrayed, particularly by scrolls and water snakes.

★ ★ ★

When examining this old culture we must remember that we have to do with enormous spans of time and space. Those races in question even in their early development stages did not lead an enclosed spiritual existence. Again and again common Indian concepts and ideas, besides a common Indian sense of form, break through, later to be guided in certain directions with the evolution of hard and fast religious systems. We can only decipher Ancient American art if we examine it as a whole and realise that it was deeply bound up both with the cultural life and the economical and social organisations of the Indians. The history of intra-American migrations and correlated influences cannot be explained dogmatically according to stylistic details, but must be viewed as far as possible in its wider aspects. The process of friction, contact and superimposed culture—a great historical example of this is apparent from the finds in the region of the Cejas de la Costa—forms one of the most interesting chapters in the history of Indian life.

The tombs which have been opened and explored in Recuay number more than a hundred, and in the Valley of Casma on the coast similar finds have been made which visibly confirm our theory of the connection between the kingdom of the Chimu and these high-lying valleys and that this whole art and culture must be viewed as a whole. It is not so much a question of a more or less arbitrary division of cultural terrains but of the apparently obvious and simple fact that the early art of the Chimu and that of Chavín must have been contemporary, as is shown in the chronological table on page 127. The Black Cordillera was in the region under survey no insurmountable obstacle and for a cultural exchange it was not always necessary to follow the Santa River since there were five other passes which all led out to the coast and into this remarkable mountain pocket.[166]

In order to give a better idea of the ebb and flow which took place in the Chimu kingdom on the Cejas de la Costa, characteristic of the whole region on both sides of the Black Cordillera, it seems pertinent to end our visit to the uplands with a glance across the White Cordillera and the 13,000-feet pass of Cahuis to Chavín de Huántar on the Rio Puccha. The site lies at about 6,600 feet, and above it on the left bank of the river are to be seen the ruins of a palace and a temple which originally formed a rectangle, not built vertically but with tapering walls of huge blocks of limestone and granite and held together with mortar.

Beneath the palace and the temple were corridors, the height of a man, built of small stone blocks running off at many angles and broadening out here and there into small cells, the roofs of which were occasionally supported by stone pillars in the shape of unequal prisms. This use of pillars was characteristic of the ancient architecture of the highlands, already in vogue many centuries before the first appearance of the Inca, and recalling the Mitla Hall of Pillars in Mexico, the so-called temple of Viracocha near Cacha being the best-known example in Peru.

The weatherbeaten sculptures of Chavín show figures ending in serpent heads with wide mouths and pointed canine teeth reminiscent of the Mexican god Tlaloc. The whole building plan denotes that the site was a shrine and not a fortress. Chavín, by its actual position, could not, as we have already remarked, have been the capital of a large kingdom, for which there was no room in this narrow valley. The character of a smaller shrine is particularly stressed by the basic form of the broad sawn-off pyramid, the presence of a flight of steps and the cells meeting on the platform.

A shallow circular sacrifical bowl of hard, dark stone was also found standing on four squat feet; it probably served to catch the blood. We cannot determine the nature of the rite, but there is hardly a doubt that it took place in the manner customary to ancient Peru. The victim was usually led to the platform of the

35 *Above:* Two examples of Huarás art. See text p. 174 *Below left:* Pitcher from Recuay *Below right:* Serpent vase with heroic figure

36 *Above:* The so-called Sun Gate at Tiahuanaco—part of the frieze with the central figure *Below:* Fortifications of Chan-Chan. Entrance to the Hall of Arabesques destroyed by flood in 1925

37 *Above:* The god with the carapace in the form of a snail man *Below:*
The art of the Cejas de la Costa

38 *Above:* View of the three bays between Santa and Chimbote. See text p. 184 *Below:* The ancient Indian fortress Paramonga on the Rio de la Fortaleza. See text p. 190

temple reserved for men and beasts where the heart was taken out and offered to the guests. Here we have the same custom as in Mexico, where the victim was laid on a slightly arched stone, held down by priests, while one of them opened his breast with a sharp obsidian stone and cut out the palpitating heart to lay it still steaming in the blood-bowl, the rim of which was decorated with stone human hearts. For human heart's blood was the divine ambrosia without which the god would not have been able to complete his course across the sky. The victim, however, became the image of the deity. Blind trust in the power of this magic inspired the Indian to subscribe to this sacred sacrificial custom and a smoking heart was willingly offered to the all-highest. The victim was by no means an object of contempt. He entered the proud ranks of heroes and warriors worthy of being worshipped.

What ensures the almost completely destroyed temple of Chavín a permanent place in the history of Ancient American art and culture, apart from all later finds,[167] is the Raimondi monolith reproduced on page 178. We have already mentioned this monument in connection with the saga of King Naymlap. When we think of its stone features we are apt to connect this magnificent memorial of a lost culture with the central figure of the Sun Gate at Tiahuanaco (Plate 36). But this analogy usually goes too far. Whereas in the Sun Gate we are dealing with a great and ceremonious scene of adoration, which sprang from a spirit born in the Andes themselves, and in self-willed asymmetry resulting from the contact of two cultures and two races creating something completely new, the figure of Chavín follows the old familiar lines in the severest symmetry and approaches far more the art of Mexico. The Indian creations constantly recur in the north to the ice flows of Alaska. Lehmann in his elements of Mexican forms, 1924, quite rightly saw in the Raimondi monolith a certain connection between the style elements of the Chavin reliefs and those discovered in Central America.[168]

In this magnificent figure there is no trace of adoration. It stands alone in its magnificence and reaches artistic perfection in its towering series of ancestral heads in the religious outlook which inspired the entire life of the Chimu. That the snakes are ranged formally in this picture, that the almost incalculable

The Raimondi monolith

variety of the symbols submit the utmost formality, makes this work unique, whatever riddle it may still conceal.[169] The snake speaks to the visitor from all the walls with hieratic power in Chavín as in Moche and Chan-Chan. But it does not necessarily form a bridge to the Inca but to another race whose language was Colla, usually incorrectly called Aymará.[170] A host of stylistic particularities in the art of the Chimu, especially the geometrical forms borrowed from the mountains during its maturity, testify clearly to a cultural contact with the Colla-speaking race, as do the previously mentioned Chulpas and last but not least the place names which appear throughout the whole Cejas de la Costa and naturally in Chavín.

None of these words has any meaning in the later Quechua language but make sense when one goes back to Colla, the speech of those Indians who presumably created the great and mysterious culture on Lake Titicaca. They cannot be dealt with at any length in this book, which deals primarily with the kingdom of the Chimu, but they can serve as a background when we mention the coastal culture just as the towering crests of the Andes rise behind the oases and the dunes. Chavín is no more than a corruption of the Colla word *chapi*, which means a thorn bush, and its locative *chapi-na* or telescoped *chapin* means 'in the bushes'. In a similar way the names of the nearby larger villages and many other terminations still have a meaning in Colla.

Whether the first Colla-speaking race represents the first settlers in the Cejas de la Costa is in any case questionable. It is quite credible that in the Raimondi monolith we can see the stone Yampallec itself, and it is thus an ancestor image or idol brought by the nomads, incorporating a great Central American artistic tradition. To corroborate this the simplicity of the rest of the temple precincts compared with the monolith gives this strange stone a somewhat alien and imported effect. The remaining sculptural finds from Chavín are in actual fact much clumsier and more primitive and display a certain lack of composition and confident stylisation. In other words they might be the creations of colonials who find themselves in a new land surrounded by influences with which they cannot so quickly come to grips.

Admittedly the Sun Gate in the ruins of Tiahuanaco reveals countless elements which recur in Chavín, but it also points quite

clearly to a far more southern coast, to the valleys of the Chincha where those close relatives of the Chimu once penetrated
from the sea into the land and following the river beds came
across an autochthonous population with which they intermarried, ultimately producing the art and culture of Nazca. The
fish and the snake coastal symbols, however, reappear at 12,000
feet on the banks of Lake Titicaca and in the so-called Sun
Gate at Tiahuanaco—that unsolved riddle of American archaeology. We know nothing of the men who created this powerful
architecture, and the same applies to the Toltecs in Mexico; they
are ubiquitous but nowhere conceivable as a people, except in
their works of art and the very weak traces hinted at in the Colla
language. Lake Titicaca, which shrinks about a yard each year,
is today twelve times as large as Lake Geneva and thirteen times
as large as Lake Constance. In the old days it covered a very
much greater area and like the sea must have afforded every
inducement to water worship.

Should we succeed in unravelling the hidden meaning of the
fish symbol and its related symbols, the question of the origin
of the Tiahuanaco culture will one day be solved by the research
spirit. We shall perhaps find that it was not a pure sun cult as is
usually accepted today but that on those heights one of the most
remarkable revolutions in religious history took place, namely
the exciting but unexplained transition from moon to sun worship. The explanation of Americanists derived from general folklore that in such cases a transition has taken place from a
totemistic matriarchal social organisation to a patriarchal one is
no solution. In this particular case we should only be trying to
explain a change in religious concepts by a change in the social
condition of the people without going back to the causes of these
changes, apart from the usual dogmatic arguments for matriarchal concepts and patriarchal society which have been
exaggerated to the point of absurdity.

Unless we merely wish to call one phenomenon by another
name the actual explanation for that culture and its influences
may perhaps be sought in the fact that on the Cejas de la Costa,
and above all in the region of Lake Titicaca, two different but
vital races met, releasing in the ensuing clash the power necessary
to create the miracle of Tiahuanaco. Possibly an original matri-

archal society existed among the Indians who previously dwelt in that land. Various details in the art of Nazca confirm rather than contradict this supposition. The patriarchal organisation must be attributed to the newcomers, the people from Central America, who in the legend of King Naymlap appear from the very beginning in clans and families.

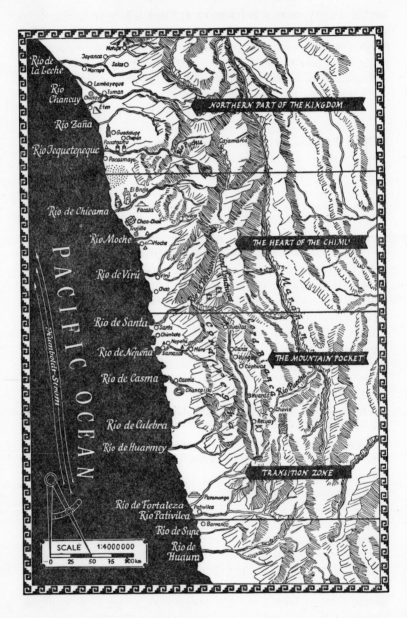

CHAPTER THIRTEEN

The Transitional Region

THE last important cultural region within the actual Chimu kingdom extends from the beautiful flat lower reach of the Rio Santa to the deep gorge of the Rio Pativilca (Map page 182). In general it is characterised by an aridity unusual for Peruvian conditions, the reason being that the Black Cordillera which runs parallel to this coastal sector is only 11,000 feet high, an altitude which in these regions is inadequate to produce snowcapped mountain chains. The little water that collects on it flows mainly from its east wall in the Santa Valley, towards which most of the streams that spring from the Black Range flow. Four comparatively insignificant rivers debouch westwards into the Pacific Ocean, these being the Nepeña, the Casma and the even smaller Culebra and Huarmey. The whole region owes its peculiar aspect less to the rivers than to its connection with the sea through the graceful terrain of the three bays to the north as well as to the grandiose desolation of the southern coast.

On the lower Santa the ruins of Cantagallo are worthy of the greatest attention. In the drifting sand we find half-buried ruins of a palace characteristic of the transitional region. For the first time we meet here on the coast the remains of pillars and columns showing the influence of highland architecture. They formerly stood round a large twin-colonnaded courtyard about twelve feet apart. Since we can still count more than a hundred plinths it must have been a very distinguished building. It can no longer be maintained with certainty from the remaining heaps of ruins whether these adobe supports stood free or supported light walls which were then adorned like a tapestry. Near the otherwise dreary village, Santa, are still to be found the ruins of an old fortress with a double ringed wall giving a magnificent view over the sea and the surrounding countryside.

South of the Rio Santa the undulating hills give the land variety (Plate 38). Three consecutive bays afford the most beautiful natural harbours to be found on the Central Peruvian coast. A few miles from the mouth of the Santa lies the first of these bays, the Bay of Chimbote. On the landward side it is surrounded by a flat crescent-shaped beach on which the waves break with a soft murmur. This friendly beach continues south at the foot of some low foothills which separate the Bay of Chimbote from the Bay of Samanco. The beach is so flat that at flood tide, although the sea normally makes little encroachment on the coast, it nearly disappears beneath the water. The rocky cliffs then look like a forbidding island.

The name Chimbote is the mis-spelling of the two Quechua words *chin*, which means silence, and *poto*, which means the same as the French word *pôt* or *port*, in other words a port or a harbour. The extensive ruined city on this bay must have once been a great cultural centre in a particularly populous region. A host of ceramics of all types have been found here and they have been distributed throughout the world. Since these clay vessels include various forms, from the earliest Chimu style to the latest, the name of the site of origin has not been given to a particular group. Millipedes appear on the designs more often than in the north and point to a gradual transition to the art of the southern coast; the whole region is less culturally hermetic and individual than the more northern regions.

The feudal system ruling on the coast in times of weakness enabled a few strong vassals to make themselves independent and at certain periods (which cannot be specified today) particularly in the coastal area, independent political communities were formed. For the duration of such a rule culture took on its own tinge. By and large, however, in the transitional zone the brilliance of the central art and culture of the Chimu proved stronger than the influence of the uplands, although the region teems with memorials of recurrent relationships, as the following pages will show.

The penetrating power of Chimu culture is often felt more strongly the more we have to take into account foreign influences and undercurrents. This is shown very plainly in the adjacent Nepeña Valley. This river flows into the Bay of Samanco and on its upper reaches where it is called the Rio de Moro, after a local village, penetrates far enough into the Black Cordillera to allow a crossing of the mountain pocket and as a result the liveliest cultural exchanges in the very earliest ages.

To start with the coast, to the right between the river and the Bay of Samanco about three miles below Nepeña village on a small granite hill stand the ruins of Panamacilla, which take their name from this spot; in Quechua *pana* means right and *marca*, as we have already mentioned, the community, while the end syllable is a Spanish diminutive. Originally a temple must have existed in Panamacilla which became more strongly fortified and also inhabited, so far as one can ascertain today after the great ravages caused to the pyramids by treasure hunters. At its side on the slope of the mountains are extensive ruined walls and court-yards and on a spur running south the remains of a rectangular building of unhewn blocks of stone. The base of the five-storeyed pyramid belonging to it measures about sixty feet in length. Its apex has today completely disappeared. Above the mountain village of Moro, on a height surrounded by two gorges, stand the ruins of Cuchipampa with its gateway partly adorned with coarsely chiselled figures. A little farther up the valley are the remains of a former twin fortress called Huancarpon. Double fortresses obviously originated in this land for the purpose of keeping contacts between widely distributed tribes. This was particu-larly intelligent when, as in the above-mentioned case, it was a question of a frontier fortress.

The most famous is the Valley of Nepeña, not on account of the ruined fortresses which lie completely forgotten in the sand, but on account of its enormous terraced buildings which provided large populations with accommodation in the days of the Chimu. Thanks to their planning, the effect of which seems to be ever-lasting, the modern inhabitants still enjoy the great expanses of fertile soil at their disposal in regions which would otherwise have been merely a sad, neglected desert.

The largest cistern alone is more than half a mile long and eight hundred yards wide. It consists of a particularly solid stone dam seventy-two feet thick above the valley which meanders through a gorge between two high mountains. For feeding these powerful dams the Indians used two independent canals, one of which was no less than twelve miles farther up the valley and the other starting at the source of the Nepeña. These different figures are inadequate to describe the achievements of this ancient culture. They are almost inconceivable when one thinks of the simple technical aids with which they were created. In this masterpiece of irrigation with its network thought out to the smallest details the builders showed an amazing ingenuity in exploiting the conditions afforded by Nature.

The canals usually wind in slow, even descents between the individual slopes, skilfully avoiding the various obstacles. Where the exploitation of the terrain does not suffice the canals are carried on aqueducts or occasionally across sixty-foot embankments over narrow valleys or hollows. For miles on end they are then hewn to perfection out of the natural cliff. Very often they run through mountain spurs in such a complicated network that even today engineers sometimes find it difficult to plot their course.

These waterworks did not have to cope solely with the regulation of necessary dampness, they also had to protect rainy regions from too much water and offset the destructive effect of water streaming down the slopes and terraces. The construction of artificial layers of earth and its manuring would have been pointless in the face of the violence of sudden storms, had not the destructive effect of the water been previously dealt with. The great firmness of the soil helped in these constructions; the dams had a host of sluices which at any given moment could cause artificial flooding. Thus these gigantic buildings, which still arouse the admiration of modern technicians, could also be used in wartime and for the defence of the country. According to Montesinos' account the diverting and closing of the irrigation canals was one of the most decisive moves on the chessboard in the defeat of the Chimu by the Incas.[21]

To return to the coast, the southernmost of the three above-mentioned natural harbours is formed by the Bay of Casma, which is nearly as large as those of Samanco and Chimbote. Into this flows the Rio de Casma, which is very shallow in winter but which at its mouth forms a five-mile-wide delta producing a coastal stretch of great fertility.

One of the wonders of the Casma Valley is the ruin of the

old fortress of Chancaillo which stands on a 600-foot crest on the left bank of the river. It is a round building with three concentric walls at varying heights, ovoid in shape. The actual fortress stood on the upper platform. It consisted of two lower round towers and a square building, either a residence or a place of worship, as will be seen in the adjacent sketch.

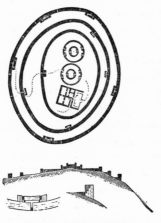

Plan of Chancaillo

That the whole site was for defence purposes is proved by the thickness of the outer wall (over twelve feet) and the roominess of the fortress precincts which with its solid towers allowed adequate movement for the defenders. The gates were staggered so that an invader could not possibly force an entrance in a direct line. The ground plan recalls certain Central American buildings and is well suited to the terrain. It would be wrong, however, to draw any bold conclusions from the appearance of a round building instead of the normal rectangle. The terrain itself gives us the key. It called for this particular type of construction.

Round buildings crop up from time to time in the other ancient Indian cultures, particularly in Central America,[171] but they are always rarer than the rectangular varieties. They represent to a certain extent the first attempts at architectural form, for where the Indians decided to build a mound—whether

for a tomb, for the purposes of worship or as living quarters—
in the embankment of an artificial hill a circle or an eclipse
resulted at the first instance. Only when they wished to perfect
the space at the top did they arrive at the square and the rectangle, which allowed far more comfortable and useful partition.
On the other hand where Nature forbade this rectangular design,
then, at least in their fortifications, they adhered to the lie of
the land. In buildings designed solely for worship a gradual
difference apparently occurred in the plan. As we have already
mentioned, we know that in Central America all round buildings
were dedicated to the god Quetzalcoatl.[126]

The material of which the Chancaillo fortress was built consists
of rough granite blocks placed together irregularly and consolidated with a clay mortar. From traces to be found on spots
protected from the weather all the walls in the old days were
covered with a fine coat of paint. In the long fortress corridors
beams of algaroba wood in the roofs and various pseudo-arches,
such as are frequently met with in Maya country, have been
discovered. The ceramics from the tombs at the foot of the ruins
are strongly reminiscent of Recuay, proving that communications
existed across the Black Cordillera into the upper Santa Valley.
When the Spaniards arrived the whole of this region had long
since been abandoned and the buildings lay in ruins. This would
suggest that they were already past their peak during the rule
of the late Chimu.

The influence of the highlands was able to dominate because
the Casma Valley represented the nearest and most comfortable
road from the coast to Huarás, today still the largest village in the
upper Santa Valley. Its ruins, which we described earlier in the
chapter, testify to its importance in olden days. In this region
we are obviously dealing with a place which changed rulers
several times. It is not surprising, therefore, that stone buildings
are to be found on the coast and sun-dried bricks in the old
settlement at the south-western end of Huarás in the mountains.
The individual tribes and their builders remained faithful to the
customs of the regions from which they originated. The granite
blocks of Chancaillo fortress were not brought from a great distance but were quarried from the hill on which it stands. We
must not, however, draw any far-reaching conclusions from the

use of stone instead of the usual brick building practised by the Chimu. Nature itself favoured this type of building in the same way as it favoured the circular form.

If we consider Chancaillo to be a particularly attractive alien fortress in the Casma Valley, the ruins of Mojeque are no less so. They lie a mile from the fortress on a low hill, separated from it only by a small depression. On the crest of the granite hill were found twelve cubic stone plinths with rectangular bases thirty-six to sixty feet long, twenty-four feet wide and about eighteen to twenty-one feet high. These megalithic blocks were set in a row running from east to west. Stone stairs led to the top of the hill, suggesting that the place was a shrine. The number twelve in the stone erection orientated from east to west and the whole spaciousness of the building plan suggest that this site stemmed from the earliest time of the Incas or their immediate predecessors and was connected with sun worship as opposed to moon worship.

The remaining antiquities in the Casma Valley are typical Chimu huacas and the actual temple of Mojeque is the usual format: all of them are stepped or terraced buildings or broad flat-topped pyramids. The remains of dark red colours on the walls recall the shrines which the Spaniards on their arrival saw gleaming on the coast of Pachacamac from the sea.

The temple of Mojeque towers above all the others in the valley. This deserted mass of ruins was obviously in its prime one of the noblest constructions on the whole coast. This must have been at the time when a powerful influence from the uplands penetrated the Casma Valley into the plain. It is the period when severe geometrical forms appear in the art of the Chimu and its clash with the art of Tiahuanaco. Much in the temple of Mojeque indicates that the mighty walls did not succumb to the ravages of time but to violent attacks from enemy troops. What followed in the Chimu kingdom was that often far weaker and featureless flirting with the old forms gave their art an effect which is known as Late Style.

Farther to the south the region undergoes a great change. After the significant Rio de Culebra we come to the narrow valley of Huarmey, earlier known as Hualmi—to an unspeakably dreary, deserted and yet intriguing landscape which can be seen to its

advantage in our aerial photograph (Plate 26). Across a large
stretch of desert, the Pampa de Mata, with its bare hills and
undulating sand dunes one of the most deserted stretches of the
coast, we finally reach the southernmost frontier of the Chimu
kingdom. This frontier is formed by the smaller Rio de la Fortaleza and the broad Rio Pativilca, which together with the Santa
and the Chira are the most important and deepest streams of
the coast. They are often very dangerous in a rainy season. The
first Europeans who had to cross them, Hernando Pizarro and
his friends, found this to their cost.

Miguel de Estete[4] confesses in his report that at the end of
January 1533 they could only swim across the raging flood with
the greatest difficulty. On account of its swift-flowing stream it
bore in those days the beautiful name Huaman, the Indian word
for falcon. Its banks, which reach a height of 150 feet in the
coastal area, caused the Spaniards to name it the Rio de la
Barranca, the river with the steep banks. Barranca is also the
name of a village to the south standing some seventy-five feet
above the stream. On the north side is a second settlement,
Pativilca, officially named today after the river and the valley.

Its whole character makes this valley the easily defended
borderline to the south. On the Rio Pativilca at the time of the
tenth Inca, the decisive battle for the Chimu kingdom began.
The frontier fortress, Paramonga, a supply and defence point as
it was in those days, does not stand directly on the fringe of the
valley but behind a second stream, the Rio de la Fortaleza. The
fortress hill rises at the northern edge of the delta-shaped broadening of the valley through which the Rio de la Fortaleza and
the Rio Pativilca flow into the sea. Both rivers debouch from
different directions out of the mountains and their mouths are
about ten miles apart (Map page 182).

The Rio de la Fortaleza is the weaker and brings down only
a small part of the Pativilca waters, but in the rainy season it is
also in spate. Presumably in the old days the whole plain around
the giant fortress could be flooded. In the course of the centuries
the ground by the coast appears to have risen considerably; the
sea has also receded.

The actual fortified hill rises more than 150 feet and lies free
and separated from the first foothills of the Cordilleras, which

after undulating gently soon rise sharply. Although in ruins the fortress is an impressive sight even in the reduced scale of the aerial photograph (Plate 38). In this photograph, the partially collapsed walls to the east at the extreme right-hand corner of which the main entrance was situated, appear as a bold line at the foot of the schist fortress. Two cubic layers of masonry enabled this to be barricaded and rendered inaccessible by deep cuts. From this outermost entrance steps led to a mighty dam at the foot of the first fortified terrace. From here a strongly fortified path with a well-defended gate led to the second terrace and the courtyard. The ground plan is reproduced below in order to illustrate the aerial photograph.

From the second terrace a fourth provided with all possible protection had to be crossed in order to reach the third and uppermost platform. This contained the main quarters for the garrison as well as various large and small rooms surrounded by corridors. As a further precaution the latter never stood in direct communication with each other and often ended blind so that an invader could be trapped. At the back of the citadel, through a forty-yard-long corridor—an apparent cul-de-sac with a well-disguised gate just before the end—one reached the battlements facing the sea through a final smaller maze. Here in the old days was the princes' dining-hall and the quarters of the commanding officer.

The innermost part of the last-named buildings consisted of

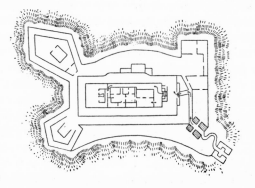

Plan of the Paramonga Fortress

two equal-sized square rooms, each twelve feet square, surrounded by a special breastwork giving a free view of the whole
countryside and the sea where an equally strongly fortified castle
once stood on the shore. The two rooms were painted in shades
of ochre and well protected from surprise attack by the blind
defence corridors, and any approaching enemy could be spotted
from a very long way off. The second deeper terrace, clearly
visible in the aerial photograph, surrounds the east, south and
west sides to a breadth of twelve feet, broadening out near the
entrance to a forty-five foot wide courtyard. This was presumably
solely for the defence of the inner citadel.

The lowest terrace is nearly eighteen feet wide on the south
and west sides, while to the north it curves along the slope of the
hill, providing a protected spot for the commissariat buildings.

From this terrace one reaches the three outer works of the
fortress, which nestle against the slopes of the hill. The largest
of these bastions embraces the west left corner. It forms an
irregular pentagon, the longest side of which measures 120 feet
and consists of a main terrace and a second smaller one on which
an open sentry post faced north-west. The south-west bastion,
clearly visible in the foreground of the aerial photograph, is
considerably smaller as a result of lack of space on the rock. It
is also in the shape of an unequal pentagon and also contains a
sentry post.

Both these outposts are joined to the terrace of the main
building by narrow, easily defended paths. The advanced fort
at the north-east corner, hardly visible in our picture, is not so
completely detached from the fortress as the other two. It forms
a large square, on which are the ruins of the casemates, and was
used by the men who had to defend the gateway and who had
to be able to move from here quickly to any spot. And finally the
south-east corner was equipped with the powerful gateway we
have already described instead of a bastion. This bulwark was
flanked by no less than three natural hills, on which, as can be
seen in the photograph, were erected defences independent of the
fortress.

In view of the grandeur of this whole site it is worth while
describing the surroundings. The distance between the fortress
and the sea is about a mile and a half. One the coast the 100-

39 Pitcher from the Pachacamac region. By the way in which the vessel is carried, archaeologists can determine the region from which the find stems

40
Vessels from the
central coast
Left: Pan pipes
player from
Pachacamac
Below left: An
ovoid vase with a
dark blue geo-
metrical pattern on
white from
Chancay *Below
right:* A spiked
vessel from
Cajamarcilla

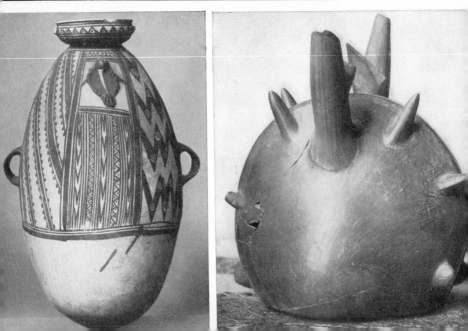

41

Right: Mask of an oracle. Gold-copper alloy with a green patina. The ears are very stressed. Fine holes can be seen in the forehead, presumably for fixing a crown *Below:* Clay figure with owl head and crescent moon above stepped pyramid, club and square in hand. See text p. 205

42 *Above:* The volcano Misti with the city of Arequipa below *Below:*
Ancient Indian huaca in a suburb of Lima, the modern capital of Peru

metre-high cliff rises sheer out of the flat sandy bank which
surrounds the valley estuary. To seaward it forms an almost
vertical wall and to landward a steep sandy slope which is joined
to the heights behind the fortress by an eminence.

On the top of the cliff we meet once more the remains of stout
walls and fortifications. This citadel and the mighty main fortress
undoubtedly supported each other mutually, and completely sealed
off the narrow strip of land between the mountains and the
coast. They also dominated the single road leading from Huaman
in the south to the valleys of the north and into Chimu country.

At the foot of the mountain on the seaward side is the huge
desecrated burial ground in which the dead of many battles lie.
When we examine the whole site we realise that for races which
knew neither gunpowder nor dynamite this frontier wall must
have been almost impregnable. It is unimportant to the issue
that the material from which these typical Chimu walls and
powerful fortifications were built was not stone but the usual
clay bricks dried in the sun. With the weapons available to
Indian warrors of those days, even a very superior force could
not have taken the walls by storm if defended by a resolute
garrison, and it would seem as though the kingdom of the last
Chimu in its conflict with Tupac Yupanqui succumbed not only
to material superiority but also to an inner political pressure.[172]

When Cieza de León travelled along the coast he saw the
fortress of Paramonga, which was already abandoned and
heavily damaged. Its walls and fortifications were richly painted
and still in their original form. This sixteenth-century Spaniard
called it a well-appointed and decorated fortress with admirably
built quarters and apartments. He was particularly struck by the
fact that the water was led up to the highest points through
special conduits.[173] There is no reason to doubt his statement,
although none of these have as yet been found. The imagination
of this chronicler who took the fortress for Inca work was not
vivid enough to invent for no apparent reason something he had
not personally seen. These conduits obviously made the fortress
the marvel it was considered in its heyday

Garcilaso, who may have seen it with his own eyes, since he
spent a short time in Lima on his journey from Cuzco to Spain,
relates that the fortress was adorned with charming paintings

G

and other rarities which made it well worth a visit.[172] Hernando
Pizarro and his twenty-five men saw it in full state of preservation on their way to Pachacamac. They rode to Paramonga and
stayed there overnight. Pizarro's secretary mentions the road up
to the gate as being well laid and describes several fine images
outside and within. Finally he drew attention to the figures
enthroned on either side of the main gate.[174] On American soil
these could at best have been jaguars but far more probably they
were the canines of Tiahuanaco art which kept watch here on
the frontier of the kingdom at the turn of the century.

CHAPTER FOURTEEN

Pachacamac

THE culture of Tiahuanaco can only be dealt with in this book in so far as it had a direct influence on the Chimu after the year A.D. 750. To follow its traces as a means in itself would simply mean to leave the coast, the entire geographical and intellectual region of moon worship and to penetrate far into the mountains among the inhabitants of the *altiplano* and the kingdom of the Sun—a task which we must leave to the author of a future work on the connections between the Inca kingdom and the ancient culture of Tiahuanaco.

Nevertheless, to round off this study of the circles which were drawn into the world of moon worship on the Peruvian coast, it is necessary to proceed farther south along the shores of the Pacific and examine in their broad outlines a few of the neighbouring cultures to the south of the Chimu. This is a most attractive undertaking because those races stood in the closest cultural relationship to the Chimu. Although closely related to them their art, above all the early art of Nazca, took its own course yet these basically identical or similar cultures supplemented each other artistically and spiritually. For comparison, this art of Nazca, described in the following chapter and so closely related to that of the Chimu yet so different in form, gives us a deep insight into the mystery of the functioning of Indian imagination and the possibilities of its artistic expression in the realm of moon worship.

The inhabitants of the *altiplano* have always felt very keenly —even at the time of the Inca—the great contrast between themselves and the people of the coast. This is not entirely due to geographical features. The difference even entered the language, because the combined coastal clans were known under the common name of Yunga. Many of the most reliable chroniclers refer to these races which had been welded into the Inca kingdom as

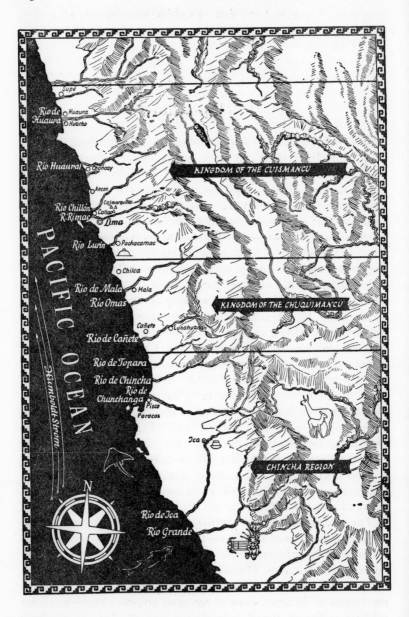

Supe

Rio de Huaura Huaura
            Huacho

Rio Huaural Chancay

            Ancon
            Cajmarquilla
Rio Chillón Callao
R. Rimac   Lima

            Pachacamac

PACIFIC OCEAN

            Chilca

Rio de Mala Mala
Rio Omas

            Cañete
            Lunahuana

Rio de Cañete

Rio de Topara
Rio de Chincha
Rio de Chunchanga
            Pisco
            Paracas

Humboldt-Strom

            Ica

KINGDOM OF THE CUISMANCU

KINGDOM OF THE CHUQUIMANCU

CHINCHA REGION

N

Rio de Ica
Rio Grande
            Nasca

of a unity. Cieza de León describes them as a degenerate people whose rulers were fantastically extravagant and obsessed with the idea of festivities and ostentatious luxury. These princes travelled only in litters, had many wives and constantly wore rich garments embroidered with silver, gold and costly gems. Each ruler had a large retinue and was served with much pomp and ceremony. They were accompanied by heralds and fools; guards stood at every corner and the host of servants demanded by the ceremonial was quite a normal phenomenon at the courts of these princelings.[175]

The temperament of any race, of course, is basically determined by the landscape and climate. Even today we still find the inhabitants of the mountains tough, serious, taciturn and melancholic, whereas the coastal dwellers have a far more frank, passionate and sensual temperament, a frivolous and lively imagination which betrays itself in so many of the pottery designs of the Chimu and in their later clay sculpture. We must not, however forget that Cieza de León's account refers to a time when Chimu culture had already passed its peak. He describes the people of the Late Style and of a culture which had already had a thousand-year-old tradition. The Mature Style of the Chimu displays magnificent reserve and it is no coincidence that in that age the severe forms of the mountains had their influence.

It would certainly be incorrect to deduce that the art of the Chimu renaissance was not an individual growth. The art of Pachacamac affords the best and most striking proof of this. It differs basically from that of the northern coast and often possesses a duality without any hard and fast character. While it can be said of the art of the Chimu that in all its stages down the centuries it expressed a united folk with a united feeling for style, the neighbourhood of Pachacamac represents the most interesting mixed region and the great crossroads for all possible styles of different ages and races not only from the coast but from the whole vast Andean cultural circle.

The realm of Pachacamac starts with the Rio de Huaura, which, with its canals, irrigates the valleys of Huacho and Masu, forming together one of the most beautiful, broadest and greenest corridors on the coast. The stream contiguous to this is known officially today as the Rio de Huaural; it reaches the sea near

Chancay, and on many maps is named from the latter place, often confused with the foaming Chancay in the north which enters the sea near Lambayeque. Farther south in the immediate vicinity of the modern capital, Lima, there followed the Rio Chillón, the Rimac with the nearby eponymous ancient shrine, and the Lurin, on the left bank of which stood the temple city of Pachacamac (Map page 196).

At the time of the Inca conquest the rulers of this region bore the name or title 'Cuismancu', which must not be confused with Chuquimancu, the name for the princes of the next states farther south. The subjection of these two feudal dominions by the Inca took place before that of the Chimu at the beginning of the fifteenth century. The fame of the Cuismancu resides above all on the fact that to them was attributed the building of the Cyclopean temple to the god Pachacamac in the Lurin Valley. Most of the chroniclers agree on this point.[176]

The whole land is strewn with huacas and the ruins of former cities. Since the end of the ninth century Pachacamac's shrine was the main and most imposing place of pilgrimage in the whole of the Andean region. Entrance to the actual temple precincts was confined to the priests and the princes when they brought their sacrifices and gifts. The large city attached to the temple was divided into two parts, one of which was inhabited by the subjects of the Cuismancu while the other served to provide accommodation for the thousands of pilgrims who streamed in from near and far. As an enduring testimony to their devotion and guardianship of this mighty temple, the most varied villages, cities and provinces throughout Peru had erected their own pyramids[177] which were later to be overshadowed by the brilliance of the Inca sun temple.

The comparatively late building period, according to archaeological finds, suggests that about A.D. 1000 the city represented the metropolis of a mighty kingdom which comprised part of the coast and a large area in the uplands. The site was ideal and predetermined by Nature. A bare twelve miles north of Pachacamac lies the Bay of Callao, one of the largest and best-protected natural harbours in the world, large enough to hold all the navies of the world. Callao therefore is also the harbour of Lima, and the latter, as Ciudad de los Reyes, founded on

January 18th, 1535 by Pizarro with great ceremony, is the capital
of Peru and its only really large city, which, together with the
harbour area today, has some 800,000 inhabitants. In the middle
of this extensive area can be seen the remains of pyramids
which contain thousands of mummies, most of which rest singly
in small chambers made of brick tiles. A new large sortie, the
Avenida del Progreso, has been driven right through one of the
largest of the ancient shrines. A second huaca which was spared
such sacrilege can be seen to its advantage in the aerial photograph (Plate 42), in one of the suburbs of Lima.

From Lima too the famous Central Andean railway[178] winds
through sixty-eight tunnels, the longest of which lies at an altitude
of 15,000 feet above the mountain ridge. The modern *autobahn*[179] opened in 1935 which leads from Lima across the Andes
at 15,500 feet to Oroya and from there farther north to Cerro
de Pasco and Huanuco, and to the south to Cuzco and Lake
Titicaca, merely follows the age-old routes of communication.

It is no wonder, then, that a cultural exchange existed at
every important point of the coast since time immemorial. A bare
twelve miles north of Pachacamac in the immediate vicinity of
modern Lima stood a second important religious centre, that of
Rimac, in which the priests, as we have already mentioned on
page 168, pronounced their oracles wearing masks. To this
oracle, whose temple was richly appointed but rather smaller
than that of Pachacamac, came the envoys of the individual
princes, presumably to ask for political advice.[180] Of the priests,
we know from Oviedo[181] that they were always garbed in white,
lived a chaste life and ate neither salt nor pepper.

In the ruins of Nieveria we must presumably see a more
ancient shrine. They are almost identical with those of Cajamarcilla (Plate 43). This city of the dead, fifteen miles east of Lima
in the Rimac Valley, must not be confused with the eponymous
place on the right bank of the Marañon, level with Cajamarca
on Latitude 7° S. in the Bolivar province. Cajamarcilla was
most probably already a dead city at the time of Pizarro. The
Conquistadors make no reference to this spot when they explored
the neighbourhood of Pachacamac in search of a site for their
new capital.

It would be pointless to look for an individual art style in such

a region. Only a practised eye can detect anything that could
be described as Chimu art. The most striking characteristic of
all later finds in Pachacamac is the strong influence of Tiahuanaco style. The vessels[182] dug up within the cones of the temple
show a comparatively direct sequence from the purest Tiahuanaco style through a later—recognisable by the use of white, black
and red—to the style of the Inca period. Even in this latter
unifying epoch of the whole land the Late Style black ware of
the Chimu is very seldom to be found along the central coast.[183]
Thus once more we have a justification for that cultural border
on the Rio Pativilca; the relations of the kingdom with Pachacamac were not nearly so active after the ebb of the Tiahuanaco
tide as those which Pachacamac held with the mountains and to
the south.

Very little can be said with certainty about the art of the
Central Peruvian coast of this age because everything in this
region was overwhelmed by the later flood of conquerors. Remarkable are the finds in Chancay, north of Pachacamac. Here
we find vessels in the form of gigantic eggs reminiscent of the art
of Amazonia.[184] Their particularly coarse clay is usually covered
with a pale yellow coating on which are traced in brown or
blue-black sober geometrical decoration, as can be seen in Plate
40, bottom left. On the ovoid form is usually set a bowl-like
collar which is then adorned with some anthropomorphic sculpture. These were often urns which perhaps had to be carried
great distances, possibly across the entire mountain range, for
here we are in a region which represents the closest contact
between the coast and those nodal points in the Andes where the
chains intersect and have made communication possible since the
earliest ages. In addition to the pottery solid little figures have
been found; these were produced in great quantities. Little clay
temples also serve here to house the ornaments.

The finds in Chancay can be divided into five different
groups,[185] of which the most modern is usually black on a white
ground while its precursor consists of three-colour geometrically
adorned vessels; the next group adds a fourth colour and then
follows a level, the fourth group, where the pottery is white on
red, and finally, at the lowest excavation levels, clay wares with
a black design on a white ground. This fifth and most ancient

group, although the utensils themselves are usually badly finished
and bear the stigma of provincial art, is particularly interesting
because it suddenly recalls early Chimu art and at the same time
that of Nazca. In this way a bridge is built between those two
associated cultures which in a later age obviously stemmed from
the uplands.

The older finds in fact show the close ties between all the races
devoted to moon worship.

To a more practised eye, provided the objects are not from
the uplands or from the coastal areas, the first expressions of
Chimu style, and in the later stages under Tiahuanaco influence,
are clearly visible in many small details of Pachacamac art.
Thus in Pachacamac were found vessels of the above-mentioned
ovoid form of Chancay enhanced by the artistic genius of Chimu.
A sculptured clay vessel like the water-carrier in Plate 40 shows
no primitive naïveté and rigidity in its outward form but the fluid
form and finer modelling of the Chimu, and in its whole essence
has the effect of a gay creative spirit. In the decoration of finds
such as the Pan pipe player illustrated in Plate 40 from the
region of Pachacamac, we find the light circles or large blobs
characteristic of Chimu art which redeem the surfaces from
archaic quietude and often endow them with a touch of gaiety.

To end this survey, we must give some thought to the great
excavation site of Ancón. Reiss[4] and Stubel dug up thousands of
artefacts from there. But since there are no ruins available it is
not known whether there was another shrine here or merely a
gigantic necropolis connected with the other shrines of the cult.
In Ancón, too, a host of different styles have been more or less
summarily classified and given a wide interpretation. Since this
was a question of obvious collecting mania it is very interesting
for individual archaeological research but less important for this
thesis, which tries to deal with the crux and the causes of things.
Seen purely formally, it is very dangerous to quote this region
when identifying styles or cultures. They are only sites where
excavations were made and no more. The stylistic characteristics
must be looked for elsewhere and incorporated into all the other
cultural patterns.

On the art of Pachacamac as a whole, it must be mentioned
that at its peak around the turn of the tenth century it expressed

G*

the Tiahuanaco spirit which in this region had mingled for centuries with coastal forms ruling farther north and south. A union between the tendencies of Chimu and Nazca art can often be observed particularly in the ceramics of Cajamarcilla.

These specimens combine the sculpture of the north and the bright colours of the south. Here will often be found delicate pale orange-yellow wares. The spouts of the vessels have been adopted from Nazca, become longer and to a certain unsatisfactory degree approach the pot-bellied form of the Chimu. In general the colours are richer than in the art of the north, but decisively more sober than in Nazca and consist solely of white, black, iron-grey, dark brown and reddish-violet hues. The figures are less imaginative than those of the south and tend more to the realism of the Chimu, inasmuch as animals and plants of the region are often reproduced and fruits with curious prickles (Plate 40).

★ ★ ★

All that we possess traditionally from the neighbourhood of Pachacamac dates from a later age when the significance of this place and shrine was so great that even the Inca did not dare to capture it and were content to introduce their own sun worship in a new temple, the remains of which still stand proudly above the sand. Even after the Spanish conquest, despite all the efforts of the victors, long columns of pilgrims wended their way to the ancient temple. According to Estete, all villages up to 300 hours' journey away furnished a yearly tribute to the shrine, individual collecting centres being erected throughout the land to receive the tribute. The tribute consisted of cereals and the usual sacrifices, but, above all, precious vessels which were used to decorate the temple.

According to Hernando Pizarro's reports to the Royal Audience of Santo Domingo[186] the coastal regions paid tribute at the time of the Inca not to the latter's capital Cuzco but to Pachacamac, and not to the Inca sun temple but to the old shrine of which Garcilaso records that the Inca Pachacutec, after he conquered the place, removed the idols which consisted of fishes and a dog or a fox. Estete, who visited the temple in 1533, mentions a wooden figure at the feet of which lay, in his opinion, very strange offerings to the god. In the anonymous *Conquista del Peru*, which has often been attributed to Xerez,[4] will be found the account of an eye-witness who after the first Spanish visit to Pachacamac wrote that this city was larger than Rome and that in its temple dwelt a devil who spoke to the Indians in a room as black as himself.

The most valuable of these reports is that of Garcilaso, according to whom fishes and a canine were the idols worshipped in this temple. This confirms that this ancient cult was also dedicated to the moon and the sea. On the find of a golden fish in the Huaca de Toledo in Chan-Chan, further details are given on page 166, and important data on the water worship of the Indians will be found on page 169, *et seq*. It is now essential to deal briefly in a general manner with this fish cult which evolved from totemism in Hellas, Latium, Syria and Egypt. Christianity, too, as we have already remarked, merely preserved ancient traditions in the fish symbol—in the catacombs, in baptism and other customs. The fact that in hieroglyphics the fish was the symbol of Christ, the initial letters of the word Jesus Christ, Son of God, Redeemer, in Greek *Jesus Christos Theou Yios Soter* forming the word *Ichthys*, a fish, means that it certainly goes back to far earlier representations. The Fish God in the religion of the Lycian Orphics in Asia Minor, who worshipped Orphos, the Sacred Fish, must be mentioned here.

Sea divinities are very well represented in Greek mythology. Apart from the ruler of the sea, Poseidon, and his wife Amphitrite, we have Oceanos with Thetis and her daughters, the Oceanides; Nereus, his wife, Doris, and their fifty daughters, the Nereides, Triton and the Tritons, not to mention individual sea spirits such as Proteus, Glaucus, Leucothea, Palaemon, Scylla and the Sirens. All of them possessed the gifts of prophecy and metamorphosis. Pictorial art showed them in a great variety of forms, and it is not only an interesting historical fact but essential in order to understand Indian culture and folk psychology to look round in the world for further such figures.

The Nixies, for example, who in Nordic and Germanic mythology inhabit the streams, rivers, ponds and lakes, were no prerogative of these races but slumbered deeply in the subconscious of the human psyche. The Nix, Neck or Waterman is usually old and long-bearded but is sometimes portrayed as a tousle-haired or curly-headed boy. The female Nixies usually appear sitting in the sun, combing their long hair like the Lorelei, with the upper part of their body of amazing beauty emerging from the waves. Long hair, whether on the head or on the chin, constantly recurs in these figures.

It is curious that despite the beardlessness of the Indians several multi-coloured vessels were found in a very ancient shrine of Moche which, in the Mature Style of the Chimu, show figures with long beards similar to the one from the Chicama Valley illustrated in Plate 30. In connection with Indian fish worship it is particularly interesting that a fish divinity also appears in Babylon as a cultural hero and teacher of wisdom and that traces of a similar concept crop up in Greece and again in the Irish myths, where a fish of wisdom when eaten by certain chosen men made them become soothsayers.

The connection between a fish divinity and the cultural hero is doubly interesting if one remembers the long-bearded figures found in the ancient capital of the Chimu. For, as we know, in Mexico there existed the myth of the culture-bringing god, Quetzalcoatl, who was always portrayed as bearded and white-faced. He presented his people with the blessing of knowledge and then disappeared to the east, where he immolated himself, or, according to other traditions, dived into the sea in order to return at a later date. The myth of this return, according to many historians, played a prominent part in the subjection of the Indians by the whites; the latter wore beards unknown to the natives and were light-skinned. The gifts which Montezuma, the last king of the Aztecs, offered to the conqueror, Cortez, clearly show that he did not look upon him as a man but as a god.[187]

The presence of a similar Mexican deity in Peru in connection with the moon worship reigning there is also very significant for the mythology of Central America, for it points to a moon worship also preceding the later sun religion in this region. In fact, Quetzalcoatl in Mexico displays a host of lunar traits, one of the most important being his role of god of the winds when he levels the path for the great rain-bringing storms, and by so doing clearly enters the realm of the moon. The reader will remember the role ascribed on page 71 to the Peruvian Conn, who, according to all accounts, like Quetzalcoatl in Mexico must have

taken a very prominent place in the beliefs of the Chimu. Just as
Quetzalcoatl's face, apart from the aforementioned beard, can
often be recognised in the Mexican portraits by the bird-like or
trunk-like protruding lips, so we find similar features in a moon
god of the Chimu on page 65. As soon as the bird-like character
becomes evident in such ceramics one recognises at once that it
is a bird of the night, the owl, which is even more precisely
indicated by a crescent moon on its head (Plate 41). In Mexico
Quetzalcoatl usually wore in addition a necklace of snail-shells
which recur in a different form in the Peruvian portraits. We
have already explained the significance of the snail-shell on page
151, and when discussing the art of Nazca we shall have cause to
return to this symbol.

In the figure of the Mexican god in the course of time, further
mythological representations entered whereby he preserves his
lunar features, above all in his relationship to the evening star.
Venus was worshipped with particular reverence by the Mexican
priesthood, and this planet's orbit later played a part in the whole
evolution of the calendar and the Tonal-amatl.[188] Since the
phases of this planet on its path round the sun cause it to disappear in the beams of the diurnal planet, as does the moon, the
figure of Quetzalcoatl, the Wanderer widdershins, can also hold
good as the expression of the movements of Venus. The same
applies to the Peruvian deity.

All these mythical figures are versatile in their whole nature.
This Indian self-sacrificing god whose return was expected,
according to Mexican tradition, is no other than the moon,
which, as it wanes in the east, is extinguished by the light of the
rising sun, at the same time burning itself up in self-sacrifice.
We can consider it to represent a natural phenomenon, but we
must still inquire into its psychological content, into the spiritual
conflicts, tensions and benefits as well as the entire intellectual
precedents which are expressed in this myth. Only modern man
can expect that an object like the moon could be expressed sym-
bolically in a rigid circumscribed form.

The conscious mind of those early cultural stages never embraced every acceptable fact in sharp, stark outlines but preferred
to combine a whole series of experiences in a single symbol. None
of these Indian myths, any more than those of other races, are

mere disguises, comparisons or conscious solutions and transla-
tions. The myth is far more the first real form of experience of
so-called primitive man. He saw reality in quite a different
manner from modern man and it was impossible that he
should realise the movements of the heavenly bodies according to
the still unknown physical laws. In the planets he also saw forces
working on human beings—love or hate, joy or sorrow.

If moon worship was connected with the worship of water, so
here in the land of the Chimu as in Mexico or in Babylon it was
the primitive concept of a golden age of purity in the far distant
past. The idea of water conjures up cleanliness. Outlook and
customs such as magic, which at one time spread throughout the
world, were preserved and developed for thousands of years and
could hardly be branded as purposeless, unnatural or even as
intentional dishonesty. By a spiritual devaluation and debasement
of earlier cultural stages one can become blind to the original
sources which were no longer valid at later stages.[189]

Long before man began to work out the sum total of his
experience from a purely logical and professional standpoint, he
had created a system of, to a certain extent, illogical science. This
race-psychological knowledge is important for an understanding
of the whole of Chimu art as well as that of Nazca with their
beautiful symbols, which until today have been given inadequate
and often impossible meanings.

On the grounds of this comparative knowledge of the significance of all mythological representations, it is not difficult to
explain the connections between dogs and the nocturnal satellites.
We have already discussed on page 64 the keen sense of observation of Nature folk who showed the dog at night in conversa-
tion with the moon. But where this portrayal becomes constant,
this explanation can no longer suffice. Quite rightly we start at
once from the premise that the moon is the ruling star of the
night. The night itself, however, is filled with its own magic and
belongs far more than the day to the irrational powers, above all
to sexual life. Now to primitive man sex was an incomprehensible
and marvellous secret. He could not possibly put it in a scientific
pigeon-hole under the title 'Reproduction' which modern man
so often does—modern man who, despite all his rationalism, is
no less a victim to his urges than his ancestors in primitive times.

Man who today, as ever, is himself the Great Unknown in the equation of existence is only an insignificant link in the unending chain of future generations. The sexual process engenders him and it is a pity that its expression in art can only be treated by serious research workers with great reservation for very obvious reasons. One thing we must make clear, however, is that sensuality not only among the Greeks but among most of the early peoples was not considered shameful and they were keen observers of the vagaries of sex. The sexual act of the canines was more readily observable than that of other animals and in ancient America it was because of the lack of other animals that the dog was introduced in so striking and such a surprising manner into Indian cults.

The dog as a bringer of sacrificial offerings.
Vase design from Chan-Chan

In addition to this there was the great part which the dog played as a hunter and therefore as a bringer of sacrifice in all races which knew him. It is certainly no coincidence that the legend of Nimrod, the 'mighty hunter before the Lord', was universal.[190] The hunter, however, in complex thought cannot possibly be separated from the fisherman. Thus the fishing dog is found in Oriental fairy-tales as an age-old tradition, using his tail as a line. The fairy story would not have recourse to this strange aid had the dog not already, mythologically, played the part of hunter and fisherman. In the same way the legend of the fox and the grapes is based on a long-forgotten myth of the wine god, Dionysos Bassareus, in the guise of a dog. Bassara, incidentally, is merely the Thracian word for fox or fox pelt, just as in Coptic Maschar or Maschor is the name for a jackal.

In addition to the dog two other beasts played important roles in the Indian cults on the Peruvian coast—the fish and the snake. They, too, stem from a great series of concepts, are interchangeable and have a strong sexual and often phallic significance. Fertility in Nature as a whole, and in particular in the life of plants, is bound up with these concepts.

Ancient Ionic philosophy which we associate with the name of Anaximander tells us that man originated from the fish. This theory can be considered as a precursor of Darwinism or as the antithesis of the latest scientific theory of organic life originating in water, even if Plutarch, to whom we owe the tradition, based his ideas more on totemistic ideas.[191]

Greek fish myth.
Vase design in Ionic style

Nor could it have escaped the notice of Indian priests and doctors, after all we have said of trepanning operations on page 93, that man as an embryo in the womb possessed four clearly recognisable gill-apertures with the intermediate gill-arch and also a host of fish-like characteristics. All in all, according to the finds, the symbol, the handed-down myths and the accounts of the chroniclers[192] in this book point to a fish cult on the Peruvian coast and a religious dogma going back to age-old concepts and experiences.

We should be completely off the trail if on account of the similarity with the fish cult of the Mediterranean in antiquity we were to attempt to fall back on the famous migration hypothesis. On page 64 we have hinted at a dog myth complex which points in a far more obvious direction. In India, where even today sacred fish are still kept, Vishnu is occasionally worshipped in the form of a fish and this applies, as the interesting word root *Vish* denotes, to the first incarnation of the deity.[193] Throughout

43 *Above:* The fortifications of the Clan palace of Tambo de Mora in
Chincha country. See text p. 215 *Below:* The ruins of the burial city
Cajamarcilla in the Rimac valley. See text p. 199

44 Nazca art *Above:* Tall beakers with vivid figured pattern *Below:*
Rubbing from an early Nazca vessel. See text p. 217

45

Above: Canine as the so-called cat demons on a Nazca vessel with forehead and beard adornment, holding a trophy head *Right:* Vase depicting a face with sealed lips

46 *Above:* The family tree. Design from a Nazca vase. The figures are all symbolised by huge heads adorned with jagged crowns. The faces are alternate pale yellow and light red while the head adornment is blood red. The eyes turned sideways are reminiscent of those on the border of fishes and serpents. Trophy heads can be seen reduced in size at various places as lip decorations suggested by three dots *Below:* Depicting the rain mythology of the Southern coast. A funnel can be seen before the face of the rain god into which carriers empty water so that the winds can have their effect

Australia the aborigines still believe that man on his death is transformed into a fish, and these primitives carefully avoid eating fish. In South America, fostered by the medicine men, there are many races which subscribe to the same belief. In the case of such an ancient and widespread belief it is impossible to say or even to suggest how far the whole fish and water worship on the Peruvian coast was introduced by nomads or whether it already existed among the autochthonous fishing population.

Although the name of the god Pachacamac, who played such an important role in the land to the south of the Chimu, was usually translated by the Spaniards as *Hacedor del mundo,* Creator of the World, the Christian concept of God as the creator was its basis, the god who conjured up the world at his command, resulting in the insuperable chasm between creating and created nature, between God and creature. The Indian noun 'Camay', however, does not mean to make, to conjure up, or to create, but to vivify, to endow with a soul, and has therefore very little to do with the Christian concept of creatures. On closer inspection the god Pachacamac reveals his title not as earth creator but as earth quickener or vivifier of the earth.

With this endowing of the earth with a soul, water as a vivifying element stands in the closest relationship to the wind. It is therefore highly significant that the other name of a deity constantly recurring in Peru, Viracocha,[194] in its second syllable *cocha* unquestionably means water. Although *Vira* in Peruvian philology has been the subject of much controversy, it is always translated as fat,[195] whereby it has constantly been overlooked that the original name of the god was taken over by the later Inca from another and far older language. Many of the old chroniclers who were in contact with Indian traditions and ideas were more circumspect. Cristóbal de Molina,[196] who perhaps penetrated deepest into the religious concepts of the Indians, avoided, as did Betánzos,[197] who married a native princess and was familiar with the speech and customs of the country, translating the word 'Viracocha' as fat lake or foam of the sea.[198] Garcilaso stoutly denied that Viracocha meant foam of the sea,[199] and the critical Santillán[200] also rejected this faulty translation. Bertonio[201] rightly tried to find another meaning for the word 'Vira' but both he and Santo Thomas,[202] under the spell of the

Christian concept of God, were more preoccupied with the philological construction of a world creator than in Indian thought. In this way arose the legend of a cultural hero who created the moon and the sun and finally created men in his own image.

In actual fact, however, the world 'Cocha' can only be translated as water while in 'Vira' we must see either an age-old speech root for man or human being, as in the Latin *vir*, the Lithuanian *viras* and the Latvian *wihrs* or in a hardly less ancient word for wind which appears in the Portuguese, a Western romance language and forerunner of the Spanish Ibero-romanch, as 'Viracao' for breeze or current of air and by analogy to the Indian word forms in the Lower Congo, meaning in particular the wind coming from the sea. In the first case 'Viracocha' would be a term for a man or the God of the Sea, and we cannot take exception to such an ancient word, which, as Garcilaso showed,[199] has taken on the character of a Christian name and in the later Quechua language forms a second main substantive from the genitive of the root word. Secondly, it is concerned with a wind, water or moon deity, as we have shown on page 204 in our description of the god Quetzalcoatl.

This new interpretation, philologically at least, is as plausible as any other hypothesis of the word 'Viracocha' and fits in far better with the general religious concept of the Indian. Even if, with the expansion of the Inca kingdom, the word 'Viracocha' lost more and more contact with its original source and spread to other regions, the ancient names of the God of other races could not quite displace it. In all these names, however, we shall invariably find the concept of a world quickener and vivifier.

CHAPTER FIFTEEN

The World of Nazca

AT the time of the subjugation of the country by the Incas, the region round the shrines of Pachacamac can be termed the domain of the Cuismancu. To the south was a state extending over various valleys the rulers of which were called Chuquimancu, the Lords of Runahuanac, Huarcu, Mala and Chilca.

Of these valleys, which, as we can see today on Map page 196, sometimes bear other names, Garcilaso[203] relates that at the time of the Inca the Chuquimancu were still respected and honoured over a vast area even by tribes which were not their vassals. This principality was smaller than that of Pachacamac, but hardly less civilised. Its agriculture was particularly progressive and in view of the obvious lack of water aroused great surprise in Cieza de León. This chronicler describes[204] in great detail the manuring of the region with fish guano, not realising that he was betraying at the same time an important detail of their worship when he relates how the fish and corn cobs were put into the soil to fructify it. One cannot help recalling the Babylonian priests on many of the clay cylinders[205] garbed as fish for their fertility incantations. In our illustration of one of these cylinders on page 212 can be seen two priests in the guise of fishes carrying out their ceremonial duties beneath a sacred tree.

The main valley in Chuquimancu country was the Huarcu Valley, adjacent to the Rio Mala, which today has been renamed after Rio de Cañete, which flows through it. Both valleys possess very extensive and excellent irrigation systems. While the upper Cañete Valley embraces the district of Runahuanac or Luna-huanac, on the lower reaches is located the former capital of the ruler, the Fortaleza of Chuquimancu. This fortress[206] testifies to the architectural skill and warlike spirit of this race. It was later built over by the Inca and by no means represents the original

211

Rubbing of a Babylonian clay cylinder showing priests garbed as fishes

fortification as Garcilaso[203] and Cieza de León[204] maintain. One can see quite clearly in the accompanying illustration the Inca shrine to the south dedicated to the sun; the remaining foundations, however, serve the old coastal traditions. This powerful defensive position originally served as protection against the savage mountain-dwellers, the Yaucu and Huarochiri,[207] of which Sarmiento de Gamboa tells.[208]

South of the Chuquimancu kingdom, where moon and fish worship were practised, lie the valleys of Chincha, Pisco, Ica and Nazca or Rio Grande. The inhabitants of this region are better known from the accounts of Cieza de León and Garcilaso as the Chincha. According to both chroniclers these people were themselves emigrants from the coast, where, on the pattern of the Chimu, they subdued at an early date an autochthonous people, introducing a more advanced social system as well as their worship of the sea. The Chincha always pursued an aggressive policy towards their neighbours inland, and one is not very far wrong in assuming them to be the issue of that early warlike uncivilised race of Nazca, of whom we possess[209] only dubious and confused details but a very great vital and colourful art.

Before examining this art we must recapitulate the geographical and chronological data. From north to south the Peruvian coast rises slowly but steadily above the sea level until finally, between Latitudes 14° and 15° S. in the region of Ica and Nazca, a plateau is formed known as the Tablazo de Ica, which becomes ever less favourable for agriculture and rises to 2,100 feet. While in the regions which we have already discussed the settlement of Chiclayo, some way from the coast, lies only

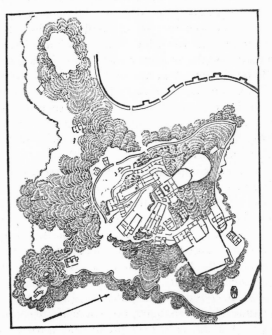

Plan of the Fortress of the Chuquimancu in the
Cañete Valley

seventy-five feet above sea-level, Trujillo is already 185 feet, Lima 500 and Ica 1,206 feet. A glance at the Peruvian-Chilean frontier completes the picture, which is one of further rise.

Travelling south the valleys cut ever deeper into the mountain; soon the the whole terrain consists of shifting sands distributed by the prevalent south-east wind. Here and there rise dark jagged hills, some quite close to the Pacific, and this landscape is not without its own wild charm. The *altiplano*, which grows ever more barren, soon rises to 3,000 feet above the sea, and rivers such as the Rio Majes or Camaná already lie at over 600 feet twenty miles from the estuary. As a result the harbour of Mollendo on this inaccessible coast has the most violent swell in Peru and shipping there is always tossed about like a cork.

Inland, however, the volcano Misti rises in its majesty to the sky, its crest covered with snow for part of the year although it does not exceed 18,000 feet. At its feet in our aerial photograph (Plate 42) can be seen the city of Arequipa with its cultivated plain, watered by the Rio Chili, while on many of the slopes in the neighbourhood the ancient terraces are still ploughed. Reaching the Peruvian frontier at last, the increasingly narrow valleys gradually take on the character of wild ravines, and it is no wonder that in gorges of this type, which extend far into Chile, no great individual culture could have matured. We have now reached the region of Tacna and Arica, where only traces of primitive art have been found.

But in the still comparatively favourable region of Ica and Nazca, the first Indian nomads who arrived on this coast were at the outset forced to wage a hard struggle like the Chimu in the north, but their aggressive spirit could not be dampened. Here in particular dwelt the tough savage South American peoples who constantly caused the newcomers great difficulty. The impressive art of the Paracas Peninsula (Map page 196), which, as will be seen in Plate 17, produced particularly beautiful weaves, must be considered the outcome of energetic friction.

At the time of the conquest the Chincha, according to the chroniclers, were still extremely proud and warlike. The most important information is to be found in the works of Cristóbal de Castro and Ortega Moréjon, who both maintain that this people never accepted sun worship but remained true to their ancient customs and cults of the moon and water.[210] The rooting out of the clan system by the Spaniards was long delayed in these inaccessible regions. The ban of marrying within their own clan continued to be rigidly enforced.

The Chincha Valley (Map page 196), so fully exploited by irrigation canals that the river no longer reached the sea but was completely used up inland, possesses a host of huge buildings from early days. The best-known ruins are the fortifications of La Centinela, of which only the western end stems from Inca days while the eastern parts are built of sun-baked bricks typical of the coast. The building[211] known today as the Huaca de Tambo de Mora (Plate 43) was formerly a clan palace with raised terraces, while a second shrine, known later to the Inca as Chinchacamac,[212] has been rechristened today La Cumbe. According to all the finds a great cultural centre once thrived in the Chincha Valley as well as in Moche and Pachacamac. With the country around the valleys of Ica and Rio Grande this area was from A.D. 1000 to 1400 a seat of culture which produced the late Nazca art. Kroeber and Strong have thoroughly investigated the fieldwork of Uhle in this neighbourhood but have unfortunately added nothing new of interest to art history.[213]

That Ica art has always been bracketed with that of Nazca is purely a geographical expedient. Only their proximity in space is taken into account; in time, however, a great difference has to be made. The early art of Nazca dried up completely towards the end of the seventh century, and not until the year 1000 can there be any mention of a new late style. The art of Ica leads directly to the art of the Inca and must be dated much later. The ceramics found in Ica differ from the rest of the region by their more simple form. Bowls with conical bases and plates are quite common. The Ica style is easily recognisable by the dominating geometrical patterns and is comparable with the art of Tiahuanaco, though with considerably reduced patterns, the former hieratic strength of which has become purely decorative. The technical execution of the glaze still lags far behind that of Nazca. For the purposes of this book neither the art of Ica nor the Late Style of Nazca are of interest. They are both descended from and related to the Tiahuanaco culture and belong in the wide circle of the Sun Kingdom. The beautiful early art of Nazca, however, shall provide the material for the closing chapter of this book on the Kingdom of the Moon, the Sea and the Fishes on the Pacific Coast at the foot of the Andes.

★ ★ ★

Hardly any other Indian art has been so greatly admired and so misinterpreted as this twin creation to Chimu art. The great similarities of technique and in the portraiture have often been

noticed. The host of strange figures which we can no longer interpret has invariably confused the observer. On the basis of the
general outlines given in this book of art and culture on the Peruvian coast and the symbols it employed, we may succeed in giving
a moderately satisfying explanation of the figures on the clay
vessels and weaves of Nazca which at first sight appear so alien.
Before making this attempt we must be quite clear as to what
in the art elements of Nazca is native to the coastal races and
what figures came over the mountains and regions to the south as
a result of communication with other races which had populated
a great part of South America from the dawn of time.

An impressive overall picture of these cultural relationships is
provided by the excavations which took place between 1925 and
1929 in the Argentine province of Catamarca—the Barreto
Mission's expeditions of Debenedetti, Weiser and later of Francisco Wolters in La Ciénega and La Aguada.[214] In the Tropic
of Capricorn, in a hitherto completely unknown valley in the
foothills of the Andes—the Valley of Hualfin—some 5,000 artifacts were dug up, including metal objects of copper and gold.
This was on the flat right-hand river bank covering an area of
ten miles long and three miles wide. The tombs, from fifteen to
twenty feet below the present surface in the yellow sand, were
found to be in good order. All around, the forest lies in its death
throes, and no houses or fortifications in this gloomy, deserted
neighbourhood bear witness to the culture of the dead. Their
bodies had almost entirely turned to dust so that it was impossible
to see in what position they were once buried. Everything perishable had also crumbled. From the remains of former wooden
objects the whole region must have looked quite different in the
old days and, as the tombs prove, must have been inhabited by
a large population. The ceramics which have come to light today
are indisputably higher in quality than anything which has
previously been found in the Argentine. Only the polychrome
pottery of Nazca approaches in refinement the delicacy of the
execution. Incidentally, the pottery is pre-eminently black, this
colour being due to its graphite content, whereas the insides show
the natural clay. What makes this find particularly valuable for
stylistic comparisons and chronology is its wealth of naturalistic,
geometrical decoration in addition to the purely geometrical. One

rarely finds two pieces alike but many analogies. The leitmotive of the curves on the neck of the vases is never repeated. In the pot-bellied vessels with barely visible curves as a result of tapering vases the main designs do not continue to the lower side. In addition to the ceramics, which often bear the sign of the cross (Plate 5), stone pots and pitchers have also come to light. Among the pictures of animals which make this art so vivid comparatively few birds appear, but, on the other hand, many monkeys, some of which smoke pipes (Plate 48). All these beasts are, for the most part, strongly stylised—the llama in a particularly graceful form. On closer examination one also finds in other parts of South America frequent portrayals of a Rain God with a trace of tears. Figures with trophy heads so popular in Nazca art (Plate 46), and which we mentioned as a rarity in the art of Huarás (Plate 35), were also found in La Ciénega (Plate 48).

This trophy head or zanca of an enemy killed in battle is very easy to recognise in the Nazca designs; they show the decapitated skull with the scalp hanging down, often soaked with blood. As a symbol it is a common and widespread Indian perquisite.[215] One cannot describe it any more than the heads with the trace of tears as an exclusive characteristic of Nazca art, since it forms part of the spiritual heritage of the Andes. The same applies to the symbol of the sealed lips, which are usually portrayed by a stripe across the mouth in the art of the southern coast (Plate 45). This sealing of the mouth, apart from its religious meaning, served a practical purpose in the case of the mummies: a thorn was thrust through the lips, preventing the chin of the dead man from falling.

The same can be said of Seler's 'feathered staff dancers'[216] which have proved such an insoluble problem in Nazca art. They, too, are not confined to this region. We occasionally find feathered staffs on Chimu pottery (page 56) similar to those on the pottery of La Ciénega (Plate 48). The feathered staff dancers from Nazca in their wild ecstasy display an almost oppressive power which far outstrips the other figures. The rubbings from these vases cannot reproduce the fantastic vitality of the dancers because they only come to life when the utensil is turning round in the hand.

Among the most interesting figures in the rich pictorial world of Nazca are those pertaining to the moon and water cult and which often recall disguises of mythical Chimu figures. Since Seler[216] introduced into scientific literature the unfortunate name of Cat Demon (Plate 45) for one of the most common figures, a whole generation of European and American scholars followed the explanation of this conscientious and important research worker because the figures in question could easily be taken for cats on account of their whiskers. Lehmann explained the protruding tongue by the habit of cats licking their young,[217] thereby contradicting himself when he wrote: 'Among the Indians of Nazca the main demon, the dappled cat, was the bringer of life and the nocturnal symbol of the male sex.'[218]

No one has ever made it quite clear why a tom-cat should lick its young. His description, however, has been passed down from book to book. This false interpretation, however, has so far prevented these figures from being reviewed in their intellectual association with the whole coast. Accepting them as cat demons one contradicts all the psychological premises for Indian creative art of that period. Even if these cats deputised for some other beast, as occurred in Chinese mythology and elsewhere in the world, their innermost nature could never be justified by this incorrect name.

Apart from the fact that for this particular animal the procedure of licking is particularly untypical and casual, there is no question here of natural realism but of a pictorial symbol-laden expression. One merely has to consider what creatures are usually portrayed with a protruding tongue to see that it is characteristic of dogs and, above all, of snakes. Snakes, one might say, almost hear with the tongue; according to human concept they are deaf and actually have no acoustic organ. Their tongue, on the other hand, is capable of picking up the subtlest shocks. The snake constantly puts out its tongue because it is picking up sound waves.

We might add that not all cats possess whiskers, and this applies to the puma. Dogs, on the other hand, without exception, have very pronounced sensory hairs. If one considers without prejudice the 'cat demons' illustrated on the following page we shall see in them rather than stylised hair a regular full beard and recall those remarkable Chimu figures from Moche or from the

Chicama valley, and in consequence the entire worship of the coast and its religious concepts (Plate 30).

The role played by canines in Chimu art (page 65) frequently recurs in the Nazca figures in the shape of the two servants of the Rain God (Plate 46), also a lunar figure. If, however, we recognise in the cat demons a relationship with the canines in Chimu art their connection with the snake need cause no surprise. This mythological association extends far beyond Peru to the Haida Indians on the Canadian north-west coast, where dog and snake are pictured together.[219]

So-called 'cat demons' on early Nazca ware

Although it remains impossible to reveal this exchange of roles in individual cases by rejecting the idea of the cat demon we return to the elements from which not only the religious concepts of the Chimu but all those of the early Nazca inhabitants were formed—concepts which were then expressed pictorially in many guises as was seemly, since they depicted the life of the spirit in a physical body. Since among the finds from Nazca there are also mouth masks of fine metal—similar to the beards shown in the pictures and which often take the shape of a moon crescent —there is also a clear-cut connection here with the cult of the coast, with the oracle of Rimac and the masks found in Moche, from behind which, at a later date, the priests practised their augury in the name of the deity.

We might be accused of tipping the baby out with the bath water if on the pretext of interpreting the art and culture of the southern coast we exploited the controversy of this misnomer to see the canines in every animal figure in Nazca art. In the south, with its strong totemistic trend, real cats were portrayed, just as they were from time to time in the north. Pumas and jaguars are not rare, particularly in the sculptured ceramics, but they are always portrayed correctly with their long, lashing tails. After the penetration of the Tiahuanaco style they appear in the more realistic later art along the whole coast. But this is hundreds of years later than the early Nazca art which produced these 'cat demons'.

Another constantly recurring phenomenon in the painted pottery of the southern coast is the frieze of heads with many jags and scrolls (Plate 46). This belongs to the conceptual world of ancestor worship and proves once more the close connection with the outlook of the north as expressed very characteristically in the Raimondi monolith (page 178) which is contemporary with early Nazca art. That the tongues of other heads as well as snakes represent ejaculation needs no special mention for the intelligent reader. But the points in the pictures will recall Neptune's trident and what we have already remarked on page 17 on the subject of the sceptre in connection with water worship. When the Maoris, the original inhabitants of New Zealand, equipped their ships they never forgot to place a trident in the bows. This idea, too, was bound up with the age-old universal worship of water. In the art of Nazca the crests of the waves are often portrayed by jags in the shape of a comb (Plate 47) and the snake is a water snake. In our illustration of a magnificent dream landscape will be seen two dogs with the white belly of a fox, while their bushy tails are reminiscent of the beaver and once more remind us of water. The stressed hump of the animals can be explained by the fox's comparatively greater capacity for arching the backbone than the dog, which is clearly expressed in the picture. Since the fox is a creature of caves it is also associated with the idea of the underworld and it appears in this form as the motive of the underside of the bowl dealt with on page 151. In any case, it is apparent how little was left to chance and how well conceived this whole magical world was. The stars by night and the three-pointed cacti, beneath which the snakes crawl, embellish the gay red, white and black design on a beautiful Nazca vase (Plate 47).

The many intellectual and formal elements from which the great coastal art originated changed only very slowly down the centuries. By the complex character of its mythological concepts one cannot reasonably expect that the moon cult could be destroyed overnight in favour of sun worship. Certain solar features must, from the very start, be inherent in any world of religious ideas since people were bound to look up at the sky. Sudden changes would only be possible at periods when lunar and solar representations were already more or less in the balance: a political *coup d'état* could, at any time, lead to a religious and cultural change. On this account alone it is of decisive importance in the study of symbols never to lose sight of the question of chronology. Frequently the symbols of the later sun worship are no less than transformed signs and modes of expression of an earlier moon worship. It is, therefore, easy to understand that the figure with the snail-shell on its back at a later age appeared as an ancient god and among the Maya would correctly be described as such as we have explained on page 151.

To explain the figures in the brilliant coloured art of Nazca individually would be a task beyond the scope of this book. Let us just mention that an earth goddess often appears and she is not difficult to recognise by her symbols of fertility. The basic motive of the bird with the snake already heralds the later art; more often, however, the bird is shown with a fish which in the later Chimu style is subjected to all manner of metamorphoses, particularly as a cormorant with a ray. The pipes of Pan in connection with fertility and keening (Plate 28), are, in common with the portrayal of burial dances, common property of the art along the coast. Finally, as particularly significant, Plate 46 shows a scene from the rain mythology in which many of the elements are depicted.

We see here the helpful dogs on each side of the god waiting with vessels full of water to be poured on to the earth. Near them, close to the rim, we see at a common turning-point chubby figures symbolising the wind which precedes the rain and reminiscent in their formation of the Mexican hieroglyphic 'four winds'.

And to close, a little more on general lines about the wonderful old vessels of Nazca. Although in this region have been found no great ruins or traces of architecture, the countless tombs lie at so many superimposed levels that this culture too must be considered as one of the oldest on the coast. The lowest strata go back to about the beginning of the Christian era. The topmost finds date from Inca times and display a mixture of Late Nazca style with the pure Inca style, recognisable in the amphorae. The objects from the deepest levels, however, display great skill and are one more proof that this race, like the Chimu, must already have been in possession of an archaic culture before they settled in this region.

Since early Nazca art by and large is less realistic than that of the northern coast, it is more difficult to find the documentary solution of their costume. However, there are enough vessels which indicate that here, too, there was no particular difference between the entire coastal population. The most striking feature is the difference in hair style : far more simple and less beautiful in the south than in the north. The use of charcoal and chewing of coca recur here as do individual items of Chimu costume. The cloak seems to have been worn with great effect.

The ceramics of Nazca art are usually very easy to distinguish from those of the remaining coast. They are characterised by the painting in several colours, by their delicacy and the resistance of the overcoat. Many of the vases have been magnificently fired and entirely coated with a brown, dark red or yellowish-white glaze. The forms are usually simple and much of the sculpture is more hinted at than actually executed. In the case of the pitchers the handle does not taper into a single spout (Plate 27), but the two pipes which lead inside are joined by a crossbar (Plate 47) and the ends are free. Moreover, in Nazca art there are many tall beakers (Plate 44) which do not occur in Chimu art and only appear occasionally in the central coastal region at Pachacamac, where they are usually decorated with symbols in Tiahuanaco style (Plate 22).

These simple forms, in particular flat plates, were admirable for painting, which is the main attraction of this art, while those of the Chimu sacrifice colour for much richer sculpture. The Nazca artist used a magnificent range of colours: white, every shade of yellow, the whole range of reds, various browns and deep greys, greyish brown and a greenish-grey. Pure blue does not exist, although some vessels show a tender bluish violet hue and many of them a bluish grey. The pure colour only appears in the weaving. Obviously the Indians had no basic material at their disposal which would have enabled them to paint their vessels blue.[220]

As bold colourists who loved colour for colour's sake they did not fight shy of bold contrasts of hues which often give surprising effects. These ancient artists knew how to combine a reddish orange with reddish violet in a masterly manner; to place grey next to pale yellow, separating it by a simple sepia or black stripe which enhances the outlines of the pattern and gives it its ultimate significance.

Thus the Nazca artist revelled in the whole range of colours while the palate of the early Chimu in general is very sober and confined to the use of brownish and blackish tones. In Nazca, too, as in the north, a light background is the rule, but vessels are also to be found in yellow, red and black grounds. On a red ground the dark outlines of the figures stand out, while on the black the patches of colour seem to be swimming. This gives the pictures a deep ethereal background and a picturesque charm of movement.

The sculptural effects on pottery, on the other hand, which represent the peak of Chimu art in the north are missing in Nazca. Bulges are more suggested than executed and can be appreciated better with the hand than with the eye. Occasionally vases portraying faces confine themselves to adding a nose while all the other parts are either drawn or painted (Plate 45). In this connection it must not be forgotten that even the earliest Nazca art is very unplastic compared with Chimu art. Thus in early times until about A.D. 1000 a great community spirit reigned on the coast.

The people of the north, during its peak, progressed from a linear style to really magnificent sculpture and ceramics while in the south a transformation took place in the trend towards ornamentation and to the style of Tiahuanaco. Not until the later period did both join again under the unifying power of the Inca. This was no new beginning but the end of a culture.

A great Indian kingdom and a spiritual world which had flowered for more than a thousand years had been engulfed in limbo.

47
Left: Magic of the
night. Symbolical
pattern on a
Nazca vase *Below:*
Detail of the
pattern. See
text p. 221

48
Black pottery from the ruined Argentine city, La Ciénega *Above:* Jugs with pipe-smoking apes *Below:* Two aspects of the same vase. Feather staff dancers with cross, trophy head and animal emblems as attributes

NOTES

The names in italics refer to the bibliography. Numbers refer to the volume when in Roman and the page when in Arabic figures. The old chroniclers and works which are available either in manuscript or translation are, for convenience sake, quoted in chapters instead of pages. L=book; C=chapter.

1. For the reader who is unacquainted with the pronunciation of the Spanish-American language the following aids may prove useful:

c before e and i=s; c before a, o and u=k; ch as in church; g before e and i=ch; gu before e and i=g; qu before e and i=k; j as the ch in loch; ll=lye; n=nye; z=s; x=sch since 1815 and ch in the old chronicles. The syllable hu is not unlike the w in word. The Spanish acute accent denotes stress; it is used in the text only for clarity in certain instances and at other times when it is customary in the modern Spanish tongue. The original orthography has been adhered to as far as possible in the bibliography.

2. On the subject of Indian navigation vide: *Cieza*, I, C 85; II, C 39; *Cobo*, IV, 220 et seq.; *Colección*, V, 198; XXVI, 259; *Frézier*, 120; *Garcilaso*, L 3, C 16; *Juan y Santacilia*, LV, C 9, 465 et seq.; *Oviedo*, IV, L 46, C 17; *Pizarro*, I, 138; *Relaciones*, I, 13; *Transactions*, XVII, 456 et seq.; *Zárate*, L 1, C 6.

3. Cabello de *Balboa* arrived in South America in 1566 and remained there until 1602. After serving as a soldier in his youth, he took Holy Orders late in life. At the outset he lived in Bogota and later in Quito, where, in 1576, he started his chronicle under the patronage of Bishop Don Pedro de la Peña, completing it on July 9th, 1586. He also made use of several manuscripts which a monk named Juan de Orozco compiled on the subject of the natives.

4. Vide Bibliography.

5. New York Public Library, MS. L 3, C 17.

6. Faquisllanga is probably an old name for the modern Rio Chancay which was usually referred to in the more ancient literature as the Lambayeque river. Cf. Map p. 182, and Text, p. 195. *Middendorf*, II, 382, suggests Facquisllanga as being the Facalda. But this was also an Indian term for the Chancay.

7. Whereas in Christian art angels were only given wings from the fourth century onwards, the portrayal of winged creatures not unlike the Greek spirits was one of the most ancient Indian designs. Cf. Illus. p. 58.

8. Still today a place name on the upper Rio de la Leche. Cf. Map p. 182, and Text, p. 146.

9. The bases of the whole saga can be found in a form slightly different from the New York version in *Balboa,* C 7, 89 et seq.

10. Antonio de la *Calancha* was born in 1584. The sources as to his birthplace are conflicting. It is immaterial whether he was born in Chuquisaca or in La Plata because this nomer refers solely to the cathedral of his birthplace, Charcas or La Plata, formerly called Chuquisaca and today Sucre. He was doctor of theology at San Marcos University in Lima and later entered the Augustinian Order, in which he held a number of high positions. He travelled the country far and wide eagerly collecting information. In 1619 he was Prior of the convent in Trujillo, where he survived the disastrous earthquake of February 14th. His chronicle was completed in 1633 and he died at Lima in 1654. For further information vide *Biblioteca* 1913, I, 497-491.

11. Twenty-two illustrations will be found in Schmidt, 426-433.

12. Cf. *Acosta*, L 1, C 19.

13. *Calancha*, L 3, C 2.

14. *Las Casas*, 108 et seq.

15. *Román y Zamora*, III, 162 et seq.

16. In addition to the above-quoted edition of *Román y Zamora*, there exists a two-volume work of the same title by Francisco del Canto, Medina del Campo, 1575; also the Republicas de Indias, edited by D. L. d'Orvenipe, in *Libros*, XIV and XV. Madrid, 1897.

17. Bartolomé de *Las Casas's* father had accompanied Columbus on his second voyage and owned a large property on the Island of Española. The son, born in Sevilla in 1474, after studying law at Salamanca, went as planter to his father's property in 1502. At the same time an eager student of theology, he moved to Cuba and entered the Dominican Order in 1521. He proved himself a true humanitarian in word and deed by opposing the enslavement of the Indians through the infamous encomiendas and tried several times to obtain protection laws for the natives from the Spanish Government. Since the Indians were unsuited for the heavy work on the plantations he sponsored the introduction of negroes. By so doing he merely encouraged slavery and founded 'black-birding' in America. He died as Bishop of Chiapas. His most important work was written in 1550. The title was: *'Apologetica historia sumaria cuanto a las cualidades, disposicion, descripcion, cielo u suelo de las tierras y condiciones naturales, policias, republicas, maneras de vivir y costumbres de las gentes destas Indias occidentales y meridionales, chuyo imperio soberano partenace a los Reyes Castilla.'* From this material the *"Historiadores de Indias"* have been published since 1909 in *Nueva*, XIII. The parts of this magnum opus referring to Peru were collected by *Jimenez* under the title *'De las antiguas gentes del Peru.'* From this easily obtainable volume *Las Casas* has been quoted throughout this work.

18. *Castro*, 206-220.

19. *Calancha,* L 3, C 1.

20. *Calancha,* L 3, C 35.

21. *Garcilaso* in a comprehensive account makes Pachacutec defeat Chimo Capac in a coastal campaign. His story in this instance contradicts many of the more reliable elder chroniclers. *Cieza de León,* II, L 2, C 58; *Balboa,* C 6, and *Montesinos,* agree that the Chimu were attacked from the *altiplano* by Tupac Yupanqui and defeated after bitter fighting. The cutting off of the water supplies appears to have played a decisive role in this victory.

22. *Humboldt,* 96.

23. Vicente Fidelio Lopez: *Les races aryennes du Pérou, leur langue, leur religion, leur histoire.* Paris, 1871.

24. Hartogh Heys van Zonteven based his findings on faked Phoenician inscriptions and the wrongly described elephant trunks in the drawings of the painter *Waldeck,* Monuments anciens du Mexique.

25. Schriftenreihe Kulturen der Erde, I, 30. Hagen i. W., 1922.

26. *Wolff,* 254 et seq.

27. *Wolff,* 227 and table of figures 35.

28. De orbe novo non novo. Altdorf, 1685.

29. Large-scale migrations are usually characterised by the transportation of plants from the homeland, even if only by weeds, the seeds of which were carried in the emigrants' belongings. Hundreds of such examples are known but not a single one in the case of the pre-Columbian age.

30. Cf. *Acosta,* L 3, C 12; and *Torquemada,* III, 7.

31. In the year 1347 an Icelandic ship visited Greenland and the present-day Nova Scotia. A glance at the map will suffice to show that here there were no vast distances involved such as exist between Phoenicia or Polynesia and America.

32. *Morley,* Papers of the School of American Archaeology, No. 11.

33. *Spinden,* 1926, VI, No. 4, and 1930, IV, No. 1.

34. *Goodman,* in *American,* New Series, VII.

35. *Martinez,* Diario de Yucatan, February 7th, 1926.

36. *Teeple,* in *Carnegie,* Publication No. 403.

37. *Thompson,* Field Museum of Natural History, Anthrop. Series XVII, No. 1.

38. *Vaillant,* Maya Research, II, No. 2. Cf. the same author's MS. thesis: 'The chronological significance of Maya ceramics,' in the Harvard University library, Cambridge, Mass.

39. Compiled by Ubbelohde-Doering in *Springer,* 612-624.

40. *Gamio, Art,* XII, No. 6, and XIII, Nos. 1-3.

41. In his famous address of April 7th: Proceedings of the Berlin Society for Anthropology, Ethnology and Primeval history, IX, 1877.

42. The typical physique of the first arrivals is perhaps seen in its purest form in those Indian races which developed very little culture. To these

races belong today the nomadic Indian tribes in the Amazon region. They are almost indistinguishable from pure Mongolians.

43. Not to be confused with the so-called Mongolian crease, that unique half-crescent formation of the upper lid by the cornea often to be seen among Indians. The Mongolian mark, on the contrary, is found at the base of the spine and consists of a conglomeration of pigmentation cells in the hide which produce a bluish tinge through the top skin. This mark is 1½-2 inches across, shows itself from five to six months before birth above the coccyx and disappears towards the age of adolescence.

44. Original text with commentary as 'Le Livre de Marco Polo,' by G. Pauthier. 2 vols. Paris, 1865.

45. Cf. *Lehmann* 1920 and his language chart (1915).

46. A short yet all-embracing study of the anthropology of this vast region is to be found only in Wissler's slightly antiquated book.

47. An account by Balboa, p. 82, particularly with reference to the later age, must be considered unreliable. We record it here merely for the sake of interest and completeness. Balboa relates that an Inca learned from some merchants who had arrived at Tumbes in balsas that they had visited the Western Islands, Aua Chumpi (Red Girdle) and Nina Chumpi (Girdle of Fire). As a result of this report he himself then sailed in a balsa to these islands bringing back black-skinned people, much gold, a copper throne and the hide and jaws of a horse. If one accepts, as Lehmann did rather grudgingly in a note to his language chart of 1915, that these islands must have been the Galapagos, we must credit the balsas with great seaworthiness, although a voyage to these islands would not be comparable with the great distances involved in a voyage to Polynesia. The whole nature of the Inca's remarkable trophies suggests booty once owned by whites, and in fact no archaeological remains have been found on the Galapagos Islands. In 1918 Buchwald, more plausibly, in Boletín, I, No. 3, 222, locates these particular islands in the Gulf of Guayaquil and gives their name from the Mochica (the Huancavillca) as the Lobos de tierra and Lobos de afuera Islands. For further information on the subject, vide H. Steffen, ZS. Ges. f. Erdk., 266-268. Berlin, 1920.

48. The original edition printed by Jose de Contreras in Lima is today exceedingly rare; for a reprint vide *Carrera*.

49. Fernando *Montesinos*, Lawyer and Licenciate, twice visited Peru on the orders of the Spanish Government. He settled in Lima from 1639 until 1642 prospecting for metals. In the course of his duties he eagerly collected the songs and legends of the Indians and at the instigation of several of his trusted men wrote his 'Memorias.' The manuscript was formerly preserved in the monastery of San José in Seville but was later sent to Madrid. From a copy, a French translation by H. Ternaux-Compans appeared in 1840. The new Spanish edition which supersedes this work figures in the bibliography. A good English translation by Means was published by the Hakluyt Society in London in 1920. Details of the Indian script in C 7, C 14 and C 15.

50. *Montesinos* for example records an unbroken sequence of 101 Peruvian rulers since the Deluge, telling of bloody wars and pestilence, of giants given over to bestial lusts, in short the whole legendary armoury of a people, in which poetry and legend can hardly be distinguished from each other.

51. Don Juan de Zumarraga, the first Archbishop of Mexico, collected all the manuscripts on which he could lay his hands, piled them into a mountainous heap on the main square of Tlatelolco and burned them. Diego de Landa in his 'Relación de last Cosas de Yucatan' describes the truly hideous *auto-da-fé* staged by himself in 1561, as does Diego Durán in his 'Historia de las Indias de Nueva Espana,' written in 1588.

52. *Sahagun:* 'C'etait fixe dans les ecrits enluminés qui furent brûles au temps du roi mexicain Itzcouatl. Car pendant son règne, les princes, mexicains tinrent un conseil, dans lequel ils dirent: il n'est pas necessaire que tout ce peuple, nos sujets et nos vassaux, connaissent les ecrits enluminés; ces derniers en perdraient leur dignité, et le pays deviendrait complètement confus.'

53. Cf. Hiram *Bingham*, C 16; and Millicent Todd Bingham's article on Peru in the Encyclopedia Britannica, 15th edition, 1929.

54. *Locke:* vide his article in *American*, XIV, 325-332.

55. The two books of *Nordenskiöld*, 1925. The most important facts from Locke and Nordenskiöld are amalgamated in *Schmidt,* 95-98.

56.—The piura (Map p. 138) is a good example of the earlier more abundant irrigation. It stretches far enough into the uplands where the rainfall is constant to have water in its upper reaches. Today once more, as it was before 1740, it is a permanent river on its lower reaches. Cf. *Alcedo,* IV, and *Raimondi,* Peru, 1, 356 et seq.

57. The word for maize is in most Indian languages completely different even in its roots; in Mochica it is called seponi, in Quecha sara, in Chibcha aba, in Colla (Aymara) tonco and in Araucanian wa, to quote merely the nearest neighbours of the Chimu. In most European languages it is known under the Caribbean name maize.

58. Cf. *Leicht*, the Canines, 286.

59. So far very few pipes have been found along the whole Peruvian coast. A few examples from Pachacama consist of 10-15 inch wooden tubes decorated with figures and, as opposed to those from the North-west Argentine in Plate 48 are perfectly straight (cf. *Schmidt*, Plate 421) like those which have come to light in the Ica Valley and in Ecuador. Many finds in Pachacamac, as we have mentioned in the Text (p. 198), could easily have been imported by pilgrims.

60. In the description of the 'Repartimiento de los Rucanas Antamarcas,' *Relaciones*, 1, 211.

61. *Montesinos*, 118.

62. Cf. *Montell*, 31.

63. Since it is usually a question of countless garments solely for burial purposes one must not classify them out of hand as everyday garb. The

mummies were very richly attired in a number of garments, including feast-day clothes and additional items specially made for their funeral.

64. Cf. the whole section in *Montell*, 37-40; also his article 'Le vrai poncho, son origine postcolombienne,' in *Journal*, XVII, 173-183.

65. The supposition put forward by *Danzel*, I, 51, that the Mexican hairless dogs were sacrificed because their hair had been singed by lightning is too far-fetched an explanation and ridiculous once we recognise the lunar nature of the dog and take into account that the lightning in this connection is no more than the herald of the rain from which it originated.

66. For details of the Temple of the Sea and the Moon at Huamachuco, north of Chan-Chan, see *Arriaga*, 10 et seq.; *Garcilaso*, IV, 32-35, for the Pachacamac region; and *Lehmann*, Sprachen, I, 51, for a similar role of the canines among the Chibcha; and finally *Cieza*, I, C 50.

67. Pedro *Cieza de León* came to Peru in 1534 as a fifteen-year-old boy and took part in La Gasca's march on Cuzco. After many voyages he returned in 1550 to Lima where he wrote the first part of his chronicle. The second part did not appear until 1560. He was a keen observer and studied the Indians so conscientiously that his chronicle is of the utmost value, although he takes much on trust and is susceptible to all manner of superstition. While the first part was printed in Seville in 1553, in Antwerp two years later and soon translated into English and Italian, the second part did not appear until 1875. This edition is very rare today and a more available version is noted in the bibliography.

68. In Peru the bird in question is the giant Andean vulture, the condor, which takes its name from the Indian word Cuntur.

69. *Calancha*, L 2, C 19.

70. Since in the chronicles, which were all written after the introduction of sun worship by the Inca, Conn can be associated with all manner of different myths, he can also be given solar attributes, cf. *Lehmann*, 1924, 17, we can safely rest here on his brief mention. The most important passages: *Velasco*, L 2, f 2, and *Zárate*, L 1, C 10.

71. In *Oviedo*, L 46, C 17, Pedro Corzo, who sailed as pilot for four years along the Peruvian coast, reports that a temple with images in wood and stone stood there on the heights covering an area of some 500 leguas. According to Corzo the principal deity was called Guatan, a word that also signifies the whirlwind. This seems to have an analogy with Wotan in Nordic mythology who was originally a storm god.

72. For the writing of the Indian "w" sound in Guatan cf. Text, p. 42.

73. The Mochica word Si corresponds with the ancient Babylonian designation Sin for a moon deity.

74. Further information about the Huacas will be found in great detail in *Arriaga*, 11 et seq., and in the works of the Dominican monk Reginaldo *Lizárraga*, XV, 485 et seq., who lived in Peru from 1540-1610 and travelled extensively for the purposes of study between 1555 and 1599. Further the Grammar of *Torres Rubio* and the work of *Gonzalez Holguin*

both contain an article on the Huacas. Of the modern authors *Jijón y Caamano* is recommended, C 1.

75. Also Agnual in the Tzental dialect of the Maya. In the case of the rulers and princes their hieroglyphs began with the first letter of the alphabet.

76. *Jijón y Caamano*, 402, derives Alec Pong from the Mochica aiplen = creator, and pong = stone.

77. *Carcilaso de la Vega*, born in 1539 in Cuzco. The son of a Spanish captain, he called himself El Inca because he was descended on his mother's side from the Inca Ayllus. His parents died young and at the age of twenty the boy went to Spain and took part in the war against the Moors. At the age of sixty he retired and began to write his commentaries, which on account of his origin and youth rank as the best historical source of Inca history. In actual fact they are full of errors and distortions. While in Spain Garcilaso had not only largely forgotten his mother tongue but took the information gleaned from his boyhood friends in Peru far too much for granted. Proud of his Inca origin he was always inclined to report only good of them and to despise other nations. A critical analysis of his work will be found in *Riva Aguero,* 53 et seq. and 204 et seq.

78. *Garcilaso*, L 6, C 10.

79. On the Huacas vide also *Cieza*, I, C 84, and II, C 49.

80. Pablo José de *Arriaga* was born in 1564 at Biscaya, studied in Madrid and went to America in 1579, at the age, therefore, of fifteen. In 1588 he was appointed Rector of the San Martin Seminary and in 1612 of the Colegio de Arequipa. On his return from Spain in 1601, after carrying out various journeys at the request of his Order, he was appointed head of the Jesuit Order in Peru and given the task of suppressing the Indians' idolatry. He began to wage a ruthless and pitiless religious war of extermination until his sudden death in 1634 brought to an end this mad rage. Of his various accounts the work mentioned in the bibliography is far the most important.

81. *Arriaga*, 12 ff.

82. Cf. also Text, p. 92, and Note 194.

83. *Las Casas*, 124 f.

84. *Villagomez*, 62.

85. Anello *Oliva* was born in Naples in 1572 and came to Peru in 1597 where as a member of the Jesuit Order he plunged eagerly into the task of converting the Indians. His activities were mostly in the large Jesuit centre, Juli, where he wrote a history of the activities of his Order which he completed in 1631. He died in 1642. The work was first printed in 1895 in Lima under the title Historia del Peru y varones insignes en Santidad de la compañia de Jesus. The parts referring to the social conditions in Peru were earlier translated from the manuscript into French and figure in the bibliography as a valuable source for the history of the Peruvian Indians.

86. *Oliva*, 23.

87. *Garcilaso*, L 2, C 11.

88. The Quechua particle -ntin must not be confused with inti, the sun. The word is composed of tahua, four, the numerical particle -ntin and the substantive suyu, meaning region or province.

89. Accurate statistics of the various regions will be found in *Relaciones*, I, 110 and 181; II, 52 et seq. and 62 et seq.

90. Bernabé *Cobo* was born in 1582 and came to Peru in 1599 where he entered the Jesuit Order. After studying the governmental organisation of the Indians he concentrated above all on the flora and fauna of the country. His work quoted in the bibliography serves as an excellent complement to the older reports.

91. *Cobo*, III, 235.

92. *Las Casas,* 153.

93. *Coleccion*, VII, 463.

94. *Santo Thomas*, 56.

95. Ordonanzas del Peru, I, L 2, 123 et seq.

96. Above all in the larger towns which afforded sufficient security. Cf. Text, p. 163.

97. *Santo Thomas* already knew that the kinship terminology of the Indians was very complicated.

98. This will explain the fact when, for example, Cieza de León reports that Atahualpa had thirty of Huascar's brothers killed, whereas the latter had only five brothers of the same flesh and blood.

99. Cf. *Cunow* and *Morgan*.

100. *Cieza*, I, C 36, C 40, C 44.

101. *Zárate*, L 1, C 8. The chronicler as Contador de Mercedes, a customs official, arrived in Peru in 1543 with the first Viceroy, Blasco Nuñez Vela. His work ends with the return of President Gasca about 1551.

102. *Bertonio*, II.

103. *Garcilaso*, L 1, C 3.

104. According to the 1851 Bosque estadistico de Bolivia, 272, there were in 1846 still only 5,033 haciendas, freehold properties, while the remaining agricultural land was the communal property of the Indians.

105. *Polo de Ondegardo* arrived in Peru in 1547 and later became Corregidor, Administrator and Judge of the Cuzco region. In order basically to study the ancient legal and economical conditions he examined all the earlier laws and governmental regulations, furnishing the Viceroy with full and valuable reports. The most important of these are quoted in the bibliography.

106. The Licenciate, Fernando de *Santillán*, after studying law and theology in Spain entered the Jesuit Order and arrived in Peru in 1568 where he was appointed by the Viceroy Judge and President of the Audiencia de Lima, the supreme judicial court in the land. His exalted position gave him the opportunity to become acquainted with the Indian civil code. As opposed to many other reporters, he checked critically all his information and compared it with other reports. His work quoted in

the bibliography refers to the original manuscript in the Escorial Library under the index No. L.j.5. folios 307-345.

107.   In *Relaciones*, I, 102.

108.   In *Markham*, Report 157.

109.   *Santillán*, 47.

110.   Cf. *Baudin*, Revue des Etudes Historiques, J. 93, 107-114.

111.   *Castro*, 215.

112.   *Garcilaso*, L 5, C 9.

113.   *Colección*, V, 280 et seq.; XXI, 160 et seq.; also Ordonanzas del Peru, 128.

114.   *Acosta*, L 4, C 42.

115.   Albrecht Dürer's posthumous writings, 47 f., edited Ernst Heidrich, Berlin, 1908.

116.   Vide *Kuhn*, 5.

117.   Cf. *Steinmann*, 3128 and 3123.

118.   According to the description in *Prescott*, Conquest of Mexico, I, C 3.

119.   Cf. *Leicht*, Tiahuanaco, 46 ff. and Text, p. 114.

120.   Cf. Chr. Fr. Weiser, Shaftesbury, 1916, 252 et seq.

121.   Treatise on the power of criticism.

122.   Cf. Edward Chiera. They wrote on Clay, University Press, Chicago, 1938.

123.   *Leicht*, Early Chimu, 38 f.

124.   Tripods are frequently found in Ancient Central American art and have been constantly illustrated, e.g. *Springer*, 604 et seq.

125.   *Doering*, I, 4 et seq.

126.   The relative passages in Codex Telleriano-Remensis, Codex Ramirez, Acosta, Duran, Motolinia, Mendieta, Las Casas, Gomara, Herrera, Gage, Torquemada, Bernal Diaz, Sahagun, Clavigero, Ixtlilxochitl, Juan Diaz, Landa, Fuentes y Guzman, Martyr. Oviedo and Bobadilla, and other sources admirably collated by *Pollock*, 5 et seq.

127.   Vide E. P. Dieseldorff in Kunst und Religion der Mayavölker, III, Hamburg, 1933, and references to Peru in his comment on Plate 48, No. 126, complemented by a stepped pattern of a vessel attributed to the Chimu.

128.   *Schmidt*, 78 et seq.

129.   *Raoul d'Harcourt*, 163 et seq., provides further reading matter for this specialised field. For later publications cf. Chronology, by A. C. Wiebel, in *Bulletin*, XIX, No. 4, 1940.

130.   Cf. M. Valette, Note sur la teinture de tissus précolombienes du Bas-Pérou, *Journal*, X, 43 ff.

131.   Cf. Charles W. Mead, Technique of some South American Featherwork, in *Anthropological*, I Pt. 1.

132.   *Nordenskiöld*, 1921, 71-108.

133.   *American*, II, 344 et seq.; *Anthropological*, II Pt. 2; *Bureau*, No. 45 and No. 53. Also *Burton, Gilman, Mead, R.* and *M. d'Harcourt*.

H*

134. Cf. *Extracto*, No. 5. Principals caracteristicas de los rios de la costa.
135. *Kroeber*, in *American*, New Series, XXVIII, No. 2, 331-351; XXIX, No. 4, 625-653; and in *International*, XXIII.
136. *Means*, New Clews, The New York Times Magazine, May 20th, 1934.
137. *Olson*, in Natural History, XXXI, No. 1.
138. *Tello*, Introduccion (English translation in Inter-American, New York, April 1922); Antigo Peru; Andean civilisation, *International*, XXIII.
139. In Maya Research, I, No. 1.
140. *Uhle*, Los principios, in *Boletin*, IV, No. 12.
141. *Leicht*, Tiahuanaco, 69 et seq.
142. *Douglas*, in *National*. Contributed technical papers, Pueblo Bonito series, No. 1.
143. *Leicht*, Tiahuanaco, 57 f.
144. *Joyce*, 113.
145. Cf. Juan de Estrada Ravago's account in Doc. de Costa Rica, III, 3; and Ynigo de Aranca, V, 100, op. cit.; also Alonso Ponce, in Relacion breve y verdadera de algunas cosas de las muchas . . . Madrid, 1873, II, 408.
146. *Las Casas*, 74.
147. *Lothrop*, Pottery, II, 406; Hdrlicka, in *Smithsonian*, LVI, No. 16, 10 f.
148. *Zárate*, L 1, C 1.
149. *Herrera*, Decada III, L 10, C 5.
150. *Cieza*, I, C 4.
151. *Zárate*, L 1, C 2.
152. *Garcilaso*, L 1, C 2; and *Herrera*, III, L 10, C 5.
153. In Relación General de las Poblaciones españolas del Peru, I, 9 et seq.
154. Richard Spruce, who studied Sec in 1863, compiled a vocabulary from which Otto von Buchwald in 1918 published 38 words in *Boletín*, I, No. 3, 231 et seq.
155. Cf. *Kroeber* in *University*, XXI, 216 et seq.
156. It is a question here mainly of a 30 cm. high, not particularly unusual triple vase (*Schmidt*, 261) which was found near Morropón. *Means* in an article written in 1919 at first classified it as Tiahuanaco style but later in 1931, 145, in agreement with Tello either as a specimen of Chavín or some similar as yet unclassified culture. *Jijón* in 1927, I, 210, suggested Ecuadorian origin, while *Uhle* in 1920, 166, insisted that on account of its typical handle form this vessel must be a coastal product.
157. Cf. *Pittard*, 21 f.
158. Cf. *Kroeber*, Uhle Pottery, 216 ff.; *Lehmann*, 1924, 22, and Note 45.
159. *Calancha*, L 3, C 1, C 2.
160. *Ubbelohde*, 50-56.
161. Cf. Debenedetti, Plates IX and IXV (*Ars*, II).
162. Presumably this is the same Huaca which *Calancha*, L 3, C 35,

calls La Tasca. Vide Text, p. 27. Further reports on the ruins in *Geographical*, Review, XVII, 36-61.

163. *Seler*, Reise, 223, and *Uhle* in *Journal*, 1913, 109.

164. *Garcilaso*, L 6, C 30.

165. Cf. *Raimondi*, Ancachs.

166. Two of them via Quillo and Yautam in the Casma Valley, one between Conococha and Cajacay, and another between Aija and Recuay— all today in the building of the well-advanced autobahns which at 12,000 feet lead to the last true footpath between Aija and Huarás.

167. In particular those made by Tello in 1919. Cf. *Tello* Viracocha, 298-309.

168. *Lehmann*, 1924, 35, 40, Note 70.

169. For further details *Enock*, C 7; *Gonzalez de la Rosa*; *Markham*; Comparison; Jose *Polo*; also *Raimondi*, Ancachs, 214 f.; Peru, I. 153 f.

170. In actual fact the Aymarás were Quechua-speaking Indians deported by the Inca into Colla country. The first missionaries made no distinction between them and the original Colla-speaking population, and the error which was perpetrated for the first time in 1583 has been perpetuated until the present day.

171. Cf. *Ruppert, Pollock*; and also *Carnegie*, Year Book No. 26, 249 et seq.

172. *Garcilaso*, L 6, C 33.

173. *Cieza*, I, 70.

174. *Estete*. Also in *Xerez*, Conquista del Peru, in Historiadores primitivos de Indias, L 2, 339.

175. *Cieza*, I, C 58.

176. *Cieza*, I, C 72; II, C 58, C 65; *Cobo*, L 13, C 17; *Garcilaso*, L 6, C 30, C 31; *Pizarro*, 209 f.

177. *Calancha*, L 2, C 19.

178. *Ministerio*, El Ferrocarril Central.

179. *Ministerio*, La Carretera Central.

180. *Garcilaso*, L 4, C 30.

181. *Oviedo*, L 46, C 17.

182. *Uhle*, Pachacamac, and *Baessler*, IV.

183. *Baessler*, IV, Plate 155.

184. Cf. *Nordenskiöld, Ars*, I, 1930.

185. Cf. *Kroeber*, in *University*, XXI.

186. In *Oviedo*, I.

187. *Leicht*, Early Chimu, 22.

188. Tonal-amatl corresponds numerically with the synodic orbital time of Venus of 584 days since eight solar years correspond with 5 orbits of Venus.

189. Cf. *Danzel*, I, 15 ff.; 35 ff.

190. Nimrod, according to Moses, Book I, a powerful ruler and hunter, and according to Josephus the builder of the tower of Babel, is also strangely enough the original name of the hunter constellation, the Greek

Orion. The largest star in this constellation, known today by its Arabic name Betelgueuse, was called by the Sumerians Kak-sidi, the hunting star, mythologically analogous with Nimrod. If, as is conceivable, the Zodiac among the ancients was merely the calendar of sacrifices projected into the sky, it is quite conceivable that we should, therefore, find not only the sacrificial beasts portrayed but that this celestial calendar should also include pictures of the priests in their function as hunters, custodians and finally as slayers of the victims.

191. Symposiaca, VIII, 730.

192. *Calancha*, L 3, C 1, C 2; *Cieza*, I, C 73.

193. Similarly the Buddhists of Nepal worshipped Avalokiteshvara under the name Matsyendranatha as 'Lord of the Fishes.'

194. The old chroniclers write the name in many forms—Huiracocha, Viracochac, Uiracochay and Uiracochan. Cocha in the Indian language does not only mean the sea but also a little lake or a fishpond; the word is often used to denote water in general. According to *Montesinos*, C 1, the god Viracocha also bore the nickname Illa Ticsi, which the chronicler translated into Spanish as the 'shining, gleaming base or fundament of things.' Although Montesinos was very often unfortunate as a translator it would be wrong to find fault with him in this case but recognise Ticsi as fundament, and Illa as 'old' in the ordinary sense of the word. According to my exposé (pp. 76 and 93) it is clear that only very seldom in the Indian language does the word 'old' refer to ancestral worship.

195. In northern Peru this meaning is conclusive. In the region round Lake Titicaca where the word Viracocha originated, Vira or huira has quite a different meaning. Cf. *Bertonio*, II, 88.

196. Cristóbal de *Molina*, of Cuzco, who was born about 1535 and was still alive after 1590, was an expert in Indian languages. As a result of his activities as spiritual guide in the native hospital of Cuzco he was able to acquire a deep insight into Peruvian daily life. His first work, the Relación de la conquista y población del Peru, was considered lost until a copy was recently discovered in Peru and published in the first volume of the Colección de libros referentes a la historia del Peru, Lima, 1916. His second most important work figures in our Bibliography.

197. Juan de *Betánzos* was born in Spain in 1510 and came with Hernando Pizarro, Francisco's brother, to Peru, where he entered the Viceroy's service. Having married a daughter of a Quito prince he acquired a knowledge of the speech and customs of the Indians, serving on many occasions as a Government intermediary and being finally commissioned by the Viceroy Antonio de Mendoza to write an all-embracing work which he completed in 1551 in Cuzco, where he lived from 1540 to 1576. Due to the premature death of his patron this valuable manuscript remained for a long time unprinted. A copy finally found its way to the Escorial Library where the Suma y Narración de los Incas, que los Indios llamaron Cappac-Cune, is preserved under the index No. L 15, and was used for the 1880 edition referred to in the Bibliography.

198. *Molina*, 6, and *Betanzos*, 7, 64, 114.
199. *Garcilaso*, L 5, C 16.
200. *Santillán*, 32.
201. *Bertonio*, II, 188.
202. *Santo Thomas*, 38.
203. *Garcilaso*, L 6, C 29.
204. *Cieza*, I, C 73.
205. Cf. *Ward*, Fig. 686 ff., and *Dolger*, I, 119.
206. Cf. *Harth-Terre*.
207. For an account of these races, vide *Joyce*, 152, and *Hrdlicka*, 7 f.; also the Chroniclers *Cieza*, I, C 73; *Garcilaso*, L 6, C 16, and *Sarmiento*, C 63.
208. Pedro *Sarmiento de Gamboa* led a rich and adventurous life. Born in 1532 he took part in the Spanish war at the age of eighteen and as a real soldier of fortune arrived from Mexico in Peru where he busied himself with geography, astronomy and magic. Severely punished in 1564 by the Archbishop of Lima and expelled from the country, he set out on a voyage of discovery in the Pacific and after a host of wild pranks was pardoned by the Viceroy Francisco de Toledo and entrusted with the compilation of a history of the Inca and various geographical works. His Historia general IIamada Indica was presumed to have been lost until it was discovered in 1905 by Pietschmann in the Göttingen University library and published in the original Spanish text with a long German introduction.
209. *Cieza*, I, C 74, C 75; II, C 59; *Garcilaso*, L 6, C 17, C 18; cf. also *Cheesman*, 240 ff., and *Joyce*, 187.
210. *Castro*, 206 f.
211. *Uhle*, Explorations, 65.
212. *Cieza*, I, C 74; *Garcilaso*, L 6, C 17; cf. also *Uhle*, Explorations, 67 ff.
213. *University*, XXI.
214. *Debenedetti*, with many good illustrations, *Ars*, II.
215. Cf. Paul *Rivet*, Revue d'Anthropologie, XVIII and XIX.
216. *Seler*, Die buntbemalten Gefässe von Nasca, in Ges. Abh. IV, 183.
217. *Lehmann*, 1924, 33.
218. *Lehmann*, 1924, 32.
219. Cf. *Leicht*, Illustrations of Canines, 299.
220. Ausführliche Farbenbeschreibungen *Seler*, Ges. Abh., IV, 172.

BIBLIOGRAPHY

The bold type numbers refer to the notes, pp. 225–237.

Acosta, José de: Historia natural y moral de las Indias. (Juan de Leon) Seville, 1590.

Alcedo, Antonio de: Diccionario geográfico-histórico de las Indias Occidentales, ó America. 5 vols. Madrid, 1786-1789.

American = American Anthropologist. Washington.

Anthropological = Anthropological Papers of the American Museum of Natural History. New York.

Arriaga **80**, *Pablo José de:* Extirpación de la idolatría del Píru. (Geronymo de Contreras) Lima, 1621.

Ars = Ars Americana. Paris.

Art = Art and Archaeology. Washington.

Baessler, Arthur: Altperuanische Kunst. 4 vols. Berlin, 1902-1903.

Balboa **3**, *Miguel Cabello de:* Histoire du Pérou. Ed. Ternaux-Compans: Voyages de l'Amérique, XV. (Arthus Bertrand) Paris, 1840.

Baudin, Louis: La formation de l'élite et l'enseignement de l'histoire dans l'Empire des Incas. Paris, 1927.

Bertonio, Ludovico: Vocabulario de la Lengua Aymará (1612). Ed. Julius Platzmann. 2 vols. Leipzig, 1879.

Betánzos **197**, *Juan de:* Suma y narración de los Incas . . . Ed. *Jiménez:* Biblioteca Hispano-Ultramarina. (Manuel G. Hernandez) Madrid, 1880.

Biblioteca = Biblioteca Ibero-Americana (de la Orden de San Agustín, Ensayo de una). Ed. P. Gregorio de Santiago Vela. Madrid, 1913-1931.

Bingham, Hiram: Inca Land. Boston, 1922.

Boletín = Boletín de la Sociedad Ecuatoriana de Estudios Históricos Americanos. Quito.

Bulletin = Bulletin of the Detroit Institute of Arts. Detroit.

Bureau = Bureau of American Ethnology. Washington.

Burton, Frederick R.: American Primitive Music . . . New York, 1909.

Calancha **10**, *Antonio de la:* Crónica moralizada del orden de San Agustín en el Peru, con sucesos egenplares en esta monarquia. (Pedro Lacavallería) Barcelona, 1638.

Carnegie = Carnegie Institution of Washington, Washington.

Carrera, Fernando de la: Arte de la lengua yunga de los valles del obispado de Truxillo del Peru (1644). Ed. Manuel González de la Rosa. Lima, 1880.

Castro, Cristóbal de and *Ortega Moréjón, Diego de:* Relación y declaración del modo que este valle de Chincha y sus comarcanos se gobernaban antes que hobiese ingas y después que los hobo hasta que los cristianos entraron en esta tierra. *Colección,* L. 206-220. Madrid, 1867.

Catherwood, Frederick: Views of Ancient Monuments in Central America, Chiapas and Yucatan. London, 1844.

Cheesman Salinas, Francisco: El distrito de Lunahuaná. Boletín de la Sociedad Geográfica de Lima, XXV, 240 ff. Lima, 1909.

Cieza de León 67, Pedro de: I. Parte primera de la Crónica del Peru. (Martin de Montesdoca) Seville, 1553. II. Segunda Parte de la Crónica del Peru. Ed. Jiménez: Biblioteca Hispano-Ultramarina. Madrid, 1880.

Clavigero, Francesco Saverio: Storia antica del Messico. 4 vols. (G. Biasini) Cesena, 1780-1781.

Cobo 90, Bernabé: Historia del Nuevo Mundo. Ed. Jiménez. 4 vols. (Sociedad de Bibliófilos Andaluces) Seville, 1890-1893.

Colección = Colección de Documentos inéditos para la historia de España. Archivo de Indias. Madrid.

Cunow, Heinrich: El sistema de parentesco peruano y las comunidades gentilicias de los Incas. Paris, 1930.

Danzel, Theodor Wilhelm: Mexico. 2 vols. Hagen und Darmstadt, 1923.

Debenedetti, Salvador: L'Ancienne civilisation des Barreales du Nord-Ouest Argentin, la Ciénega et la Aguada. Paris, 1931.

Dölger, Franz Jos.: Ichthys. 5 vols. Münster u. a. O., 1910-1927.

Doering, Heinrich U.: Altperuanische Gefässmalereien. Sonderdruck aus Marburger Jahrbuch für Kunstwissenschaft, II. 2 Teile. Marburg, 1926.

Douglass, Andrew E.: Dating Pueblo Bonito and other ruins of the Southwest. Washington, 1935.

Eisler, Robert: Orpheus—The Fisher. Comparative Studies in Orphic and Early Christian Cult Symbolism. London, 1921.

Enoch, C. Reginald: Peru. London, 1910.

Estete, Miguel de: La relación del viaje que hizo el señor Hernando Pizarro . . . desde el pueblo de Caxamalca a Parcama y de alli a Xauxa. (Bartolomé Perez) Seville, 1534.

Extracto = Extracto Estadístico del Peru, Preparado por la Dirección Nacional de Estadística. Ministerio de Hacienda y Comercio. Lima.

Falcón, Francisco: Relación sobre el gobierno de los Incas. Ed. Horacio H. Urteaga and Carlos A. Romero. Lima, 1918.

Frézier, Amédée François: A Voyage to the South Sea, and along the Coasts of Chili and Peru. (John Bowyer) London, 1717.

Gamio, Manuel: Cultural evolution in Guatemala and its geographic and historic handicaps. Washington, 1926-1927.

Garcilaso de la Vega 77, El Inca: Primera Parte de los Commentarios Reales, que tratan del origin de los Yncas, Reyes que fueron del Peru. (Pedro Crasbeeck) Lisbon, 1609.

Geographical = American Geographical Society. New York.

Gilman, Benjamin Ives: Hopi Songs. Boston, 1908.

González de la Rosa, Manuel: Les deux Tiahuanaco, leurs problèmes

González de la Rosa, Manuel
—continued
et leur solution. *International,*
XVI, 405-428. Vienna, 1910.
González Holguín, Diego: Vocabulario
de la lengua general de todo el
Perú llamada lengua Quichua . . .
2 vols. (Francisco del Canto)
Lima, 1607.

Harcourt, Raoul d': Les Textiles
anciens du Pérou et leurs
techniques. Paris, 1934.
Harcourt, Raoul and Marie d': La
musique des Incas et ses sur-
vivances. 2 vols. Paris, 1925.
Harth-Terré, Emilio: La fortaleza de
Chuquimancu. Revista arque-
ológica del Museo Larco-Herrera,
No. 2. Lima, 1923.
Herrera, Antonio de: Historia general
de los hechos de los Castellanos
en las islas i tierrafirme del mar
oceano. In Decadas. Madrid,
1726-1730.
Hrdlicka, Ales: Anthropological
Work in Peru in 1913. *Smithsonian,*
LXI, No. 18. Washington, 1914.
Humboldt, Alexander von: Vue des
Cordillères et Monuments des
Peuples Indigènes de l'Amerique.
Paris, 1810.

International = International Con-
gress of Americanists. New York,
unless indicated to the contrary.

Jijón y Caamaño, Jacinto: La religión
del Imperio de los Incas. Quito,
1919.
——Puruhá: contribución al conoci-
miento de los aborigenes de la
provincia del Chimborazo, en la
república del Ecuador. 2 vols.
Quito, 1927.
Jiménez = Don Marcos Jiménez de
la Espada.

Journal = Journal de la Société des
Américanistes de Paris. Paris.
Joyce, Thomas Athol: South American
Archaeology. London and New
York, 1912.
*Juan y Santacilia, Jorge and Ulloa,
Antonio de:* Relación histórica del
viaje a la América meridional
hecho de orden de S. Mag. para
medir algunos grados de
meridiano terrestre. 4 vols.
Madrid, 1748.

Kingsborough, Lord: Antiquities of
Mexico. 9 vols. London,1831-1848.
Koppers, Wilhelm: Der Hund in der
Mythologie der zirkumpazifischen
Völker. Sonderdruck, Wiener
Beiträge zur Kulturgeschichte
und Linguistik. Vienna, 1930.
Kroeber, A. L.: The Uhle Pottery
Collections from Moche.
University, XXI, 191-234.
Berkeley, 1925.
——Culture stratifications in Peru.
American, n.s. XXVIII, No. 2,
331-351. Menasha, 1926.
——Coast and highland in pre-
historic Peru. *American,* n.s.
XXIX, No. 4, 625-653. Menasha,
1927.
——Cultural relations between
North and South America. *Inter-
national,* XXIII. New York, 1930.
Kühn, Herbert: Die Kunst der
Primitiven. Munich, 1923.

Las Casas 17, *Bartolomé de:* De las
antiguas gentes del Perú. *Libros,*
XXI. Madrid, 1892.
Lehmann, Walter: Die Sprachen
Zentral-Amerikas. 2 vols. Berlin,
1920.
*Lehmann, Walter and Doering, Hein-
rich:* Kunstgeschichte des Alten
Peru. Berlin, 1924.

Leicht, Hermann: Tiahuanaco and the Ancient Civilizations of the Peruvian Coast. Paris, 1938.
——Early Chimu and Early Nazca. Some Problems of Peruvian Chronology. Paris, 1939.
——Die Caniden in der Mythologie und Kunst der altamerikanischen Kulturvölker. Zs. Schweiz. Kynolog. Ges., LIX, No. 18. Zürich, 1943.
Leicht, Hermann: Abbildungen von Caniden bei den Indianern in Nord- und Sudamerika. Zs. Schweiz. Kynolog. Ges., LIX, No. 19. Zürich, 1943.
Libros = Colección de Libros Españoles raros o curiosos. Madrid.
Lizárraga **74**, *Reginaldo de:* La descripción y población de las Indias. Ed. Don Manuel Serrano y Sanz: *Nueva,* XV, 485-660. Madrid, 1909.
Locke, L. Leland: The ancient Quipu or Peruvian Knot-Record. New York, 1923.
Lothrop, Samuel Kirkland: Pottery of Costa Rica and Nicaragua. 2 vols. New York, 1926.

Markham, Clements R.: Report by Polo de Ondegardo. London, 1873.
——A Comparison of the Ancient Peruvian Carvings and the Stones of Tiahuanaco and Chavín. *International,* XVI, 389-395. Vienna, 1910.
Martínez Hernandez, Juan: Paralelismo entre los calendarios Maya y Azteca. Merída, 1926.
Mead, Charles, W.: The Musical Instruments of the Incas. New York, 1903.

Means, Philip Ainsworth: Una nota sobre la prehistoria peruana. Lima, 1919.
——Ancient Civilizations of the Andes. New York, 1931.
——New Clews to early American culture. New York, 1934.
Middendorf, E. W.: Peru. Beobachtungen und Studien über das Land und seine Bewohner. 3 vols. Berlin, 1893-1895.
Ministerio = Ministerio de Relaciones Exteriores del Perú, Oficina de Propaganda, Publicaciones y Cultura. Lima.
Molina **196**, *Cristóbal de:* Relación de las fabulas y Ritos de los Ingas. Santiago, 1915.
Montell, Gösta: Dress and Ornaments in Ancient Peru. Gothenburg and London, 1929.
Montesinos **49**, *Fernando:* Memorias antiguas historiales y politicas del Perú. Ed. *Jiménez: Libros,* XVI. Madrid, 1882.
Morgan, Lewis Henry: Systems of Consanguinity and Affinity of the Human Family. Washington, 1869.
Morley, Sylvanus Griswold: The correlation of Maya and Christian chronology. Papers of the School of American Archaeology, No. 11. Archaeological Institute of America, 1910.
Museum = Museum of the American Indian, New York.

National = National Geographic Society. Washington.
Nordenskiöld, Erland: The Copper and Bronze Ages in South America. Gothenburg, 1921.
——The Secret of the Peruvian Quipus. Gothenburg, 1925.
——Calculations with Years and

Nordenskiöld, Erland—continued
Months in the Peruvian Quipus.
Gothenburg, 1925.
——L'Archéologie du Bassin de
l'Amazone. Paris, 1930.
Nueva = Nueva Biblioteca de
Autores Españoles. Madrid.

Oliva **85**, *Juan Anello:* Histoire du
Pérou. Ed. H. Ternaux-Compans.
Paris, 1857.
Olson, R. L.: Old empires of the
Andes. American Museum of
Natural History. New York, 1931.
Ortega Moréjón, Diego de: vide
Castro.
*Oviedo y Valdés, Gonzalo Fernandez
de:* Historia general y natural
de las Indias, islas y tierrafirme
del mar oceano. 4 vols. Madrid,
1851-1855.

Pittard, Eugène and *Lobsiger-Dellen-
bach, M.:* L'empire des Incas,
les collections précolombiennes.
Musée d'Ethnographie. Geneva,
1943.
Pizarro, Pedro: Relation of the
Discovery and Conquest of the
Kingdoms of Peru. Translated
and edited by P. A. Means. 2
vols. New York, 1921.
Pollock, H. E. D.: Round Structures
of Aboriginal Middle America.
Carnegie, Publication No. 471.
Washington, 1936.
Polo de Ondegardo **105**, *Juan:* vide
Markham.
Polo, José Toribio: La Piedra de
Chavín. Boletín de la Sociedad
Geográfica de Lima, IX, 191-231,
262-290. Lima, 1899.
Prescott, William Hickling: History of
the conquest of Mexico. 3 vols.
Boston, 1843.

——History of the conquest of
Peru. 3 vols. Boston, 1847.

Raimondi, Antonio: El departamento
de Ancachs. Lima, 1873.
——El Perú. 6 vols. Lima, 1874-1913.
Reiss, Wilhelm and *Stübel, Alphons:*
Das Totenfeld von Ancon. 3 vols.
Berlin, 1880-1887.
Relaciones = Relaciones geográficas
de Indias. Madrid.
Riva Aguero, José de la: La Historia
en el Perú. Lima, 1910.
Rivero, Mariano Eduardo de and
Tschudi, Juan Diego de: Anti-
güedades peruanas. 2 vols.
Vienna, 1851.
Rivet, Paul: Les Indiens Jibaros.
Revue d'Anthropologie. Paris,
1908.
——Les origines de l'homme
américain. Revue d'Anthro-
pologie. Paris, 1925.
Robertson, William: History of
America. 2 vols. London, 1777.
Román y Zamora **16**, *Jerónimo de:*
Republicas del mundo. 3 vols.
(Juan Fernandez) Salamanca,
1595.
Ruppert, Karl: The Caracol at
Chichen Itza, Yucatan, Mexico.
Carnegie, Publication No. 454.
Washington, 1935.

Saavedra, Bautista: El ayllu. La
Paz, 1913.
Sahagun, Bernardino de: Historia de
las cosas de Nueva España.
Trans. and ed. D. Jourdanet and
R. Siméon. Paris, 1880.
San Pedro, Juan de and *Canto, Juan
del:* Relación de la religión y
ritos del Perú, hecha por los
primeros religiosos agustinos que
allí pasaron para la conversión de
los naturales. *Colección,* III, 5-58.
Madrid, 1865.

Santa Cruz Pachacuti-Yamqui Sal-camayhua, Juan de: Relación de antigüedades deste reyno del Pirú. Ed. *Jiménez:* Tres relaciones, 231-328. Madrid, 1879.

Santiago Vela, Gregorio de: vide Biblioteca.

Santillán **106**, *Fernando de:* Relación del orígen, descendencia política y gobierno de los Incas. Ed. *Jiménez:* Tres relaciones, 3-133. Madrid, 1879.

Santo Thomas, Domingo de: Grammatica o Arte de la Lengua general de los Indios de los Reynos del Peru. Valladolid, 1560.

Sarmiento de Gamboa **208**, *Pedro:* Historia general llamada Indica. Abhandl. der Göttinger Kgl. Ges. d. Wissenschaften, Neue Folge VI, No. 4. Berlin, 1906.

Schmidt, Max: Kunst und Kultur von Peru. Berlin, 1929.

Seler, Eduard: Archäologische Reise in Sud- und Mittelamerika. Zs. f. Ethnologie, 201-242. Berlin, 1912.

——Gesammelte Abhandlungen zur Amerikanischen Sprach- und Altertumskunde. 5 vols. Berlin, 1902-1923.

Serrano, Antonio: Los primitivos habitantes del territorio Argentino. Buenos Aires, 1930.

Smithsonian = Smithsonian Miscellaneous Publications. Smithsonian Institution, Washington.

Spinden, Herbert J.: The reduction of Maya dates. Peabody Museum Papers. Harvard University. Cambridge, Mass., 1926.

——Maya dates and what they reveal. Science Bull., Mus. Brooklyn Inst. of Arts and Sciences. New York, 1930.

Springer, Anton: Handbuch der

Kunstgeschichte, VI, Die ausser-europäische Kunst. Leipzig, 1929.

Spruce, Richard: The Cultivation of Cotton in the Piura and Chira Valleys of northern Peru. London, 1864.

Squier, E. George: Peru, Incidents of Travel and Exploration in the Land of the Incas. New York, 1877.

Steinmann, Alfred: Maske und Schamanentum in Amerika. Ciba Zs., No. 89. Basle, 1943.

Stephens, John Lloyd: Incidents of travel in Central America, Chiapas, and Yucatan. 2 vols. New York, 1841.

——Incidents of travel in Yucatan. 2 vols. New York, 1843.

Strong, William Duncan: The Uhle Pottery Collections from Ancón. *University,* XXI, 135-190. Berkeley, 1925.

Stübel, Alphons: vide *Reiss.*

Teeple, J. E.: Maya astronomy. *Carnegie,* Publication No. 403. Washington, 1931.

Tello, J. C.: Introducción a la historia antigua del Perú. Lima, 1921.

——Inca. Wira Kocha; Revista Peruana de Estudios Anthropologicos, I, No. 1. Lima, 1923.

——Antiguo Perú. Primera epoca. Lima, 1929.

——Andean civilization. *International,* XXIII. New York, 1930.

Thompson, J. Eric: A correlation of the Mayan and European calendars. Field Museum of Natural History. Chicago, 1927.

Torquemada, Juan de: Los viente i un libros rituales i monarchia Indiana. 3 vols. Madrid, 1723.

Torres Rubio, Diego de: Grammatica y vocabulario en la Lengua general del Peru, llamada Quichua. Seville, 1603.

Transactions = Transactions of the Connecticut Academy of Arts and Sciences. New Haven.

Tschudi, Johann Jakob von: Reisen durch Sudamerika. 5 vols. Leipzig, 1868.

Tudela y Varela, Francisco: Socialismo peruano. Lima, 1905.

Ubbelohde-Doering, Heinrich: Auf den Königsstrassen der Inka. Berlin, 1941.

Uhle, Max: Pachacamac. Museum of the University of Pennsylvania. Philadelphia, 1903.

——Los principios de la antiguas civilizaciones peruanas. *Boletín,* IV, No. 12. Quito, 1920.

——Apuntes sobre la prehistoria de la region de Piura. *Boletín,* IV, 165-167. Quito, 1920.

——Explorations at Chincha. *University,* XXI. Berkeley, 1924.

——Excavaciones arqueológicas en la region de Cumbaya. Anales de la Universidad Central, XXXVII. Quito, 1926.

Ulloa, Antonio de: vide *Juan.*

University = University of California Publications in American Archaeology and Ethnology. Berkeley.

Urteaga, Horacio H.: El Perú. Bocetos históricos, Lima, 1919.

Vaillant, George C.: Chronology and stratigraphy in the Maya area. Maya Research, II, No. 2. New York, 1935.

Valdez de la Torre, Carlos: El ayllu. Mercurio Peruano, V, 187-209. Lima, 1920.

Valesco, Juan de: Historia del Reino de Quito. Ed. Don Augustin Yerovi. Quito, 1841-1844.

Villagomez, Pedro de: Carta pastorale de exortación e instrucción contra las idolatrias de los Indios. Lima, 1649.

Villarán, Manuel Vicente: Condición legal de las comunidades de indígenas. Lima, 1907.

Viteri Lafronte, Homero: La Historia del Reino de Quito. Revista de la Sociedad Jurídico-Literaria, XIX, 162 ff. Quito, 1917.

Waldeck, J. F. de: Pittoresque et Archéologique dans la Province de Yucatan pendant 1834 et 1836. Paris, 1838.

——Monuments anciens du Mexique. Ed. Brasseur de Bourbourg. Paris, 1866.

Ward, W. Hayes: Seal-cylinders of Western Asia. Washington, 1910.

Wiesse, Carlos: Las civilizaciones primitivas del Perú. Lima, 1913.

Wissler, Clark: The American Indian. An introduction to the Anthropology of the New World. New York, 1917.

Wolff, Werner: Déchiffrement de l'ecriture Maya. Paris, 1938.

Xerez, Francisco de: Verdadera Relación de la Conquista del Perú. *Libros,* I. Madrid, 1853.

Zárate **101**, *Augustín de:* Historia del Descubrimiento y Conquista de la Provincia del Perú y de las Guerras y Cosas, Señaladas en Ella, Acaecidas hasta el Vencimiento de Gonzalo Pizarro y de sus Secuacos, que en Ella se Rebelarón contra su Majestad. (Martin Nucio) Antwerp, 1555, and (Alonso Escrivano) Seville, 1577.

NOTES ON THE ILLUSTRATIONS

IN the choice of the illustrations for this volume every effort has been made, where several copies were at our disposal, to choose the one that represented the best angle for viewing. Wölfflin's criticisms of illustration in his *Gedanken zur Kunstgeschichte*, Basle, 1941, merit the attention of anyone reproducing works of art. So-called art photography in its own field may be as uninhibited as possible and from a point of view of taste follow whatever direction it pleases; for the science of art, however, in which the plates are only a means to an end, photography must first and foremost be of documentary significance and the choice is often extremely difficult since complete falsifications of the original print often exist. The primary rules, as laid down in the journal *Photo-Berater*, No. 5, Basle, 1944, should not normally be broken.

To elucidate the true proportions of the objects illustrated, in the following complete table of illustrations, dimensions are only given when for some reason they are of particular interest or depart from the expected norm. Most of the clay vessels range from between 16 and 30 centimetres high. Large vases of 1 metre, however, also exist such as the one in the Museum of Lima University, illustrated in Greslebin's *El Arte prehistorico Peruano*, Buenos Aires, 1926, Plate 5.

Apart from the particular information given about the plates, the table of illustrations furnishes the provenance of the objects and the collections which served for their original classification. Only in exceptional cases are the present whereabouts named, since many of the most famous collections have been dispersed in various cities and countries. The examples from the Rietberg Museum in Zürich originate without exception from 199A Depot Seenhauser, Trujillo. In the assembling of this collection of plates our thanks are due to the Sammlung für Völkerkunde der Universitat Zürich, the Kunstgewerbemuseum der Stadt Zürich, the Musée d'Ethnographie de Genève, the Museum für Völkerkunde, Basle, and the Franklin Institution Records as well as the International Institute of Art and Letters. These bodies have kindly made available to the publishers the very latest photographs.

PLATES

1 Clay vessel with broad spout. Little painting. Lines of colour fired. Trujillo. Rietberg Museum, Zürich

2 (*a*) Small brown clay vessel with spout attachment. Rietberg Museum, Zürich

(b) Clay vessel from the Huaca del Sol. Moche. Musée du Trocadéro, Paris

(c) Spoutless clay vessel probably from the Chicama Valley. Gaffron collection

3 (a) Brown clay vessel with spout. Chimbote. Zürich University

(b) Clay vessel with painted modelling. Trujillo region. Gaffron collection

(c) Clay vessel with spout, face unpainted, Chicama Valley. Gaffron collection

4 (a) Peruvian balsa, according to Alexander v. Humboldt

(b) and (c) Carved leeboards
The remains of bright paintwork. The length, including the decorated rudder blade, totals more than 6 ft. Ica. Gretzer collection

5 (a) Zoomorphic vessel in black clay. Lambayeque. Museum für Völkerkunde, Basle

(b) and (c) Black clay vessels. La Ciénega. Baretto collection

6 (a) Ancient Peruvian gold jewellery. Musée d'Ethnographie, Geneva

(c) Jewellery worked in heavy gold leaf. Pattern of snakes. Trophy heads and further symbols from the coast and Tiahuanaco style. Pachacamac. Baessler collection

(b) and (d) Hand mirror with pyrite surface and wooden frame. Ica. Gretzer collection

7 (a) Metal jewellery of the Chimu. (1) Bronze pin. Paita. Gretzer collection. (2) Silver pin. Pachacamac. Baessler collection. (3) Bronze chisel. Trujillo. Macedo collection. (4) Bronze work. Piura. Baessler collection. (5) Bronze ornament. Provenance unknown. Bastian collection

(b) Various gold beard-pluckers. Length 5 to 7 cm.; length of chain, 14·5 cm.; length of the pluckers on the upper right with decorated handle, 11·3 cm. Ica. Gretzer collection

(c) 5 different combs, 6 to 13 cm. wide; comb with handle, 24 cm. Southern coast. Collections: (1) Gretzer; (2) Bastian; (3) Gretzer; (4) Bolivar

8 (a) Clay vessel in the form of a house. Lima. Sutorius collection

(b) Carved wooden box, 20 × 8·5 cm. Pachacamac. Baessler collection

(c) Wooden stool, 37·5 × 11·5 cm. San Ramon. Bolivar collection

(d) Woven shirt with embroidery. Ica. Gretzer collection

(e) Shoes and sandals. Ica. (1) Leather shoe with bright coloured wool trimmings. Gretzer collection. (2) Silver shoe. Macedo collection. (3) Bast sandals. Bolivar collection

9 (a) Zoomorphic clay vessel. Chimbote

(b) Mask in copper and gold alloy with three clawed paws also of gold leaf. Length of mask, 25 cm. Teeth of mussel shells. From the moon pyramid of Moche. Sutorius collection

(c) Zoomorphic clay vessel. Chimbote. Barbet collection

10 (a) Stone figure of reddish lava. Height, 1·14 m. National Museum, Mexico

(b) Clay vessel painted brown on a white ground. Trujillo. Macedo collection. (Detail of the drawing on the side of the vessel, p. 141)

(c) Clay vessel with zoomorphic design on a light ground. Trujillo. Baessler collection

11 Clay vessel. Three-coloured painting in white and black on red. Provenance unknown. Zürich University

12 (a) Clay beaker with polychrome design. Ratinlixul, Guatemala. University of Philadelphia

(b) Clay dish with reddish-brown pattern on a white ground. Diameter 38·5 cm. Chimbote. Gretzer collection

13 Clay vessel. Face and neck unpainted. Head-dress pale yellow. Design and spout in Indian red. Chicama Valley. Gaffron collection

14 (a) Trachyte head. Copan, Honduras. Museum of Harvard University, Cambridge, Mass.

(b) and (c) Clay vessels. Chicama Valley. Gaffron collection

15 (a) Work basket. Tomb artifact found together with female mummy. Provenance unknown. Musée d'Ethnographie, Geneva

(b) Shoulder bag in carmine wool and white cotton. Nazca. Schmidt collection

16 (a) Blanket of white cotton with stepped pattern and figured design in various pale red and brown tints. 1·42 × 1·66 m. Ancón. Musée du Trocadéro. Paris

(b) White feather cloak with pale red and dark brown stepped pattern and animals. 85 × 85 cm. Nazca region. Gaffron collection

17 Two strips of red cotton tissue. Figures in red, brown, blue, green, yellow and white. Paracas. (a) Ratton collection. (b) Hein collection

18 Scale beam and scale with nets. Ica (?). Musée d'Ethnographie, Geneva

19 (a) Clay vessel surmounted by seated figure and bas-relief on the side. Trujillo region. National Museum, Lima

(b) Anthropomorphic clay vessel. Trujillo region. Jahnckee collection

(c) Vessel with skull and reed pipes. Chicama Valley. Museum für Völkerkunde, Berlin

(d) Clay vessel with brown design on a white ground. Chicama Valley. Museum für Völkerkunde, Berlin

20 (a) Loom with unfinished work. Marquez. Baessler collection

(b) Woven tissue, foundation of cotton, embroidered with wool. Provenance unknown. Musée d'Ethnographie, Geneva

(c) Indian knotted cords (quipus) (1) Spiral hanging in the form of a tassel. (2) Attached to a carved wooden beam. Both from Ica. Bolivar collection

(d) Blue cotton fabric. Pattern in white and yellow threads. Pachacamac. Musée du Trocadéro, Paris

21 (a) Double vessel of blackish clay. Chimbote. Baessler collection

   (b) Anthropomorphic clay vessel. Chimbote. Musée d'Ethnographie, Geneva

   (c) Zoomorphic clay vessel. Chimbote. Rautenstrauch-Joest-Museum, Cologne

22 (a) Zoomorphic clay vessel. Chimbote. Baessler collection

   (b) Two clay beakers with polychrome painting in Tiahuanaco style. Pachacamac. (1) Baessler collection. (2) Gretzer collection

23 (a) Zoomorphic double vessel in clay. Trujillo. Rietberg Museum, Zürich

   (b) Zoomorphic vessel in black clay. Lambayeque region. D'Harcourt collection

   (d) Phytomorphic vessel in black clay. Lambayeque region. Musée du Trocadéro, Paris

24 (a) Twin vessel in reddish-brown clay, with cross-bar and zoomorphic decoration. Pachacamac region. D'Harcourt collection

   (b) Phytomorphic vessel in black clay. Lambayeque region. D'Harcourt collection

   (c) Quadruple vessel in reddish-brown clay with zoomorphic sculptured ornament. Trujillo. Rietberg Museum, Zürich

25 (a) Clay vessel with spout. Reddish-brown painting on a light ground. Trujillo. Rietberg Museum, Zürich

   (b) Tripod bowl with polychrome painting. Height 13 cm. Pachacamac. Baessler collection

   (c) Hafted semi-closed clay bowl. Painting red-brown and pale yellow. Trujillo. Rietberg Museum, Zürich

26 (a) Huanchaco with the River Seco. Photograph G. R. Johnson

   (b) The coast south of Huarmey. Aerial photograph. Geographical, special publication

27 (a) Spouted clay vessel. Black painting on a white ground. Chicama Valley. Musée du Trocadéro, Paris

   (b) Three clay vessels with spouts. Pale yellow ground. Painting of the outer vessels Indian red, and the centre vessel dark brown. (Detail of the design of this vessel, p. 68.) Chicama Valley. Museum für Völkerkunde, Munich

28 (a) Ancient Peruvian mummy in its original burial garb. Heavily patinaed damaged copper mask with the remains of the former gilding. Wrap of Gobelin-like woven, patterned material. Hanging by a string a beard-plucker with two copper discs on a common clasp. Museum für Völkerkunde, Vienna

   (b) Clay vessel with sculpted figures. Reddish-brown painting. Trujillo. Baessler collection

29 (a) Anthropomorphic clay vessel. Head probably set at a later date on a pot-bellied pitcher. Height of the whole vessel, 32 cm. Trujillo region. Linden Museum, Stuttgart

   (b) Spoutless vessel. Moche. Städtisches Museum, Bremen

(*c*) Spoutless vessel. Trujillo. Alexander collection

30 Anthropomorphic clay vessels:
    (*a*) Chicama Valley
    (*b*) Provenance unknown. Museum für Völkerkunde, Berlin

31 Anthropomorphic clay vessel. Painting dark red and yellow tints. Trujillo. Rietberg Museum, Zürich

32 Huaca del Sol. Moche. General view and section. Length of the southern side, 136 m.; east side, 228 m.; height of terrace, 18 m.; height of pyramid, 23 m. Total height, 41 m. Franklin Institution Records

33 The first and second palaces of Chan-Chan. Aerial photographs. Geographical, special publication

34 Three clay vessels. Colours dark brown, red and white. Recuay
    (*a*) Macedo collection
    (*b*) Sokolowski collection
    (*c*) Gretzer collection

35 (*a*) and (*b*) Two vessels of whitish clay. Huarás. Lima University
    (*c*) Clay vessel with black, red and yellow design on a white ground. Recuay. Zürich University
    (*d*) Anthropomorphic vessel in brown, white and red. Incised contours of the eyes. Recuay. Macedo collection

36 (*a*) Section from the centre of the frieze of the Sun Gate at Tiahuanaco. Lava. Height of the frieze, 82 cm.
    (*b*) Masonry from the ruined city of Chan-Chan near Trujillo. Fragmentary ornaments on sun-dried brick walls. Photograph A. Bandelier. New York. Franklin Institution Records

37 (*a*) Polymorphic clay vessel with spout. Chimbote (?). Museum für Völkerkunde, Hamburg
    (*b*) Anthropomorphic vessel in black clay with a simple spout. Provenance unknown. Musée d'Ethnographie, Geneva
    (*c*) Anthropomorphic clay vessel in pale yellow and brownish red. Trujillo. Musée d'Ethnographie, Geneva

38 (*a*) Landscape between Santa and Chimbote
    (*b*) The frontier fortress Paramonga and its surroundings. Aerial photograph. Geographical, special publication

39 Anthropomorphic vessel in white clay. Grey and on the back a little red paint. Height, 41 cm. Circumference, 82 cm. Central Coast. Zürich University

40 (*a*) Anthropomorphic clay vessel with dark brown and white painting on a reddish ground. Pachacamac. Zürich University
    (*b*) Egg-shaped clay vessel with geometrical pattern and relief of animals. Colours blackish-blue and white. Chancay. Baessler collection
    (*c*) Clay vessel with spiked protrusions. Cajamarcilla. National Museum, Lima

41 (a) Mask of gold copper alloy with a green patina. The ears particu-
     larly stressed. Small holes in the forehead. Height, 26 cm. Found
     in a subterranean chamber of the Huaca de la luna. Moche.
     Sutorius collection
    (b) Polymorphic vessel of reddish clay with white and reddish-brown
     painting. Chimbote. Baessler collection
42 (a) West prospect of the volcano Misti and the city of Arequipa
    (b) Huaca in a suburb of Lima. Aerial photograph. Geographical,
     special publication
43 (a) Huaca de Tambo de Mora in the Chincha Valley
    (b) The ruins of Cajamarcilla
     Both pictures from the Franklin Institution Records
44 (a) Tall clay beaker with figured pattern. Nazca. Museum für
     Völkerkunde, Berlin
    (b) Beaker with polychome pattern. Nazca. D'Harcourt collection
    (c) Pattern of a tall clay beaker. Black, white, yellow and dark red
     tints on a pale red ground. Nazca. Gaffron collection. After
     Doering
45 (a) Clay vessel with two spouts joined by a crossbar. Polychrome
     figured pattern. Nazca. Zürich University
    (b) Clay beaker with sculpted nose. Nazca. Zürich University
46 (a) and (b) Polychrome painting on clay vessels. Nazca. Gaffron
     collection
47 (a) Hump-backed clay vessel with polychrome design. Nazca.
     Gaffron collection
    (b) Detail of the same vase
48 Vessels in black clay:
     (a) and (b) Pitchers with incised zoomorphic representations
     (c) and (d) Two aspects of the same vase. La Ciénega. Baretto
     collection

ILLUSTRATIONS IN THE TEXT